"WILLINGLY TO SCHOOL?"

The story of nine hundred years of education in Warwickshire

**The book is dedicated to learners and teachers past and present
in Warwickshire, and to all who have supported them.**

*"........the whining schoolboy ....
.......creeping like snail
Unwillingly to school ...."*

(Shakespeare "As You Like It" Act Two)

Note: The Cover combines two pictures; pupils outside Hatton C.E. School around 100 years ago, and pupils today outside the same buildings, now called The Ferncumbe C.E. School. It illustrates the two themes of change and continuity.

Also written or edited by David Howe

"Towards a School Language Policy"
"Better School Libraries in Primary Schools"
"Better School Libraries in Secondary Schools"
"Into the Classroom"
"Absent from School"
"Working Successfully with People"
"Carnival : A Poetry Anthology"
"Becoming a Writer"
"Bringing Learning to Life" (with Joan Wilson)
"Education for Democracy" (with others)
"Schools and the Police"
"Sensitive Issues : Drugs Guidance for Educational Settings"
"A History of Coten End School"
"A History of Exhall Grange School" (in draft)
"Literacy ICT and Numeracy: A Handbook of Ideas"; (with Maggie Wagstaff)

Warwickshire Publications
Official publisher to Warwickshire County Council
Libraries, Heritage and Trading Standards
Head Office: Barrack Street, Warwick CV34 4TH

Contents

Foreword

This book sets out to tell the story of almost 900 years of schooling in Warwickshire. It also celebrates in particular the centenary of Warwickshire County Council as the Local Education Authority. Both the earliest documented examples of a school in the county, and the development of the education authority took place close to one another: Northgate Street, Warwick. As I sit in my office at one end of that street, I have been reading about and reflecting on the momentous and tumultuous events and achievements of the last millennium in education.

The county's schools have educated trailblazers who have left an indelible mark on the country's history: William Shakespeare and Sir Frank Whittle are just two famous examples. It has been intriguing to learn something of their schooling in Warwickshire, and of many more, including poets, politicians and world champions in sport.

Our schools have fostered many lasting initiatives: the first Parent Teacher Association, the first School Council, the first Teacher Consultative Committees and more. These three highly significant creations have all contributed to a key informing principle of Warwickshire County Council's work in education: working closely with our partners, a tradition valued highly to this day, and one which will endure.

One of my predecessors, Bolton King, Director from 1904-28, began this tradition with his determination to develop education policies based on a simple philosophy "trusting the teachers and reducing officialdom to the minimum." His successors have enabled the creation of an authority with both traditional virtues of courtesy and consideration together with responsiveness to change. Messrs. Perkins, Yorke-Lodge and Chenevix Trench all worked tirelessly in their distinctive ways to improve the education of all pupils, not just the academic successes, important though they were and are. Michael Ridger and Margaret Maden led the authority's schools through major reorganisations which were characterised by both principle and by the according of the highest priority to consultation and co-operation: with parents, teachers, governors, local councils and the diocesan authorities.

I am particularly proud of the work we now do, but have been fascinated to discover that OFSTED's praise for our relationships with our schools sums up a long and eventful history. The phrase used in our 1999 inspection report described Warwickshire as being "principled, fair and honourable" which encapsulates a long tradition. It is both humbling and intriguing to read of the high standards of professional conduct developed and sustained throughout the last century. But, above all, it has been illuminating to glimpse moments in the daily routine of literally hundreds of thousands of pupils and teachers ..... moments both funny and tragic.

From the visits of myself and colleagues across the county, I can paraphrase Perkins' words: "We've done our damnedest", or Bolton King's characteristically modest response to fulsome tributes: "We have tried hard to do what we could for Warwickshire children." That is true of our County Councillors, of all parties, who have always highly valued the importance of education to individuals and their communities within the County. It is also true of our headteachers, teachers, inspectors, officers, non-teaching staff, governors and many more.

Together we hold in stewardship a great responsibility to the citizens of Warwickshire and this book is a testament to our enduring values of tolerance, equality and mutual respect - our striving to fulfil the individual potential of every young person. The theme of our millennium celebration was: "Look to the future - but learn from the past." As we look forward, with confidence and optimism, this book outlines our rich inheritance.

I would like to pay tribute to David Howe, the author of this book, for his scholarship, his hard work and his ability to retain a sense of fun - which can be seen throughout the text. David is a former, distinguished Inspector and Chief Inspector of Schools in Warwickshire and his educational insights coupled with his local knowledge have combined to produce a book which will educate, entertain and amuse. Like the values Warwickshire espouses, I believe that this book will stand the test of time.
But only you, the reader, can judge!

Eric Wood
County Education Officer

Introduction

The idea for this book came to me as I walked my dog round Warwick Racecourse one Saturday afternoon in 1995. Earlier that day I had been browsing in the 'Local History' section of Warwick Library and I was reflecting on how much more likely it was that independent schools such as Rugby, Warwick and King's High would have their histories written than most state schools. One glance at the relevant shelves confirmed that. Since then, I have discovered that many more school histories have been written, usually to mark a centenary or a half century. But their typically more flimsy binding, their pamphlet-like nature and their limited circulation had meant that they were much harder to find.

Even within the local education authority family, an unofficial hierarchy exists. I have traced histories of all of our grammar schools. But few secondary modern school histories survive, and I know of no special school histories that exist, except one I have written on Exhall Grange. In fairness, it should be noted that most of our special schools are of relatively recent origin.

If one adds in the existence of preserved sets of school magazines, local historians would find more in print on the history of the education of the 'top' five percent of its pupils than on the remaining ninety five percent.

This was why I approached Eric Wood, the County Education Officer, with the proposal of a history of Warwickshire Schools - all of them. The original intention was a millennium history. But my early researches suggested 2003 as a much better date. The Act that created counties such as Warwickshire as a local education authority became law in December 1902. Warwickshire asked for a little more time to assume its responsibilities, which it finally did on July 1, 1903. A centenary commemorative edition would be much more appropriate, and give me three extra years to finish it. Hence its appearance in 2003.

The Scope of the Book

The book is about Local Education Authority schools but includes some reference to the independent sector. Schools such as Warwick School, Kingsley and King's High once worked closely with the authority. Bolton King's retirement party took place at King's High, for example. Rugby School has been closely involved with the work of schools in Rugby. Its heads have chaired and served on local committees and have served as governors in local schools. In particular, the school works closely with Lawrence Sheriff School.

Other independent schools in the county have, quite understandably, functioned entirely separately. Where there are no obvious 'cross-overs', I have not included them.

I have normally confined myself to the compulsory years of schooling, currently five to sixteen. Valuable services with an honourable history supporting school life such as the Youth and the Careers Service I have neither the space nor the qualifications to tackle. They will deserve a history of their own. I do not cover nurseries; I do make occasional reference to Colleges of Further Education where there is something unusually distinctive to say. They, too, deserve histories of their own, and the colleges at Rugby and Nuneaton are partially written up.

I had intended originally to cover only the history of the last one hundred years. But it soon became apparent that one can only understand Warwickshire schools as they are now by reference to the L.E.A.'s 'inheritance' in 1903. In particular this is true of church schools. One might wonder why there is currently an impassioned debate about the development of new single-faith schools in England, while Coventry-born Mo Mowlam works for the development of integrated schools in Northern Ireland. To answer this question takes us back into the eighteenth and nineteenth centuries, or even earlier. There is also the notion of the 'pendulum' in educational fashions. I later argue that the closest parallel to what passes for a "philosophical" basis for current thinking on education can be found in the second half of the nineteenth century.

So, I have, probably unwisely, had a go at nine hundred years rather than a hundred.

Like Vivian Bird in his "Short History of Warwickshire and Birmingham" (but unlike Slater or Tasker in their histories) I make no claim to include Coventry in my concept of Warwickshire. I make an occasional reference to schools in Solihull and Sutton Coldfield, until 1974 part of Warwickshire. Essentially, my concept of Warwickshire is the county we have at the time of writing.

Qualifications for Writing the Book

I studied History as a supplementary subject in my degree, but I cannot claim to be other than an amateur historian.

My association with the area is extensive and varied. I was born and brought up in Warwickshire and attended three local schools. On my mother's side, I can trace members of the family attending local schools at least as far back as 1870. My children attended between them four different local schools, and an F.E. College.

As a teacher, I taught in a county secondary school for nearly five years, and, while at university, did vacation supply teaching in two primary schools. I also taught evening classes at the "tech" (the local College of Further Education).

As county adviser, then inspector, I visited every school, college and nursery in the county, some of them many times. Since starting this book, I have returned to 145 schools

So, I know the county's schools well. But my real qualification is that I volunteered. Many have said that it seems an over-ambitious project. I now agree. But if H. G. Wells could write a history of the world, and Simon Schama a history of Britain, surely a history of Warwickshire schools is achievable ..... though I know of no other L.E.A. history so wide in its scope.

Notes on Procedure

I have made extensive use of quotation, hence much use of verbs like 'recalled'. In so doing, I have normally reproduced original quotations exactly as written. Thus, capital letters have at times been used in ways that are no longer accepted practice, because conventions in their use have also changed; they were used more liberally in the past. Quotations have been used either to illustrate generalisations, or because they encapsulate what I consider to be an intringuingly idiosyncratic moment or view. In other words, they have been used for two almost exactly opposite reasons! When used to illustrate the typical, I have resorted, probably too often, to phrases like 'for example'. I have striven to ensure consistency in the use of punctuation. For example, I have decided to punctuate rather than leave unpunctuated initials and acronyms. If any unpunctuated examples appear, it could be that they appear in a quotation and have been reproduced as originally written. Or, I just missed them. My concern to make explicit links between past and present has led to much use of phrases like 'to this day'.

I have normally retained names, except where I have thought that their use might cause embarrassment or hurt. I have deliberately used an informal style. One effect of this is some use of abbreviations like C.E.O. and H.M.I. in sections where their use is repeated.

I have checked sources as far as I can. However, many sources: school logbooks, personal reminiscence etc. are by their nature the only source I have and events, or versions of events, cannot easily be verified.

Reading the Book

I envisage the book as one to be dipped into rather than read as a story from start to finish. It is drenched in detail and is much more an anthology than a narrative, though it does tell a story. An issue that pre-occupied me throughout was whether to write chronologically or thematically. Some topics: the nineteenth century or the second world war, for example, seem better written chronologically. Others, like 'Inspection' or 'Special Events', are rather like motifs that run throughout the history. In the end, I have compromised. After all, the history of education is often one of compromises! The book is mainly chronological, though in zig-zag fashion, as one tries to cover a number of simultaneous developments. A few sections are thematic.

I have adopted a policy of trying to mention at least once as many different schools as possible. The extent to which schools are mentioned will depend on one or more of a number of factors:

a) availability of relevant documents e.g. logbooks
b) availability of a school history.
c) invitations by heads to visit and peruse documents.

And some schools simply seem to have been particularly newsworthy, or well documented.

I do scincerely apologise that I have not been able to identify the source of all quotations, although the title should be listed in the Bibliography. I shall be pleased to rectify omissions in any future issues.

Enough preamble! On with the story.

David Howe (March 2003)

Acknowledgements

The number of people who have helped me is enormous. To list them all would turn this book into some kind of directory, or the script for a nightmare awards evening.

Apart from the lengthy list of names that I have included below, I would add:

a) Heads and secretaries of schools whose documentation: logbooks, minutes etc. I have consulted. Invariably, I have been provided with a warm welcome, a warm room and a cup of coffee, even in schools where I arrived as a stranger.

b) Staff at all our town and village libraries across Warwickshire. They rarely knew who the somewhat tentative, dishevelled man was who asked them about their local history collection, but every single one combined efficient help with kindness.

c) The staff at the County Record Office and at Warwick Library have been particularly helpful, not once daunted other than momentarily by my enigmatic requests or my frequent visits.

There follows a further roll call of honour which, believe it or not, has been edited:

Those named below were particularly helpful in providing information and/or correcting my errors:

Gill Ashley-Smith
Peter Ashley-Smith
David Beaumont
James Bolton King
Peter Bolton King
*Miss Broadley
*Joan Browne
Lynda Carnes
*Eileen Carter
Ted Cockerill
*Seamus Crowe
*Adrian Dilworth
*Martin Dunne
*Janet Eaton
Glyn Essex
*Barbara Evans
Sarah Evason
*Janet Eyre
Jean Field

Janice Fielden
*Barbara Gibson
Alan Griffin
* Trina Gulliver
*Pete. Guppy
*Gerald Haigh
*John Hancock
Michael Henry
* Arthur Hunt
Ian Jackson
Bob Jelley
David Jones
Mary Jones
*Eleanor Joynes
*Derek Leeson
Jan Perry
* Rex Pogson
Deirdre Powell
Angela Raby

Martin Robinson
Wendy Robinson
*Sam Sharma
Christine Thompson
*Peggy Thornton
*Ralph Thornton
*Norman Turrell
*Bruce Turton
Marie Twomey
Paddy Wex
Paul Williams
Rod Williams
*Cavin Woodward
*Malcolm Wray

* indicates those I
interviewed.

I would also like to thank the following organisations and their representatives:

Keith Draper, Alan Kirby, June Fairbrother and staff at the Coventry Evening Telegraph, for access to files; Christine Cluley, and various committee members of FWCRO (Friends of the Warwickshire County Record Office); Lesley Chatwin and the Coventry and Warwickshire Local and Family History Society; Nash Meghji and the County Music Service; John Olorenshaw and the Bulkington Family History Society; Canon John Eardley and the Church of England (Coventry Diocese); The Headmaster and Librarian of Warwick School; Andrew Morris and the Diocesan Schools Commission, Archdiocese of Birmingham

The following spent some time reading and tactfully commenting on chaotic draft chapters: Sheila Bean, John Burton, Angela Hewins, Margaret Maden, Merlin Price, Michael Ridger and 'Bill' Wilson.

Particular thanks to my editorial committee over many years: Lisa Blunt, Chris Jeens and Eric Wood, and, more recently, Sam Tame.

Their willingness to meet me regularly kept me moving through quagmires of self-doubt.

My long-suffering wife donated our dining room as a long-term extension to my office, the latter hopelessly overcrowded with books and papers. She also joined me on countless forays into far-flung villages and around half a dozen exhibitions.

Dorothy Macfarlane typed and retyped the manuscript, working evenings and weekends with saintly patience. Apart from me, she may prove to be the only person to get through the whole book.

Spike Milligan once memorably concluded an acceptance speech for a lifetime achievement award thus:

> "I'm not going to thank anybody because I did it all by myself."

I have so many to thank. But for whatever wrong that remains:-

> "I did it all by myself."

1

The First Schools

Which was the first school ever to be opened in Warwickshire? The strongest claim is that of Warwick School, with only three other existing schools in the whole country probably able to exceed its number of years in existence; St Paul's London, St. Peter's York and the King's School Canterbury may be older, but A. F. Leach in his history of Warwick School asserts that only Warwick has documentary evidence of its existence at the time of Edward the Confessor: a royal writ headed 'Confirmation by King Henry of the customs and ordeals of iron and water and of the School of Warwick', in which the church had its right confirmed to keep the school "as fully and lawfully as it used in the time of King Edward".

Although the writ is undated, other names and details in the document indicate a date of around 1123. The Venerable Bede in his 'Ecclesiastical History' suggested 598 AD as a starting date for the school in Canterbury, which would appear to give the edge to the King's School in its claim to be the first. Colin Chapman cites evidence of a school in Galloway, Scotland at the start of the fifth century, but whether conjecture or not, these debates are an early distraction from matters in Warwickshire.

The early history of Warwick School was closely linked to the development of St. Mary's Church, Warwick. This mirrored what happened elsewhere, for schools such as King's School, Canterbury were attached to the great monasteries and cathedrals. On a smaller scale, the chantry schools began to provide an education. A chantry was a church or chapel endowed by a wealthy person with a priest who often taught at a school or in a room linked with the chantry. From Saxon times onward and throughout the Medieval period education was the preserve of the church. It was the needs of the church, for example a need for adult males who were well educated in Latin, that gave rise to grammar schools. Such schools often began as chantry schools and they enabled boys who sought to enter the priesthood to study Latin grammar.

What is a 'School'?

One problem with determining chronology of schools is that documents often refer to a 'scolemaster', leading to assumptions that a school therefore existed. But much early education took part in a 'scoleroom' at the back of a church. Thus, there is reference on the flyleaf of the parish register at Lapworth to John Wight, Schoolmaster in 1662, but the date of the first 'school' is uncertain. The same can be said of the reference to Peter Bishop at Kineton in 1662 who was licensed 'to teach school'. The Vicar of Claverdon wrote in 1673: "I doe teach by the importunity of my neighbours a few children of my parish." Again, it is not sure whether he taught in anything like a purpose-built school.

In Henley there was mention of a schoolmaster in 1707, but again, origins of the first school are questioned. An advertisement in the Birmingham Gazette informed local residents that: "The Revd. E. Jones respectfully informs his friends and the public that he has fitted his house up at Beaudesert in the most commodious manner for the reception of twelve boarders." He talked of "a regular plan of education and a strict attitude to the morals of his pupils." Would this be counted as a 'school'?

Even in villages as small as Pillerton Hersey and Pillerton Priors, there were references to "various little dame schools", often no more than a room in a house. Claims for the existence of schools sometimes stem from bequests to establish such schools, as, for example, in Long Itchington (1641), Barford (1677) and Priors Marston (1711). But provision of money did not necessarily ensure a rapid start to building.

The first reference to education in Kenilworth traced by its historian Joyce Powell was in the writings of William Best, local vicar, in 1718:

"There is no public or charity school maintained in the Parish but for the want thereof out of kindness and charity to my neighbours being generally very poor and not able to pay for their child's schooling I have myself for about ten years taught them gratis in the church vestry to read English well and to write and copy accounts …. whereby I have had an opportunity to instruct them often in the principles of the Christian religion."

In these early developments we can discern the elements of a curriculum which was to dominate the nineteenth century and which is urged on us even in the twenty-first: the "three Rs" plus religious education.

The Grammar Schools

Just as Warwick School can claim to be one of the oldest in Great Britain, so the Grammar School at Stratford upon Avon can claim to have probably the oldest surviving school buildings still in use. The Pedagogue's House, built in 1426-7, even in 1906, was described as "the oldest school building used for the same purposes today as at the beginning of the reign of Henry VI". The register of the Diocese of Worcester makes reference to a schoolmaster or 'rector scholarum' in Stratford back in 1295, and there are further references to a schoolmaster throughout the fourteenth century, probably one who rented a room. From 1403 onwards documents enable the history of the school to be traced without interruption to the present day.

All sorts of claims difficult to test can be made for origins of schools at the end of the fifteenth century and onwards, but G E Saville, well known local historian, has traced the history of a grammar school at Alcester at least as far back as 1490.

Nicholas Carlisle's "A Concise Description of the Endowed Grammar Schools in England and Wales" (1818) gives some information on the next few grammar schools to open in Warwickshire. However, his evidence for dates is not always clear. He wrote of: "The Free Grammar School at Nuneaton …. founded by King Edward the Sixth in the year 1553. The school is open to the boys of the Town and Parish indefinitely, free of expense." Pupils could be admitted at nine years of age. As the school grew and became a local institution, so stories of troubled relationships emerged …… of parental complaints such as the one that alleged his son had been whipped "till the blood dript down from his tayle to his shoes."

A grammar school existed at Coleshill for hundreds of years and its origins could be earlier even than the Reformation, but precise dating seems problematic. There is some evidence to suggest that 'The Free Grammar School at Coleshill' opened in 1520, but Carlisle was unable to help us here. He reported bleakly: "The Author is not able to give a description, as no answer has been received to his letter."

The origins of Rugby School, indebted to Lawrence Sheriff: "Citizen and Grocer of London" are well documented in its many histories. Sheriff's will, dated 22nd July 1567, left: "Fifty pounds towards the building of a school, House and Alms-houses in Rugby". The recorded cost was of £54.41 for a building "stopped with straw to keep out rain and wind."

For the first hundred years its existence was precarious and its headmasters not always fully paid. The school was originally for <u>local</u> boys: "the children of Rugby and Brownsover and next for such as bee of other places thereunto adjoyneing." The original foundation was very modest, and Sheriff clearly intended no more than the creation of a small local grammar school to serve a small market town. Even in 1874, the Times thundered in its January 31st edition: "Except for a succession of distinguished and powerful administrators, it would have been nothing but an ordinary Grammar School."

Next to arrive appears to have been 'The Free Grammar School at Atherstone', founded by a Royal Charter of Queen Elizabeth, dated December 22nd 1573. This was to be " ….. for the education, instruction of boys and young men in grammar in Atherstone." To ensure efficient management of its funds, the Queen's Charter directed that: "Twelve of the more discreet and honest men of the Town should be, and be called Keepers and Governors." This was an early reference indeed to a school governing body.

The names of King Edward, Nuneaton's first "governours" are inscribed on the old school wall, now the parish office for the nearby church. Even then, they could be removed for "mismanagement, neglect or bad behaviour."

Carlisle wrote in less precise terms of other grammar schools, for example, the 'Free Grammar School at Monks Kirby, near Atherstone' about which he told us that it was " .... founded prior to the year 1625; but there is no history nor tradition of its origin in the Parish."

Why it was described as 'near Atherstone' is unclear, unless it was because it was sited close to the Watling Street on which Atherstone stands. It was clear from the will of Thomas Wale that this was the Monks Kirby we know today, for he specified that free education be available only to scholars in the village and in the neighbouring villages of Stretton-under-Fosse and Brinklow, and "none other". It may have struggled to survive; it certainly had trouble in recruiting graduates.

Mentioned not by Carlisle but in local histories are references to grammar schools in Long Itchington, Brailes, and in the north chapel of Coughton church, but there is little or no precise information. There is documentary evidence also of so-called 'grammar schools' at Kingsbury and Salford Priors, all in the seventeenth century. Carlisle did make mention of 'The Free School at Dunchurch', founded by Francis Boughton in 1707, whose trustees were to appoint "a sober, grave, orderly and learned schoolmaster". The original school building, now a private house, still stands by the entrance to the churchyard.

Another intriguingly vague reference is to "The Grammar School at Hampton Lucy" which, apparently, by 1818 "is now sunk to nothing .... it is nothing more than an ABC school for the parish boys". No dates are suggested for its opening.

Other Examples of Early Schooling

I make no claim to have identified and authenticated every school opening in the county during the seventeenth and eighteenth century. What follows is a somewhat cluttered account of a proliferation of school openings.

As early as 1611, there is reference to a school at Harbury for "poor boys", founded by one Thomas Wagstaff. Probably as early as 1638, but certainly by the middle of that century, Sir Francis Nethersole endowed a school in Polesworth, devoted to teaching reading and writing and imparting a Christian education. This initiative was most unusual in that "dual" schools were opened : that is for boys and girls, educated separately, but in the same building. The Nethersole family was just one example of several whose names would be linked with schools over many centuries; the Verney Family was another. There is reference to a free school for all the children of Combroke and Compton Verney, opened in 1641.

From then on, the pace of growth began to accelerate, though not all claims have been substantiated beyond doubt. In Kingsbury there were reports of a school operating in a local chapel as early as 1637: "a locke and caye for the scoole house dore" was part of the churchwarden's accounts for 1637, and also of a school in

Snitterfield in 1661. George Abbott, who died in 1649, left £4 10/- per annum to provide a free school at Baddesley Ensor.

Soon afterwards Thomas Dugard provided in his will money for the children of Barford to enable them to "read and reckon and for poor girls to sew." This was another very early reference to the education of girls whose education, if it happened at all, did so usually at home.

Minute books of a Free School in Long Marston are preserved from 1656, but with a focus on administration rather than children. Further schools or rooms were mentioned by A. F. Leach in his contribution to the history of the county: at Leamington Hastings (1665), Middleton (1672), Long Itchington (1674), Fillongley (1690) and Budbrooke (1701). All were designed for children of the poor; all owed their start in life to local philanthropists.

In the late seventeenth century, schooling was provided in Leamington Hastings for " .... all children of qualified parents .... to teach to read and say the catechism". We have this statement by the school 'Correspondent' of Shustoke: "The school, it is interesting to note, was founded in 1699. The present mistress is doing all in her powers to make the children worthy of this historic foundation."

1707 was to be a busy year. Apart from the previously mentioned school at Dunchurch, barely two miles away, a local benefactor opened 'Elborowe School: a charity school for 30 boys and girls in Hill Street, Rugby', although its earliest existence was apparently in the south aisle of the parish church. At the same time another local benefactor, Nathaniel Newton, a Quaker, endowed a school in the village of Hartshill near Nuneaton.

In 1715 Nicholas Chamberlaine, rector of Bedworth for more than 50 years, left money in his will to found "two public charity schools". Where and when these schools opened is uncertain, but his munificence benefits local schools to this day.

Education Spreads

By now many relatively small villages had their own school. Thus, for example, Stoneleigh gained a school in 1710. Norton Lindsey employed a schoolmaster in 1749 at £10 p.a. In subsequent years, there were regular payments for upkeep of the school and schoolhouse. A "charity" school was opened in Southam in 1762 and in Tachbrook in 1771. Another for "poor children" was opened in Leek Wootton in 1776. Cubbington reportedly followed in 1780. Nearby, Leamington at this time was still no more than a village, its rapid growth not due until after the discovery of healing waters there. It was not until the population had grown to 2000 that the first day school for the poor was opened in 1822.

Saville has used local directories dating from 1792 to show how, even in a small town like Alcester, schools began to spring up in profusion as the nineteenth century arrived. As schools were often short-lived, detail is lacking, but there were references in the early part of the century to boys' and girls' day and boarding schools, with ages of pupils as young as four and as old as twenty. Mrs Treslove's Boarding School at King's Coughton, for example, received one mention only. How long it lasted and what it taught is unknown. The same was true of literally dozens of other schools.

Educating the Poor : National Initiatives

Through the second half of the eighteenth century and the first half of the nineteenth century there was to be a growth in the number of schools for poor children. They were generally called charity schools, and they developed in haphazard fashion. This was because they usually depended on local initiative or on a bequest. Nevertheless, they often influenced the pattern of provision right up to the present day. Many schools were established by the Church of England or by nonconformist groups, especially the Methodists. The S.P.C.K. (Society for the Propagation of Christian Knowledge), a Church of England organisation, was founded in 1698 to open and advise on the running of day schools. It was replaced in 1811 by the National Society for the Promotion of Education of the Poor in the Principles of the Established Church. This, not surprisingly, was usually shortened to the National Society. The Society had an ambitious aim: a school in every parish in England and Wales. Its inheritance today is the large number of Church of England schools in all parts of Warwickshire from Clifton in the east to Salford Priors in the west .... from Newton Regis in the north to Kineton in the south. The Nonconformists set up the British and Foreign Schools Society in 1814, but lacked the funds to match the National Society.

Funding the Schools

This, then, was the national background. At local level there continued to be countless examples of these diverse origins of schools. In Kenilworth, for example, a local surgeon, Dr William Edwards, provided in his will in 1723 for two free schools, one for the boys of Kenilworth, the other for Hatton, Shrewley and Beausale. (The Edwards Charity has continued to help schools to this day.) In 1790, a local schoolmaster, William Turner, left £100 to aid the founding of a 'Free School'. Another school nearby had begun early in the eighteenth century, supported by a nonconformist charity. The first 'National School' in Kenilworth did not, however, open till 1836 and not until the second half of the nineteenth century was there any provision made for Roman Catholic children.

It was the National Society also that enabled the building of a school in Cherington, with a donation of £169 0s 9d. The Church reserved the right to stipulate entry conditions. At Tanworth-in-Arden in 1806 children were accepted by the church only if they could "read words of one syllable".

A relatively small village like Brinklow had at different times during the nineteenth century evidence of three private schools, together with a 'dissenting' (nonconformist) school, and a National School (opened in 1828). The National Society also opened schools in nearby Harborough Magna (1845) and Pailton (1848).

In Fenny Compton, a purpose-built school opened in 1833. There were schools before then, but no records appear to have survived. A full account of the donations towards erecting the schoolroom has survived, and it illustrates how church, charitable institutions and local generosity could combine. The school received a grant of £54 from the National Society and £10 each from the Rector and the Dean and Chapter of Christ Church College, Oxford. The curate "and friends" chipped in with £5. Twenty-seven citizens subscribed one shilling each; 24 more gave six pence each and one Widow Hirons increased the final tally by one penny. Soon afterwards in 1839 a school opened in Snitterfield, also with money from public subscription and a grant from the National Society.

Urban Development

However, even as education in villages began to develop, towns often lagged behind. Leamington, Rugby and Nuneaton had scant provision until later in the century. Leamington was a small village until the discovery of the medicinal waters that would give it 'spa' status and therefore tourist potential. In 1801 its population was 315, smaller than that of nearby Radford Semele, but by 1840 it was nearly 13,000. Rugby's population grew only slowly until the arrival of the railways, from 1838 onwards. Between 1730 and 1830 it rose from 900 to 2300 (approx). By 1901 it was 17,000 and by 1971 it had reached 60,000.

Education for Girls

For girls there was little provision. It was assumed that they would be educated at home. However, there were notable exceptions to this negligence. In 1790 the Countess of Warwick created a School of Industry "to provide for the education of poor girls and to form habits of virtuous order and industry." Sixty girls aged 9-14 attended: their curriculum was a familiar combination of the three Rs and preparation for their future role: Reading, Writing, Arithmetic, Sewing, Knitting and Spinning.

The State Takes an Interest

All this activity happened without any formal support from the Government. Education was not then seen as a national responsibility. This would change dramatically during the nineteenth century, and an early sign of a government beginning to acknowledge its responsibilities was an Act of Parliament introduced in 1802 by Sir Robert Peel. Peel was M.P. for nearby Tamworth and lived in Drayton Manor, close to the Warwickshire border. His Factory Act required employers to make provision for reading, writing and arithmetic during at least the first four years of a seven year apprenticeship. The instruction had to form part of the apprentices' twelve hour working day, a day that could not begin before 6.00 a.m., nor end later than 9.00 p.m.

Two key dates in the history of state provision of education were during the 1830's. First, in 1833, Parliament made a grant of £20,000 towards the building of schools and school houses. Thus was born the notion that the State should fund education. Secondly, in 1839, inspectors were appointed to monitor the use of state money. Thus were born school inspectors, and state scrutiny of local initiative.

2
The Nineteenth Century:
Towards Education for All

Frances O'Shaughnessy has given us a meticulously researched account of the growth of educational opportunities in Leamington. No other county town has received such detailed treatment. Her book, thus, provides an instructive case-study of the rapid growth in urban education. Two hundred years ago the "town" was "a village of the humblest kind" with fewer than 300 people, living in thatched cottages around the church. By 1822 the population had risen to 2000, and a local vicar opened the first voluntary day school for the children of Leamington's poor. The town then had to wait 16 years for its second such school: a Wesleyan day school. Denominational competition then began to flourish with a Congregational day school in 1840, and Catholic schools in 1848 and 1850. The Baptists followed in 1860, by which time the Church of England had six schools. This rapid growth, largely nourished by rival church groups, was to typify expansion of provision elsewhere.

So, opportunities increased rapidly, although often in conditions enough to dismay all but the most hardy. The Leamington Congregational school, for example, was in the basement of the chapel " ..... it was a capacious basement, half of which was to house tombs. The schoolroom .... had two windows on its outside wall, each with only 18 inches above ground level ..... the boys worked in semi-darkness in the cold, damp atmosphere of a school below ground and stone-floored."

An H.M.I. wrote rather more positively about the nearby Roman Catholic boys' school in 1853: "Schoolroom excellent ..... offices good ..... playground sufficient ..... furniture - 2 cupboards, 2 grates, desk, table. Instruction careful and intelligent."

Throughout the century the challenge was first to provide, then to resource adequately, a basic level of schooling. Progress was often so slow as to be indiscernible. An inspector noted at Polesworth Nethersole Infants in 1857 " ..... an undue proportion of children over seven for whom there is no desk accommodation."

Nearly 40 years later, in 1893, another inspector tartly observed that: "This (Polesworth) is a very good infant school but it ought to be twice as large as it is."

There may have in reality been much more progress in providing school places than is evident here, for the nineteenth century saw rapid increases in population throughout the county. The arrival of coal mining in Polesworth ensured an increase nearly fourfold from 1365 to 4665. Coal mining plus growth in the ribbon trade almost doubled Nuneaton's population between 1850 and 1901.

Rugby's growth provided another example of population explosion. Thomas Hughes was able to get away with a dismissive description of early nineteenth century Rugby by a stagecoach guard as a "werry out-o'-the way place and is off the main road you see" in his novel of the 1830's "Tom Brown's Schooldays".

But the arrival of main railway lines from 1838 on turned it into a "railway town" in that its size, location of industry and housing all stemmed largely from the coming of the railways. The arrival of the railway in Rugby rapidly transformed it from a market centre of 1,500 people to an industrial centre of 21,000. Elsewhere, the development of coalfields rapidly increased the population of Bedworth. Southam and Coleshill almost doubled their population over the century. Only Henley experienced a reduction, owing to a decline in coaching. Simply trying to keep up with the numbers, never mind extending and improving provision, was to be a major pre-occupation for potential and actual providers from the start of the nineteenth century to the 1970's.

Funding the Schools: the Churches

The development of schools continued to depend on the generosity of local philanthropists and of the Church of England or of a religious group. At Aston Cantlow, the Reverend Hill put up £1000 of his own money to start a school. At nearby Shottery, the Reverend Collis stumped up £450. The Reverend Thomas Lane spent more than £700 on the school at Wasperton. In Marton, aided by local subscription, the Reverend B. Hulbert raised £480 for a local school.

The Willoughby Charity funded the erection of a school in 1816. However, such local largesse could be linked closely to peremptory policy. The Charity Trustees minutes of 1842 show that at a meeting on December 8th: "Mr William Cleaver and his wife, the school master and mistress, received notice to quit the school on 25th December." The thirty year old Charles Dickens, who was shortly to write a short story entitled 'Mugby Junction' about nearby Rugby, could surely have turned this laconic minute into a harrowing tale. (Dickens, by the way, did visit Warwickshire from time to time to give readings. One such reading was at Bath Place School, Leamington. He could well have spent time on Rugby Station awaiting a connection to Leamington.)

A year later the same school, Willoughby published rules drawn up by the trustees. One illustrated the expected attendance at church: "That every Sunday the children be required to attend school at nine in the morning and two in the afternoon and to proceed from the school with the master and mistress to the morning and evening service at church." At Harbury, rule six stated: "Any complaints must be made to the Vicar. And to secure the school from interruption no person will be allowed to visit without an order from the vicar, who daily inspects the schools himself."

Religion often took priority over everything else in the curriculum. Educationists such as Hannah More wanted literacy to be confined to the ability to read, particularly the Bible. Writing was not part of the deal. Indeed, rudimentary reading was widely taught even in the first half of the century. Joan Allen, drawing on 1841 Census material, estimated that over two thirds of the children in Hartshill and Oldbury were having tuition in reading either at day or at Sunday school; over half were attending both.

In the 1860's, entries in the Little Compton logbook suggested that the Vicar was prepared to horsewhip children who were tempted by a rival establishment and there were references to "children regularly being molested in the streets by clergymen." Elsewhere, one head wrote this: "Received a complaint from the Dissenter's School that the children of this (National) School have 'insulted their children and thrown stones at the door'. Investigated the affair and found it to be of a not very serious character. Cautioned the children upon stone-throwing etc." (Bishop's Itchington 1884)

The emphasis during the nineteenth century, whether in government funding or in local endeavour, was emphatically on education of the poor. When St. Matthew's Parochial School opened in Rugby in 1853 it declared its target group unequivocally: "For the education of children only of the labouring, manufacturing and poorer classes …. and for no other purpose." Among many diverse starting points for schools was that in Bilton, near Rugby. A school there was said to have developed from 'The Magnet', a club so named because it was intended to draw men away from the public house.

As the nineteenth century gathered pace, so did another movement to promote education among the poor: that of the Sunday School movement. Though its origins and originators are contested, most experts agree that it began in the second half of the eighteenth century. An early example was the Baptist Sunday School in Alcester in 1813. A minute book from 1823 to 1852 tells of classes starting at 8.30 a.m.(summer) and 9.00 a.m. (winter), and 1.30 p.m. Classes were segregated, and there was an enviably high pupil-teacher ratio : two teachers to fifteen pupils, the teachers often being ex-pupils. Rules for the teachers urged them to " ….. excite emulation in remembering the contents of Scripture ….. avoid corporal punishment as much as possible, especially during the time of public worship."

Education of Girls

The education of girls was even more piecemeal than that for boys. This was partly because many questioned the need for them to be educated at all, except perhaps at home or in the household of a family of standing. The "luckier" ones (e.g. in Bishop's Tachbrook and Tanworth-in-Arden) were typically offered the "three R's" plus sewing and needlework.

Wasperton House promised in 1821 the head's unremitting attention to "the Education, morals and domestic comforts of her pupils." As Leamington became fashionable, families would come to stay for the season. Advertisements in local papers would offer education for "young ladies during the bathing season." Improvements came slowly, but provision remained rudimentary. In Harbury, in 1856, toilet facilities for all girls were described thus: "For girls there are two closets, each containing two pupils side by side." But things were on the move, albeit slowly. King's High School, Warwick opened in 1879 and Clarendon House Ladies in Kineton in 1882.

Opposition to schools for girls came from all kinds of sources. A notice in the "Courier" (May 10 1884) publicised objections to a scheme proposed by the Principals of Ladies' Schools. The first (of many) objection was: "This meeting considers that a Public High School for Girls is not needed in the town. That all educational requirements are fully met in the existing schools ...."

When Leamington High School for Girls opened in small premises near the top of the Parade in 1884, a letter to the Leamington Spa Courier summed up much local and national feeling. It lamented the dangers of "those high pressure schools" and urged all concerned to be "content with the old-fashioned seminary presided over by a refined and cultivated woman".

A speech delivered by the Reverend Edward Thring (Headmaster of Uppingham School) at the school's prize-giving some years later suggested some ambivalence in his perception of the aims of education for girls: "We are to be trained for the battle of life. And if there is no battle practice, no drill, what sort of soldiers shall we be?" but: "Don't despise cookery; remember, cookery to the vast majority of mankind means home .... Be winsome, loveable, above all, helpful."

One end of century initiative was a college at Studley where young women were trained in agriculture and horticulture.

Even by 1915 there was no state provision for the secondary education of girls in Stratford. The choice was a daily train journey to Warwick or a private girls' high school. Similarly, girls from Rugby had to travel to Nuneaton to receive a state education. It was a long day: arriving at 7.50 a.m. and leaving at 5.40 p.m. Not till 1919, when the County purchased a private school, was there L.E.A. secondary provision for girls in Rugby.

Inter-Church Rivalry

Catholic schools tended to open later in the century than National schools. An exception was in Princethorpe, where, to this day, the only school is a Catholic one. This was probably due to support in various forms from the nearby Priory, formerly a Benedictine monastery, now Princethorpe College. Francis Newdigate, M.P. for North Warwickshire, successfully urged a government committee to enquire into "monastic institutions" such as Princethorpe to fire a warning shot. He spoke of dark rumours of "seven underground cells with very strong doors and very good locks". Subsequent enquiry established that these were merely for storing apples and coal.

Children's loyalty to their church schools was often flimsy, as recorded by the head of Atherstone Boys English School: "Noticed that the Roman Catholic children come here for a while and then go back to their Chapel School, and then after a while return to our school again."

Competition between denominations often did hit attendance. The head at St. Mary's Leamington noted this when he wrote of "competition of other schools with greater teaching power, better apparatus and attractions in the shape of magic lanterns." The purchase of a 'magic lantern', an embryonic slide projector, had lured children away to a nearby Congregationalist school, even though by now the lantern was an invention nearly 200 years old. At Bedworth Central Girls "31 children stayed away from school to see the Foundation Stone of the R.C. Church laid." But retribution was swift, albeit not divine: "All children who stayed away yesterday without leave were kept in this morning till 1 o'clock."

Rudimentary Provision

Some children received what education they did in workhouses such as those at the Union Workhouse at Shipston-on-Stour. Children were often placed there because they were illegitimate; they were taught by a resident schoolmistress. Once again, the curriculum would be the 3R's plus religious instruction. Reading materials included maps, bibles and Isaac Watts's 'Scripture History'. But those who were educated in designated schools may have fared little better in accommodation and resources. Even later in the nineteenth century, newly-opened buildings were depressingly cramped. In Exhall near Alcester: "The village school opened in 1872. It was a tiny building, 25 feet long, fourteen feet wide and fifteen feet high."

At Radford Semele (1859) "….. the school was so dark that the children could not see their slates." The school at Ilmington was dismissed as "a wretched hole of a room" (1851). At Ullenhall, two small rooms were lit by oil lamps with a fire in each room. The flooring comprised wooden blocks, and boys and girls were segregated by a wooden fence. At Churchover: "The school-house, though roomier, was little better than a cottage, the street door opening directly into the living room." A school built in 1814 in Hillmorton near Rugby was known as 'The Dump'. Tolerance of individual needs was limited: "Edward Vernon has given me a great deal of trouble because he will write with his left hand. I made him stand by the easel with his left side against it." (Vicarage Street, 1868)

A New Intake

After the Education Act of 1870, schools for the first time contained children who had previously received no formal teaching and who came from families who had never attended school. The Rector of Rugby recorded his alarm thus: "Another problem we had to face was that the whole social structure of Rugby was threatened by the coming of the first big works, in whose wake a new type of urban population came flooding in. Both day school and church accommodation threatened to be hopelessly inadequate." John Drew of Kenilworth claims: "It was not unusual for boys to wear petticoats and hobnailed boots, for clothes were handed down from the older to the younger children irrespective of sex."

Attendance

Many heads lambasted the parents for lack of support. Here is the head of the Cubbington C.E.: "It is my opinion the labouring classes care very little whether their children are educated or not. They ask for leave to do the most frivolous work ...." Things were no better at Stoneleigh: "School almost empty this morning. Children gone acorning after the frost and the winds."

At Pailton, the Head was clearly losing patience: "I despair of obtaining regularity of attendance, unless the committee adopt some rules and have them adhered to ......" (1864). Yet years later his successor was still noting such unsatisfactory causes for non-attendance as "peeling willow" (1867) and "following the hounds through the village" (1881). The head of Atherstone North Boys listed seven boys who "make a habit of staying away on fair days".

Some parents then, as still today, disliked 'part' weeks when schools reopened midweek after holidays: "Several parents do not think it worth their while to send their children until Monday next, today being Thursday." At Brinklow, "Parents will keep children away for such reasons as 'Not up in time' and 'Had no time to wash them'. On other occasions the Head might have welcomed more attention to cleanliness, however dilatory: "Sent boy home to be cleaned. Made some of the dirtier children wash at the pump, but this child too bad to remedy himself."

Sometimes, the reason was simply financial hardship: "Called on some of the parents this morning. Several said they could not send their children because they had no work. I gave them permission to send them and pay when they get work." (Vicarage Street, 1867), and "There has been a thin attendance of the children all the week. The Weavers and Miners being out of work, the parents have been unable to pay for their schooling." (Bedworth Central Girls, June 20, 1879)

At Shrubland Street, Leamington, the Head observed more dispassionately: "On account of the entrance of the Circus, attendance very poor ...." (1885). Other reasons over the years for non-attendance, noted in logbooks, included "cattle plague in Curdworth"; "Sale at Water Orton of Christmas Fat Stock"; "Excuses of the usual kind .... 'minding baby' ..... 'gathering acorns' ....."; and the rather morbid " ..... the body lost yesterday being dragged from the water, many obtained leave from their parents to go and watch" (St. Mary's, Leamington).

Local dignitaries were often accorded the same respect as the high and mighty, thereby providing legitimate chances to escape school: "Funeral of G. H. Nelson Esq. Half-day holiday"   (Emscote, Mar 1898);and "Half holiday for funeral of Queen Victoria" (Emscote, Feb 1901).

At Radford Semele pupils truanted because of: "Indian and Colonial visitors to Leamington." At Atherstone Boys' English School the Head noted in 1870: "Several boys away today, owing to their parents killing the Christmas pigs." The Hampton Lucy logbook recorded plaintively in 1876: "It seems strange, but I find many of the children's parents are averse to them learning at home, and even go as far as to order them not to do so."

Royal Visit

Queen Victoria visited Leamington in 1856. A special platform was erected for schoolchildren: "On this stage were placed 2300 schoolchildren, under the management of Messrs. Baker and Coles, schoolmasters." Messrs. Baker and Coles surely deserve their footnote in history for supervising that lot! One idly wonders how many and how near the available toilets were.

The State Investigates

From 1850 onwards there was a series of investigations which "comprehensively anatomised the conditions of the nation's schools". The list included:

<u>1861:</u> The Newcastle Commission - an enquiry into 'The Present State of Popular Education in England'

<u>1864:</u> The Clarendon Commission - enquiry into the revenues, management and the nine chief public schools, including Rugby.

<u>1867:</u> The Taunton Commission - to cover the remaining schools, i.e. other than elementary and the public schools.

The Clarendon Commission specified responsibilities for governors not so different from some of their responsibilities today. They were to be " ..... the guardians and trustees of the permanent interests of the school" and should include people ..... conversant with the world and with the requirements of active life. " They had to decide what should be taught, and they were responsible for the appointment of the head. They often included examples of "the great and the good". Even at elementary schools such as Rugby's St. Matthew's at this time the managers included the vicar, a captain and a lieutenant colonel, and their early agenda items ranged from requests for increases in salary to unsatisfactory water closets.

(I note in passing that my own governing body recently devoted much time to a pay policy ..... and to the state of the boys' toilets.)

Payment by Results

The Newcastle Commission produced a report in 1861 critical of the teaching and standards in elementary schools. The outcome of the report was a decision that would greatly influence the daily lives of schools into the next century. The decision was to make a school's grant dependent on how well its pupils performed in an annual examination. This scheme became known as 'payment by results' and was introduced in 1862. In the same year it became obligatory for schools to keep a logbook.

It is salutary to reflect on the 'payment by results' policy, because it is similar in many respects to what we currently have: annual tests on "the basics" etc. The only difference is that, instead of a direct link between results and grant, we now have published league tables based on test results whose explicit intention is to encourage parents to "shop around". If parents do move their children to another school, money follows the children. Thus, schools performing less well are likely to lose income.

Clever children then were able to take the tests earlier, while "dull" children were often held back. The result was that each standard was taken by children of a variety of ages. The laconic, ledger-like content of logbooks revealed little of the strain that "payment by results" caused, but the head of the Borough School in Warwick showed stresses not unlike those reportedly induced by present-day OFSTED inspections.

"Examination Day yesterday and today, and from the way we have worked, and the overtime and overpressure expended we ought to do well. Only those who have attained 90% or over can understand the amount of screwing and overpressure used to produce such results. On an average I have spent three hours overtime in school daily for three months ...."

In 1889 - Dr Fenton, Medical Officer in adjacent Coventry, referred to the "prejudicial effect" of the grant system: "The probability of ..... producing disease is lost sight of"

The gradual growth in freedom from the 'payment' by results era was reflected in more freedom in heads' use of logbooks. Ernest Castle, head of Little Packington School (1905-15) used his to criticise his managers for lack of interest, the cleaners for throwing rubbish over the hedge and his daughter (a teacher there) for regular unpunctuality. He felt able to use red ink to underline a point about which he felt strongly.

Punishment

Punishment then obviously extended to pupils' behaviour <u>outside</u> school, as is confirmed by entries in a punishment book for Polesworth Nethersole: "Hitting girls on the way home" and "Misbehaviour after school hours." At Marston Boys, pupils were caned for "setting traps in the wood and snaring rabbits" and "pulling turnips out of the field" and even "playing in the standing hay."

At Exhall, the logbook recorded the phenomenon of the recidivist through 1888 and 1889: "John Smith stole a quantity of chalk from the school ....." (12th Nov, 1888); "John Smith received a caning for very bad behaviour." (26th Nov); "As usual, John Smith continues to give a great deal of trouble. ..." (22nd Jan, 1889); "..... he seems altogether incorrigible ....." (5th Feb); and finally " ..... John Smith has been expelled ....." (18th Feb)

Parents were by no means always tolerant of caning: "Mrs Hayes visited school to object to caning of her 2 children. She will withdraw them if it happens again." The Head of the Borough School, Warwick offered an early example of doubts of the morality of caning children: "Been making an effort to do without the stick but only partially successful. Might if I had no young teacher."

Children Run Wild at Wolvey

Wolvey had a church school, and therefore was provided for. But denominational clashes in the 1890's caused the head in anger to close the school because so many parents exercised their 'conscience clause'. The school remained closed for eight months, causing "a hundred children to run wild through the village." Fortunately, a temporary school was opened in the Baptist Rooms for some by now "desperately backward" children.

Salaries

There seem to have been considerable variations in the salaries paid to headteachers. In 1806, Thomas Tibbetts at Claverdon received ten pounds per annum. Compare this with the eleven guineas given to Esther Hudson at Charlecote in 1868 and no rapid pay-rises were to be seen, apparently. There was evidence of considerable variety: £15 p.a. to the head at Grandborough but £40 p.a. to the head at Willoughby, both at roughly the same time. Nationally agreed pay scales were a long way off.

The Creation of School Boards: 1870

The 1870 Education Act was a significant moment for the creation of local education authorities. The Act was the work of W.E. Forster, a man with local connections; his wife was the daughter of Dr. Arnold and, therefore, sister of poet and H.M.I. Matthew Arnold. It ordered an audit of elementary school places in each parish. Where a local voluntary school already existed, no further action was taken. But where voluntary agencies had failed to provide a school place for every child, the government decided that its intention to provide universal education would need action. The Act therefore established School Boards - in effect, the first local education authorities. They were directly elected by ratepayers and they were charged with providing such schools as were necessary to supplement local voluntary initiative. They had powers to enforce attendance at all schools, voluntary and board. The larger boards had committee and sub-committee systems. They could, if they wished, pay the fees of the poorest children. To avoid conflict with nonconformists and others, a compromise was reached over religious teaching whereby they could withdraw their children from scripture lessons if they were sent to a Church of England school. Thus, a dual system emerged : church schools and board schools. To this day the same duality can be seen in small towns such as Polesworth, Southam and Whitnash.

Boards could be established in villages as well as towns. The villages of Newbold-on-Avon and Long Lawford shared a very active Board which generated much local interest. One of its elections in 1897 attracted thirteen candidates, and the turnout was high : 74% in Lawford and 82% in Newbold. The Board members took their responsibilities seriously. An evening meeting that same year lasted four hours, with the reading of minutes and correspondence occupying one hour.

Water Orton School, opened in 1878, was then part of the district of Aston and the first school to be opened by the Aston School Board at a cost of £300. School openings were often accompanied by much celebration in the community. Water Orton School opening triggered a 'tea and entertainment', the latter including "a pianoforte duet, stylishly played ..... a very clever and gentlemanly entertainment in the art of conjuring and legerdemain ..... the entertainment concluding with a description and an exhibition of the Telephone" (Coleshill Chronicle). This last item must have been quite an event: Bell did not perfect his telephone system until the year before. The school from its outset was presented as a community resource. It would be available for "lectures, entertainments, public meeting and such like."

Bath Place School in Leamington was just one of many to be opened with what the local press called "full Masonic honours". A procession included representatives of various lodges and was preceded by the Warwickshire Yeomanry Band, playing "the gay notes of 'The Entered Apprentice'."

England and Wales thus became divided into school districts which were based on the existing municipal boroughs and parishes. All ratepayers were eligible to stand for Board elections, including those working men who had recently gained the vote after the 1867 Reform Act. Votes could be distributed among candidates or allocated to a single candidate, a system known as "plumping". The first such election in the country was in Manchester in December 1870. Much of Warwickshire was slower to respond, encouraging the Church to make desperate attempts to increase the number of school places: "There is scarcely a village in our County which is not putting its school house in order and ascertaining if they have sufficient accommodation." (Leamington Spa Courier 17th December 1870)

Nuneaton and its surrounding villages successfully fought to retain their church dominated voluntary system. Haselor reportedly had a School Board but no school. Leamington and Warwick both procrastinated. Even in January 1881 the Courier was able to report that in Leamington " ..... the prospect of a School Board is not quite so imminent as was imagined", but the first Board was elected in April that year. Approximately half of those eligible actually cast a vote, although many voters declined to take part under the erroneous impression that not voting would excuse their having to pay the School Board rate. At the time of the election, the local paper asserted " ..... respectable and intelligent members of the working classes will inevitably feel some repugnance at sending their children to sit side by side with the children of the idle and dissolute, brought in by compulsion from the gutter ....." Though the churches had opposed the establishment of a Board, they had representatives on it, for example the Vicar. Elections engendered much interest: two large public meetings containing "heated harangues".

Warwick too delayed. It did elect a School Attendance Committee in 1876, but it was not until adverse H.M.I. reports on St. Nicholas Infants' Schoolroom and the buildings of the School of Industry in 1880 that impetus to establish a Board developed. The Inspector had claimed that of the 2045 children requiring places in Warwick, there was accommodation for 1383 only. The Warwick Board finally began on 1 June 1882. Until 1888, places on the Warwick Board were not even contested; the 1888 elections were the first, with eleven candidates contesting seven seats. Once the Board was formed, schools such as Coten End and Westgate opened at each end of the town, in 1884 as new schools, and the Board began to respond to despairing cries such as that of the head of the Borough School: "Present classrooms are almost valueless to me - only able to use them for collective lessons and then one half must stand while the other half sits."

At Henley-in-Arden, the first School Board Election also had to wait until 1881, but it did then generate enough enthusiasm for a poem to be written eulogising one of the candidates:

"In Henley Town there now does dwell   But like all men of sense and truth
A man with honest heart,   Has enemies quite a horde,
Who, in the question of the day,   Who try with all their might, and main
Must play a noble part.   To keep him off the Board .... "

There was much more.

Atherstone was another example of a procrastinating town, electing its Board only under government threat, but subsequently protesting to its M.P. in 1902 when the

Board was under threat, and managers were envisaged as no more than "invoice clerks". Once established, Boards more than compensated for initial apathy. At a riotous meeting in Stratford Town for elections to the Board, there was booing, hissing and chairs were thrown.

The Boards would continue until July 1903, when the Warwickshire Local Education Authority would replace them.

Standards: of Work and Behaviour

Standards, then as now, whether of building or of children's learning, dogged the efforts of schools. The Warwick and Warwickshire Advertiser (14th October 1884) reported: "The Coten End Board Schools will be opened on Tuesday next. It was originally arranged to open them last Monday, but this was afterwards found impossible in consequence of the whole of the arrangements not having been completed."

Soon after the delayed opening, the Headmistress, one Emma Jones, decided to examine the children in Standard One. The results dismayed her:

Arithmetic
Number who could add up to 10 mentally   :   3
Number who have no notion   :   20

Writing
Number who can write or form letters   :   2
Number who have no notion whatever   :   21

More Problem Pupils

Meanwhile, problems persisted, no matter what the kind of school. Suggested remedies for ill-health offered simplicity but little sympathy: "Attendance very poor owing to several being away with sores on their heads and faces. I strongly recommend to several of their parents a regular application of soap and water every day" (Sept 29 1884, Cubbington C.E.).

Other offences recalled in logbooks of the late nineteenth century included " ..... annoyance caused by knocking at school doors late at night. Caught William Owen in the act" and "John Gill insubordinate - refused without the slightest cause to take down a sum upon his slate and work it." These were both recorded at Brinklow, where the Head also made a familiar complaint: "Bad spelling attributed to local speech. Children do not hear a correct pronunciation."

Illiteracy remained rife. In Ansley in 1882, one third of the signatories to the marriage certificate could not sign their name and had to make their mark. Railway vandalism was evident even then. Ernest Carter had to deal with a complaint that two

Little Packington pupils had "thrown stones and a half brick onto the engine of the M.R. train at 8.35."

Even when the cane was ubiquitous, some heads agonised over its use. Carter wrote despairingly of " ..... Kate the pest (who) suffers slightly a form of imbecility and it is useless to cane or punish her." Some heads cast about for different punishments " ..... another punishment was to stand in a corner and hold a pile of slates above our head" (Ex pupil of Borough School, 1890's).

Object Lessons

Object lessons were intended to arouse the natural curiosity of the children and to develop their interest in the world around them. Sessions made use of the senses, observation and new vocabulary. They made much use of discussion and questioning and were in some ways reminiscent of our current Literacy Hour, except that in the latter the 'text' is or should be the 'object' of the children's attention.

A sample list from Wilmote (1883) illustrated the eclectic mix of topics:

Paper	Colour green
Candle	Potato
Bird's Nest	Salt

At Birdingbury the list included salt, but added butter, grass and slate.

The curriculum at St. Paul's, Stockingford included lessons to Standard V on famous people. They included leaders such as Pitt (both Younger and Older), Walpole (our first Prime Minister) and the Duke of Wellington (both military leader and Prime Minister). In the following year Raleigh, Cromwell and Nelson were added. The only woman to make the list was prison reformer Elizabeth Fry, though Standard 6 would also learn of Mary, Queen of Scots and Lady Jane Grey. The songs chosen by schools such as St. Paul's were a bizarre mix of the patriotic: "Our Country's Flat" and the traditional: "A hunting we will go."

Resources

Meanwhile, elsewhere education was moving into a period of technological innovation. Many L.E.A. schools would not receive electricity for another forty or more years. But Rugby School formed its 'Electric Light Company' before the end of the century, with its housemasters as principal shareholders.

Schools became adept at maximising such resources as they had. The logbooks of Ilmington School reported temperatures so cold in 1894 that " ..... the master borrowed a ladder so that he could place sandbags against the East wall." Two years later sandbags (the same ones? We are not told) were being deployed in "the teaching of avoir du pois."

School Treats

Few accounts survive of the 'fun' if any in nineteenth century schooling. Here is one exception. An event that enlivened the daily routines of many children was "the school treat". Edward Lovesey described a typical example at Gaydon in August 1884. There would be tea, games, and a talk by the vicar and then more games, all outdoors if the weather was good. The Gaydon event was enlivened by a glass of cowslip wine for each pupil, the recipe for which is thoughtfully provided:

One gallon cowslip flowers	3 pounds white sugar
One gallon water	Two oranges
One lemon	Half an ounce of yeast

Perhaps not so potent as its name might have suggested!

Conclusion

It had taken 750 years to take Warwickshire from a time when schools were unknown to a point where they were almost ubiquitous. The next 100 years would take universal schooling forward rather more rapidly.

3

Warwickshire becomes a Local Education Authority

The name of Arthur James Balfour, Prime Minister of Great Britain from 1902-5, is seldom recalled these days. In a recent B.B.C. poll of historians he came near to the bottom in a league table of Prime Ministers. Yet the Education Act, passed in 1902, established a system of education that is still largely intact one hundred years later. The 1902 Act placed education in the hands of county and county borough councils. Commonly known as Balfour's Act of 1902, it was inspired by a well known civil servant of the day: Sir Robert Morant. Its chief objectives were to unify and to improve elementary and secondary education, and it was deemed to be sufficiently important for Balfour personally to pilot the Act through the House of Commons.

Ironically then, as now, part of the agenda for educational reform was to endeavour to bring educational standards up to the level of those achieved in the countries of European competitors such as Germany. The Warwick and Warwickshire Advertiser for 30th January 1902 reported a lecture by Dr. Macnamara, M.P. in which he warned that defeat in the markets of the world was " ….. more serious than one on the field of battle. The danger of this country is that British people have a notion that they are divinely endowed with a model of supremacy."

The Act enabled the new local authorities to plan and co-ordinate policy across a much wider area than the erstwhile School Boards had been able to do. An indication of how controversial it was is the length of time it took from first reading (March 24th 1902) to becoming law. It did not finally leave Parliament until December 18th, and then only after the government had been forced to use the guillotine procedure. The Liberal Party, given its close links with the nonconformist movement, opposed the bill, as most schools likely to benefit were Church of England or Roman Catholic. Lloyd George spoke 138 times on the Bill in just one parliamentary session. Corrie Grant, Liberal Member of Parliament for Rugby, was prominent in debate, challenging Balfour directly, and moving delaying amendments. But there was also widespread support, from local branches of the National Union of Teachers for instance. The N.U.T. was also concerned to impress its demands on government as L.E.A. control became imminent. The union recommended in 1903 new salary scales which included "£100 (with house) for a Headmaster, £115 (without a house) and, for headmistresses, £10 below that suggested for masters."

The rapidly developing Labour Party movement opposed the Bill. It wished to prevent destruction of the School Boards and the local control they afforded. It also sought secular rather than "clerical" control of schools, with subsidised denominational teaching. The Social Democratic Federation asserted in its 1902 Manifesto " ….. that education in public schools should be secular, free from the teaching of any form of theological creed or dogma ...."

The practical effect of the Act nationally was that 2568 school boards were supplanted by 328 local education authorities. In Warwickshire, this was translated into the replacement of school boards in places such as Atherstone and Rugby by one authority. Leamington and Nuneaton became what were called part 3 authorities as a result of a concession to local feeling. Such boroughs with a population over 10,000 retained responsibility for elementary education only.

The new Act did not begin to operate until April 1903, the delay being deliberate to allow nonconformist anger to cool. They resented the notion of church education "on the rates". Warwickshire sought a further delay till July 1, to give themselves more time to prepare. Meanwhile, local church initiative had not abandoned effort. Our Lady's R.C. School, Alcester, opened in 1902, just before it would join the L.E.A. family as an infant.

An Embryonic Education Committee

An Education Act Committee began to meet on 5th November 1902. Its task was to prepare Warwickshire for its new role as Local Education Authority. The Chairman, J.S. Dugdale informed them that he and his vice-chairman, Bolton King, had been considering the question of the organisation of the staff once the Bill became law. He explained that he had heard of a retired H.M.I. who might be a desirable officer to lead Warwickshire into its new responsibilities.

The Committee met again on Saturday 29th November 1902 to meet this gentleman: one Gerald Fitzmaurice who had led inspections in Derbyshire but also had exercised supervision over Cheshire, Staffordshire and most of Lincolnshire. He explained the matters that would require rapid decisions by the authority. If he were to become Director, he would want a day a week to himself for correspondence, a sub-inspector, a clerk, a "boy" and he would prefer that financial matters be taken off his hands.

The committee was reportedly impressed, and met again on 12th December to agree a job description including staffing, curriculum, furniture, pupil teachers and office organisation. The Education Act Committee then voted unanimously to recommend his appointment to the County Council. The County Council met on 4th February 1903 to recommend that one Education Committee be appointed and that it be called the Warwickshire Education Committee. Early in May, the County Council met again for a crucial meeting, as Warwickshire was due formally to commence its duties as an L.E.A. on July 1st 1903. This was to be the last County Council meeting before that historic event. The meeting was the longest on record. The Warwick Advertiser spoke of "an instructive although not very pleasant scene" with "members impatient to catch their train when 3.30 arrived."

Fitzmaurice's appointment was "stubbornly contested". Councillor Bowen spoke acidly of: "this superannuated gentleman." Councillor Blackham urged them "not to engage a lame horse." Councillor Johnson replied tartly: "There's too much despising of grey hairs already Mr Blackham. I don't think we should have a brainless man because he's young."

On May 9th 1903 the Warwick Advertiser helpfully compiled what would now doubtless be called an "audit" of the L.E.A. responsibilities:

"Provided" or Board Schools	39
Roman Catholic	16
National & Church	141
British	2
Parochial	38
Wesleyan	1
	237

Teaching then and now was a predominantly female profession. Three quarters of elementary school teachers were women, earning an average 25% less than their male counterparts.

The first full meeting of the "Warwickshire Education Committee" took place in the Grand Jury Room, County Hall on Tuesday 12th May 1903, and it met quarterly thereafter. Bolton King was elected Deputy Chair. It began to work its way through a formidable agenda: contracts for coal, books and furniture, procedures to dismiss two headteachers, a memorandum on children with defective eyesight, epileptic children in Rugby, extra accommodation needed at Hillmorton, Polesworth and Amington ... and the purchase of bikes at £12 each for attendance officers (one schedule on 'Rules for Enforcing School Attendance was dated 'May 1203'!)

Warwickshire Takes Control

Warwickshire assumed its responsibilities on July 1st 1903, having pleaded successfully for extra time to prepare for its new role. However, its powers in respect of elementary education excluded the more populous boroughs such as Leamington, Nuneaton and Sutton Coldfield. There had, of course, been preliminary 'auditing'. On June 17, a W.C.C. lawyer visited faraway Long Compton School to inspect the buildings and make an inventory of the furniture. Many schools recorded the change of management, though in characteristically terse and objective style: "The school this day comes under the control of Warwickshire County Council" (Curdworth, July 1, 1903); "Today the Warwickshire County Council undertook the Management of Schools" (Leek Wootton, July 1, 1903); "The schools from this date are under the New Local Education Authority, a result of the Education Act of 1902" (Fenny Compton, July 1, 1903); "First day under the County Council" (Wolston, July 1, 1903).

At Stretton-on-Dunsmore some sense of a momentous occasion was generated by the previous day's entry "last day that the school is under the Trustees of the

Stretton Charities" followed by: "From today, the school is under the Education Committee of the Warwickshire County Council."

Further from Warwick, schools might be less impressed: "Ordinary routine throughout the week" (Austrey, July 3, 1903).

At the opposite end of the county, the head of Quinton had his own view of what was the significant event of that week: "Punished Sam Russell for talking." There was no mention of the new 'bosses'.

The New Director Moves On

Fitzmaurice did not last long. Not only was his contract not renewed, but Bolton King was persuaded to renounce his political affiliations and his position as Alderman and to take over as Director three months before the end of Gerald Fitzmaurice's contract. This, in spite of the fact that Bolton King had been a controversial candidate in a by-election in Stratford on Avon in 1901 where the police were called to restore order in several election meetings.

Clearly Mr Fitzmaurice's period of office had not gone well. Why the hasty departure? County Council minutes are not helpful on matters such as these. They tend only to report decisions, rather than the reasons for these decisions. The Warwick and Warwickshire Advertiser of January 23rd 1904 provided some clues. In its report on the proceedings of the Finance Sub-Committee, as it considered the staffing of the Education Office, it quoted Alderman Lakin as saying of Fitzmaurice: "It has been found that attendance on the various committees and supervising of the staff of clerks in the education department was work for which he was not suited."

The agreement to terminate his appointment prematurely seems to have been amicable. Mr Fitzmaurice was said to have entered it "voluntarily" and he was praised as a man of " ..... sound judgement, immense technical knowledge of elementary education and was overflowing with tact," though there were enigmatic references to "the little troubles we have had all around the county."

Bolton King became Director of Education in February 1904. Mr Fitzmaurice immediately became County Inspector of Schools, still on a salary of £400 per annum. Alderman Newdigate opposed this "multiplication of officials", and the Honourable Mabel Verney raised "a white-gloved hand" against the committee's recommendation of Bolton King, saying: "I told Mr King this morning I would not vote for him (laughter)."

She also opposed the possible appointment of another official (nameless), writing that she would not "borrow half a crown to get drunk with him." She claimed that a great deal of the education department's work had been "manufactured".

Other key officers included an Assistant Director (Clement G Bone: £250 p.a.) and Chief School Attendance Officer (Major Reger: £150 p.a. but to rise by annual increments of £10 to £200). There were 9 people listed under 'Education Office Staff' including three typists at £58.10s a year, and an office boy at 7/6d per week. There were additionally three clerks listed under Education Finance.

As an indicator of the growth in volume of business to be dealt with, by 1905 the bound volume of Education Committee and Sub-committee minutes contained an index of 15 pages from 'Accounts, Payments of ....' to 'Wroxall, Caretaker's Salary'. By June 30th 1905 the various sub-committees set up had met often, "Staffing and Salaries" 30 times for example. However, Cookery, School Gardens and Manual Instruction had met only 6 times.

An Inspector Called

Gerald Fitzmaurice held his new position until he resigned on June 30th 1907. Many of his reports on schools, often no more than a dozen lines of largely factual information, survive in the bound volumes of committee papers. He reported on schools all over the county from Hillmorton to Studley, from Bedworth to Stratford. His reports had little to say about the curriculum, and their emphasis on the factual may have prompted some elected members to wonder whether collection and dissemination of information needed such a relatively well paid official. There is evidence in logbooks that his advice carried weight in schools. New Bilton School in 1905 re-organised its classes "based on Mr Fitzmaurice's suggestions". However, another entry in February 1907 (he appears to have visited the school annually) indicated the low-level nature of matters the school felt deserving of his attention:

"Gerald Fitzmaurice visited the school ..... his attention was drawn to the great difficulty the teachers had in opening the swing doors, it being an impossibility for the little ones to do so. Consequently the teacher in the babies' room was continually running in and out during winter."

The Finance Sub-committee met in July 1907 to consider how to replace him. As an epitaph, their views were less than fulsome: "We think that the work of this office can be done efficiently without any addition to the staff beyond a new office boy."

Shortly afterwards one was appointed - at five shillings a week. Bolton King's salary was raised from £400 to £500. Thus Fitzmaurice's departure enabled a saving of £299 15s a year to be made. The Education Committee, also in July 1907, did express appreciation. The Chairman moved a motion expressing gratitude, but it was passed 'nem con' rather than unanimously.

After all this excitement, the committee was able to turn its mind to less political matters : deciding against the provision of Noah's Arks but for a tender for 'non-flam' flannelette, for example.

The Warwickshire Education Committee

The first Education Committee was an assemblage of some of "the great and the good" from throughout Warwickshire. There were two earls, two 'honourables', one professor, one M.P., six clergy, the headmaster of Rugby School, and a co-opted Knight. Another councillor, William Johnson, was shortly to become an M.P. If there were any doubts as to the importance of many of these personages, their addresses would have clinched their prestigious credentials: Blythe Hall Coleshill, Wroxall Abbey, Ragley Hall Alcester, Fillongley Hall Coventry for example. This was the committee with which first Fitzmaurice and, rapidly, Bolton King would endeavour to establish an education system in Warwickshire.

It is perhaps not surprising that the newly formed Labour Party was suspicious of county councils and their hierarchical nature. "The new education authorities will be whatever the squires and parsons ..... choose to make them." ("Justice" May 24 1902).

An elaborate system of main and sub committees was established. They included main committees such as Attendance, Sites and Buildings and Finance, and sub-committees such as Staffing and Salaries, Prizes and Medical Questions. To take the example of just one committee member: Reverend V. K. Fortescue, he is listed as a member of twenty-one committees of different kinds. Of the total of 374 meetings that ran between 1903 and 1905, the committees he served on met 279 times. I have not examined the records to see how many he attended, but this gives some idea of the potential commitments of an Education Committee member.

During 1904-5 the Committee worked to develop the teaching of practical subjects such as Cookery, Needlework, Gardening and Woodwork in its elementary schools. Cookery was introduced into schools from Polesworth in the north to Kineton in the south of the county. Rugby was particularly well provided with six centres, three of them church schools: National, Wesleyan and R.C. In Kenilworth, Warwick and Stratford opportunities were available in both National and R.C. schools. A maximum of 54 scholars was set as a rule for any demonstration lessons. Opportunities for "Manual Instruction" (woodwork) were more limited with two centres at Kenilworth: St. John and St. Nicholas, but none at Rugby. Practical gardening was more widely available, though only to boys aged over eleven. The pupil-teacher ratio was high: "There must be at least one teacher for every fourteen scholars," was the regulation. Provision was also made in some village schools, often in quite small centres such as Amington, Haselor and Lighthorne.

The need to provide places to eliminate overcrowding led the Committee to announce ten new schools, mainly in the north and east of the county. Meanwhile, five "temporary" schools were opened. Additional accommodation was provided across the county from Warton in the north to Salford Priors in the south. Notwithstanding overcrowding, the Committee strove to reward high attendance. Any school with 95% or more attendance for three successive weeks could claim a half holiday as a reward.

Two Years' Hard Work

By 1905 the Department had a Director (£400 per annum), a County Inspector (£400 p.a.) and an Assistant Director (£250 p.a.); the first two could travel first class, but the Assistant Director only second class; a County Surveyor with responsibility for sites, buildings and repairs (£250 "additional remuneration" p.a.), a Chief School and Attendance Officer (£150 p.a.). To support their work there were two accountants, two clerks, three typists and an office boy, the last mentioned earning seven shillings and sixpence a week. To complete the personnel there were Mr. and Mrs. Paynting who performed the functions of "resident storekeeper and caretaker". The growth in department personnel that would continue, with few checks, throughout the century, was already well underway.

Bolton King decided to take stock after the first two years of the Education Committee. The 1905 Handbook contains a summary of its work. One of the Committee's early pre-occupations had been with a lack of provision for the secondary education of girls highlighted by the Bryce Commission in 1895. The report stated that: "There are at present in the County only two Girls' Schools recognised by the Board of Education." One was Leamington High School, then sufficiently small to be located at 19 The Parade.

As a short-term measure, the Committee allocated "£450 for: "assisting existing private schools for girls." Gerald Fitzmaurice inspected "at their own request" a number of these schools including Arnold High, Rugby, antecedent of the present Rugby High School (a selective school for girls). By 1908, a decision was taken to open a girls' school in Nuneaton, then known as Nuneaton High.

In general the Committee was anxious to extend secondary education and, to this end, it increased scholarships from 27 to 56. Fifteen of these were reserved for pupils in parishes with a population of 2000 or less to ensure that pupils from rural schools were well represented.

There were attempts to increase Pupil Teacher numbers and new centres were opened at Warwick and Nuneaton. Then, as now, there was a shortage of teachers, at least at pupil level, estimated at about 150. Then, as now, recruitment among girls was much better than among boys. At the 1905 examinations for Pupil Teacher Candidate Scholarships 168 sat (33 boys, 135 girls). Eleven boys and fifty-eight girls failed.

By 1911 Bolton King had gained another assistant director. There was an Assistant Director for Higher Education and one for Elementary Education, both on salaries of £275 per annum. Bolton King's job description remained the same, but his salary stood at £500 per annum. He was still allowed first class travel expenses but the two Assistant Directors only second. Major Reger, Chief School Attendance Officer, had received annual incremental rises of £10, and his salary now stood at £200. However, his allowances remained unchanged from 1905 " ….third class railway fare when required, the necessary trap hire if found necessary, an allowance of 1/6d if compelled by his duties to be absent from Headquarters between 4.00 p.m. and 7.00 p.m. but if absent all night an additional amount of 5/-." The number of clerks had risen from two to five but typists had dropped from three to two. There is no mention of an office boy.

Thirty-three "Major and Special Scholars" won scholarships and exhibitions in universities, twenty-eight of which were to either Oxford or Cambridge.

Another L.E.A. development was to recruit eleven permanent supply teachers (four men and seven women) to help schools to deal with long-term absence of staff. From 1910 the Committee had begun to offer a limited number of bursaries of £5 to enable teachers to attend vacation courses at the Oxford University School of Geography. The Committee also "appropriated the sum of £50 for bursaries to enable Assistant Teachers at Secondary Schools …… to attend courses abroad in Modern Languages during the summer holidays."

Bolton King was an early exponent of accountability to elected members (through reports) and to the public. He introduced the idea of exhibitions of pupils' work, held centrally and open to the public. According to Elizabeth Meaton, in an exhibition in Leamington 1907, there were between 35,000 and 40,000 exhibits.

A subsequent one in Windsor Hall, Leamington attracted more than 15,000 visitors, though most of them with free tickets. Lady Mabel Verney sustained her role as committee sceptic, attacking some of the items on display. She was particularly scathing about needlework items; too much of it was "fancy work, disfigured by twopence halfpenny lace."

Games and Leisure Activities

Whether it was the disappearance of the Revised Code, or the replacement of the austere Queen Victoria on the throne by the fun-loving Edward VII, but memories of childish leisure pursuits became much more plentiful as the twentieth century moved into its stride. Marbles, hoops and whips with wooden tops were popular all over the county. The hoop might be no more than an iron band from a barrel. At Kenilworth, there were informal competitions to see who could whip a top furthest along the road from St. John's School to the Clock Tower. There were money-earning pastimes too. Boys collected acorns from Crackley Woods in the autumn and sold them to farmers for twopence or threepence a bag. There were other examples of a 'barter' economy: "Sometimes on the way to school we saw the "rag-man" who collected your old rags and in return gave you a balloon." (Wood Street, Rugby).

Leisure activities tended to be simple, cheap and diverse. Children from Bidford remember catching the train to Broom, and back, eating a penny bar of Nestlé's chocolate bought from a machine on the platform. Children living in Oxhill spent hours " ..... playing at houses with dust for sugar, dust mixed with water from the pump and decorated with wild-flower heads for puddings ....." At Haselor, youngsters played with "hob" shooters made from pieces of hawthorn with unripe berries used as ammunition. Of course, the time of year made a difference: "There seemed to be different seasons for different games. Winter time marbles under the street lights ....." (Collycroft, Bedworth). At Chesterton and Kingston the local boys played football on the green until "chased off by a farmer with a gun." The village green was often the location for cricket and football: 'You didn't need to cut the grass. It had no chance to grow.'

These games and leisure activities invariably contributed to learning of some sort: "I learned more by watching and collecting on my way to school than I ever did inside school. Sometimes the culverts would be full of frogs and toads ....." Lillian Bowen's journey to school had its educational value, including as it often did a pause to watch the blacksmith at work.

The children of Stratford had much cause to be grateful to novelist Marie Corelli. She paid for the whole of King Edward School to go to the circus, and on New Year's Day 1900 invited 1000 children from the National Schools to a party at the Memorial Theatre.

Mary Robertson recorded the popularity of rounders in Eathorpe and Wappenbury "as long as there were not too many cowpats around." In the same area, paper chases were popular, though she noted resignedly that reading indoors was not encouraged: "What are you doing sitting there? Get out in the fresh air." Perhaps just as well, for she was limited to fewer than a dozen books : Grimm, Hans Andersen, "The Water Babies", "Little Lord Fauntleroy" etc.

The earliest cinemas were opening, even in the smaller towns. The Electric Picture House, Shipston was opened in 1913 by Miss Elizabeth Ryder, also the proprietress of the Wisteria House School for gentlemen, situated opposite the cinema. Local children, including inmates of the workhouse, were invited to the opening.

Many reminiscences recall respect for the village policeman, backed by his ultimate informal sanction: 'a clip round the ear'. Not a moment's unpunctuality was tolerated: "The headmaster used to stand at the gate till 8.55 a.m. precisely and even if you were a minute late you got the cane which he carried with him" (Clapham Terrace). Chasing possible truants was a high priority, as an obituary of David Buchanan, Chairman of the School Attendance Committee in Rugby illustrated: "He personally called upon the parents of delinquents and emphasised the need for regularity."

Winter Time

Innocent pleasures then would horrify Health and Safety officials today: skating on the pond, swimming in the canal, sliding across icy playgrounds etc.

Then as now, pleasure and horror often arrived within minutes of one another. At Lapworth on Ash Wednesday in 1907 four pupils, returning from school on an icy day, decided to try to skate on a pond known as Spring Pit. All fell through the ice and drowned. One died trying to rescue the others, including his own brother. A simple memorial to this distressing event stands to this day in the lower part of the tranquil churchyard. As one stands at it, one cannot but reflect on the two or three hundred years of potential living that were destroyed on that spot in seconds ..... of marriages, children and grandchildren that might have been. Both the head and his wife (who taught there too) were very distressed and never fully recovered. They left the school and the area soon afterwards.

Winter was in any event often a test of endurance: "The school rooms were wretchedly cold this morning, temperatures below 40F and the ink frozen in the inkwells." Even in better weather, accommodation was evidently basic. Witness this L.E.A. report on Baddesley Ensor: "Behind the door is a primitive lavatory and there is a sheer drop of 3 feet to the floor of this ..... the one towel in this lavatory is very filthy."

Official Guidance

It is salutary to compare government advice then and now. In 1905, the Board of Education published its Handbook of Suggestions for Elementary School Teachers. It had this to say:

"The only uniformity of practice that the Board of Education desires to see .... is that each teacher shall think for himself and work out for himself such method of teaching as may ..... be best suited to the particular needs and conditions of the school."

Some fifty years later, Ronald Gould, General Secretary of the N.U.T., quoted this approvingly. This new freedom to determine the curriculum prompted debate about teaching methods across the county. Stratford N.U.T. held a lengthy debate on "new methods of teaching reading" as its contribution.

The Warwickshire Code of Regulations for Teachers

In 1913, The Committee published its first-ever 'Code of Regulations for Teachers' in Public Elementary Schools in the county. In a short preface, Bolton King thanked a student teacher for the suggestion that the various regulations for teachers needed codifying and to be assembled in one place rather than scattered among "the many circulars that have been issued." It is instructive to compare beliefs and practices then and now. In its 136 pages the Code covered everything from supply teachers to fire drill to opening of windows and ink. It had an 'A' list of subjects: Arithmetic, English Subjects (including History), Geography, Nature Study and Writing. Note the importance then attached to Geography, and the absence of any reference to Science in its broadest sense.

The 'B' list contained: Physical Exercises, Needlework, Drawing, Handwork and Music. Thus, there existed an embryonic division of subjects into what we might more recently have called 'Core' and 'Foundation'.

Its tone was often terse and dictatorial: "Certain lessons should never appear on any Time Table. There should be no such entries as "Object Lessons" "General Information" etc. Apparently, these should be subsumed elsewhere. Orders, presumably then as now controversial, were issued without amplification: "Formal lessons in grammar should not be given, except occasionally to the oldest pupils." (This statement makes it quite clear that neglect of the teaching of grammar was not as is often claimed an innovation of the sixties. A subsequent report on English teaching made it clear that such local instructions were replicated nationally.)

The Code gave unequivocal commands on timetabling: "Lessons in Music and Physical Exercises should be 20 minutes in length, but in the case of the former, 15 minutes is often enough." For under-fives it discouraged "all formal lessons in the 3 Rs."

It is never clear what the source of thinking for these edicts is, though there are clues. For example, the section on 'Handwork' is headed: 'Extracts from Report of Teachers' Committee on Handwork'. The Code struck early blows for equal opportunities "..... all girls should receive instruction in drawing as well" and "We are of the opinion that light Woodwork is suitable as a rule for pupils between the ages of 9 and 11, and we see no reason to restrict the subject to boys only." But work remained to be done on equal opportunities in staffing "..... in the post of Head Teacher of a school with less than 90 average attendance .... it is the Committee's practice to appoint a Head Mistress ....."

Some injunctions are so brief as to be puzzling: "In large schools Fire Drill should be practised." Why only large schools, given that many classrooms were over-crowded and most had stoves?

Though written in the name of the Committee, Bolton King's strong influence was in evidence, for example in the section on "Prefects". "The Committee attach great importance to the establishment of an effective system of Prefects or Monitors, and will consider the successful working of such a system as one of the chief indications that a school is satisfactory."

The onset of performance-related pay was evident in this short statement on heads' pay: "The Committee may, at their discretion, after considering H.M.I.'s reports on the school and all the other circumstances of the case, transfer Head Teachers .... to scale c above."

A five page section on the Education Office library explained eligibility and borrowing procedures. It subscribed to a wide variety of journals both generic ("Journal of Education") and subject-specific ("Journal of Geography"). There were no signs of subject journals for Maths, Science or Religious Instruction. Its opening times included Saturday mornings and both lanterns and slides could be borrowed.

The 1926 Code

I do not have a copy of the second edition of the Code, but a third edition, published in 1926, contained much that is similar but some significant additions. The first five pages were devoted to the responsibilities and membership of Teachers' Consultative Committees. Many of their duties would eventually form part of the job descriptions of advisers: advice, promotion of co-operation between different phases, encourage exchange of ideas etc.

There were now details of "Standards of Attainment" for children aged eleven in English and Arithmetic, another innovation not unlike the attainment levels we have today. The tone continued often to be brusque and dictatorial: "Elementary schoolchildren should not be entered for an external examination, except with the consent of H.M.I. and the Director of Education." There was now a section on "Central Schools" with an injunction to Heads to "prepare a three years' syllabus"

These new regulations went further than their predecessors on caning. The former merely stated the law. Now: "Corporal punishment should be avoided as much as possible and should very rarely be inflicted on girls and infants. The Committee will always consider that frequent infliction of it points to weak discipline." Given that caning was alive and widely used fifty years later, one can surmise that this was a bold statement, ahead of its times.

Its section on Science (new this time) testified to the more laissez-faire approach then advocated for a broader curriculum. "It is difficult of course to teach much science at schools without special equipment, but <u>where there is a teacher interested in the subject</u> (my underlinings), a few simple general principles should be taught." That was the total advice, apart from one more sentence, on a science curriculum for 5-14 year olds. Seemingly even more relaxed and idiosyncratic, given the times we now live in, was a section on "Hobbies": "If a teacher has any special hobby in which educational value can be found e.g. poultry-keeping, informal carpentry, fruit and bee culture, study of wild flowers, meteorology and so on, a place should be found for it in the Time Table."

Was it coincidence, or the pendulum theory of curriculum fashions that flexible position statements like that were being promulgated almost exactly half-way between the introduction of "payment by results" in 1862, and the "National Curriculum" in 1989? If the pendulum theory is valid, then those teaching in the first half of the twenty-first century can expect to see a return to more local autonomy in determining what is to be taught - and how.

The Teachers' Consultative Committees

One of Bolton King's early, pioneering and controversial decisions was to support the establishment of a Teachers' Consultative Committee, followed soon afterwards by district sub-committees. He consulted the committee on a range of policy issues including books, equipment and salaries. Key members were asked to mediate in difficulties between teachers and the school managers. Good teachers were invited to write essays in which they described their methods. Seven examples survive at the Record Office. An H.M.I. of that time, T.A. Stephens, asserted that nothing similar existed anywhere else in the country.

The Committee's duties required them to:

a) exchange educational ideas.
b) consider proposals on methods of teaching from the Director and from H.M.I.
c) advise and assist teachers in distress.
d) arrange interchange of visits of teachers.

Sometimes, heads and/or teachers were sent to schools where standards were low to try to help to improve practice. So, the current and seemingly innovative practices of sending 'superheads' or 'advanced skills teachers' to rescue schools deemed by OFSTED to be failing were in fact present in embryonic form in the county nearly a century ago. Minutes of an account of how the Rugby Committee supported Frankton School in the 1920's survive today. Key figures in the deliberations on Frankton were Henry Hinde and Herbert Kay, both honoured subsequently by schools named after them. Their recommendations were, again, not dissimilar from current practices, and were subsequently repeated for schools in Wolfhampcote and Hillmorton. They included a week's programme of visits to schools where practice was deemed not to be good, and a follow-up visit in six months to ascertain the extent of any progress. These visits were not gentle. Here is the Committee reporting on a follow-up visit to Wolfhampcote C.E.: "They found that matters had improved little, if any." On a visit to Hillmorton they found that the weakness "lay with the headmistress."

The committees produced guidelines on content and books for the syllabi in "small decapitated schools." They continued to work with the newly-appointed Director Mr Perkins who, in 1930, asked them to devise: "Some kind of scheme by which there is co-ordination of curricula and some system of reporting on children who are transferred from junior to secondary school." Precisely the problem that the National Curriculum and its associated procedures sought to address some sixty years later.

League Tables

It would appear that league tables ranking local education authorities are not such a recent phenomenon. In 1910 the Chairman reported to committee that Warwickshire " .... stood very high indeed amongst administrative counties in regard to instruction in special subjects. With regard to handicrafts it stood 2nd, and in cookery it actually stood 1st. In gardening, however, it came 20th."

Moral standards were an issue then as now, but this time, apparently, Warwickshire fared less well. The Committee set as an essay title for a competition "Honesty is the best policy". The report on the entries rebuked the writers: "The majority quote this maxim ..... but as nothing more than a cold, calculating policy to get on in the world." This led to lengthy exchanges in committee on moral education.

There were hints in the minutes and in logbooks that the office and the schools clashed from time to time, or at least skirmished. In January 1906 the managers of Henley Council School resigned en bloc after receipt of a letter from the Sites and Building Committee because of "interference of the correspondent with certain works ordered by the Committee." At Budbrooke, the Parish Council complained about the new school's proximity to "seven water closets and the same number of pigsties."

The Prefect System

On January 1st 1913, Bolton King was invited to present a paper on a particular enthusiasm of his: 'The Prefect System' to the annual conference of teachers arranged by London County Council at Birkbeck College. He explained that the whole system was based on "the simple principle of trust" and made great claims for its successes, not least in terms of its moral virtues. "The prefect is constantly called on to face some new moral problem ....." and "His moral sense is always growing with exercise."

Indeed, so moral is the experience that: "There is the danger that the children may become uncannily virtuous." One advance of the system was the development opportunities it offered to: " ..... a certain child who might shine in neither work nor play."

School Medical Inspections

Education that was for the first time free and compulsory had the effect of drawing public attention to the poor state of health of many children. Towards the end of the nineteenth century, more and more publications appeared on this subject, including

"Health at School" (1882), written by Dr Clement Dykes who was Medical Officer at Rugby School.

In Britain, the London School Board was the first to appoint a school doctor : in 1890. But the idea spread rapidly, and by 1905 school doctors had been appointed by eighty-five local education authorities. The reports of these doctors and the publication of influential and disturbing government reports such as the Interdepartmental Committee on Medical Inspection and Feeding of Children attending Public Elementary Schools (1905) galvanised the Government into action. An Act of Parliament : the 1907 Education (Administration Provisions) Act gave L.E.A.s the duty to provide for the medical inspection of children in public elementary schools. The Act was supported by Circular 576 from the Board of Education, published later in the year. That gave general guidance to L.E.A.s and stressed the importance of parental involvement: "One of the objects of the new legislation is ...... to enlist the best services and interests of parents."

Bolton King was later (1913) to report that 41% of medical inspections in the county were carried out with a parent present. Thus, medical inspections proved to be an effective way of encouraging parents to come into school. The Leamington Medical Officer reported that initially 90% of parents attended but "as their suspicions were allayed, their response was not so general." According to the Guinness Book of Records, the first parents' association anywhere in the country began in Lawrence Sheriff School in 1908.

The workload of the small teams working for the Medical Officer was considerable. The 1919 Report from Leamington's Medical Officer of Health listed the work of the School Nurse as follows:

School Visits :   893   Children examined for Verminous Condition :   6413
Home Visits   : 1676

Whether this formidable programme of visits was undertaken with the aid of a bicycle is not detailed.

4

First World War

I have gone into some detail on the activities of schools and the authority during the First World War. I go on to argue that this is because it is a period largely neglected or briefly dismissed in educational history. Unlike the Second World War, it was fought almost entirely overseas. Britain in 1914 was a very different place even from the post-war Britain of 1945. Women did not have the vote. Military service was optional. Only 8% of national income was taken in taxation. People could travel, emigrate or immigrate without limitation other than finance. As A. J. P. Taylor put it " ..... a sensible, law-abiding Englishman could pass through life and hardly notice the existence of the state, beyond the post office and the policeman."

The mobilisation of people and resources to fight the war was to require unprecedented intervention at national and local level. It also impeded the growth in money spent on education. Yet most logbooks make little or no reference to what was clearly a major preoccupation of not only local and national government, but of schools and of families.

Closer examination has shown that information does exist in the form of lots of pieces that go to make a giant, albeit incomplete jigsaw-like picture. The story illustrates how Bolton King led the authority with his characteristic blend of personal conviction and loyal patriotism. The story lacks the raw and imaginable immediacy of stories of evacuation, of bombardment and of nights in air-raid shelters, but war presented the authority with unprecedented challenges, and paved the way, as did the second world war, for a major Education Act that would set the course of education for decades.

Meanwhile, Back in Warwickshire

Most school logbooks made little or no explicit reference to the war. Hampton Lucy, Eastlands and St. Austin's logbooks for example, contained no reference. In his history of Stratford Boys' Grammar, Watkins noted only two consequences of war. He attributed a rise in boarders to being: "aided, perhaps, by the outbreak of war". The Old Boys' Association was suspended because " ..... war service occupied the attention of all the officials."

Leamington College appeared almost to brush away war as a mere nagging irritant: "Despite the setbacks and initial difficulties such as frequent changes of staff and shortage of funds occasioned by World War I, the school continued to grow and flourish." At Arnold High School for Girls there were references to " ..... War conditions pressing on everyone .... supplies were difficult to obtain and costs were rising steeply".

One source of more detailed information is in contemporary school magazines. The Leamingtonian was published termly. One can trace through these editions the story of how perceptions moved from proud excitement to sorrow and dismay as more and more deaths were reported. The Christmas edition of 1914 conveyed some of the almost eager anticipation: "To know all about the War, it is necessary only to come into the Form Common Room for about five minutes before the bell rings. There you will hear in a short space of time all the fresh news summarised, freely discussed ....."

Subsequent editions invariably contained articles from old boys: 'The Life of a Recruit in Kitchener's Army' etc. The Summer 1916 edition noted: "The War has unfortunately been responsible for further changes in staff." All noted were, unsurprisingly, of men being replaced by women. Empire Day 1917 included a peroration from the headmaster Arnold Thornton against waste: "Today we are learning what can be obtained from things previously considered to be useless." A visiting speaker to the school ended his speech with a short poem: "Man am I grown and man's work must I do. Follow the deer? Follow the Christ. Live pure, speak pure, right wrong, follow the King."

The Ilmington log book recorded pupils excused for absence when their fathers were home on leave. There were passing references in Clifton, Leamington High and St. Mary's logbooks, Southam to staffing shortages and to Belgian refugees who were billeted nearby. Clearly, families of refugees were moving in around the county for the Headteacher of Fenny Compton noted the admission of five Belgian children in October 1914, but such references were few. However, the problems they raised were considerable as many spoke only French and Flemish.

Abbey C.E. School, Nuneaton was just one of a number of schools to cancel its annual distribution of Christmas tree plus presents so that the money could be sent to the fund for distressed Belgians. At Austrey, the children were dismissed early on November 14 "as the room was required for a dance given in aid of the Red Cross."

Bolton King was determined to maintain close monitoring of staffing standards, and minutes of a managers' meeting at Clifton in December 1916 reported discussion of a letter from him about the qualifications of a teacher appointed for the refugees. The managers were reportedly "entirely satisfied", however.

There is little sense of impending disaster in any source of educational history that I have studied. Scrutiny of weekly newspapers throughout 1914 showed that the first three months of the year passed relatively peacefully. An editorial in the Warwick and Warwickshire Advertiser (Jan 24 1914) lamented the lack of secondary education in places such as Southam, or the continuing shortage of county provision for girls in Rugby: "With another 2d in the pound for higher education purposes, the amount levied by Cumberland, we could greatly strengthen our secondary education in Warwickshire." A further editorial on July 18 congratulated the Committee on establishing a high school for girls at Sutton Coldfield but went on to compare its level of funding unfavourably with Shropshire.

Routine business continued in full Education Committee as a petition to save Knightcote School from closure signed by twelve persons was debated at length. Average school attendances were reported in the Warwick and Warwickshire Advertiser each month in league table form. The March 7th edition reported that the County Association of the National Union of Teachers elected its first woman president, a Miss Dix, whose "policy" included smaller classes, a higher leaving age and earlier optional retirement for teachers.

It was not until March that anything out of the ordinary occurred, but then a little local drama began.

Strike!

On March 21 Bolton King had to deal with the aftermath of a strike by hundreds of Bedworth schoolchildren in opposition to their being kept at school till fourteen. He promised to suspend all legal proceedings against parents till Education Committee had considered the matter and "to do what lay in my power to obtain examinations for labour certificates of exemption". However, he repeatedly stressed that he could only act "according to any instructions that may be given to me."

Nearly 6000 parents signed a petition in North East Warwickshire in support of an earlier leaving age. From an editorial in the Warwick and Warwickshire Advertiser of April 25 1914 it appeared that the County Education Committee had altered the byelaws on school attendance, raising the leaving age in parts of the county to fourteen, and the paper chastised it for appearing to back down in the face of pressure. This byelaw had been approved by the Board of Education and had come into effect on 1st February. It was debated at length at Education Committee on February 25th and it prompted an impassioned debate, though often informed by scepticism: "A strike of children is not like a strike of workmen. The children just delight in it" (Councillor William Johnson), and by sceptical pragmatism: "It is no good doing these wonderful things when we know perfectly well that they won't go down outside" (Hon. Mabel Verney).

The issue inevitably also attracted national interest. 'The Schoolmaster' of May 1914 weighed in with its own strictures, under the heading: "Running Away From their own Bye-laws." It described the reaction of the Education Committee as "thoroughly disappointing" and the strike as "absurd" and "fatuous". At Hartshill, apparently, some children could leave at thirteen and others at fourteen according to where exactly in the village they lived. The paper concluded indignantly: "Is that a satisfactory state of things?"

At Education Committee on 14th July, Bolton King was attacked by local councillor William Johnson for visiting Bedworth to consult parents without informing him of his visit. "Is this to be a precedent for the future?" he asked intemperately? But resolution of the affair was to be overtaken by the larger issue of war and its own demands for labour of all kinds.

Declaration of War

It was while schools were on holiday in August that matters came to a head and war was declared on Tuesday August 4th. The next few editions of local papers were full of appeals for funds and of news of recruitment to the forces. The Catholic schools in Southam put on a patriotic concert in aid of the British Red Cross Society, for example.

General Douglas Haig, later Field Marshall Earl Haig, left his home at Radway Grange near Edge Hill to go to war. Alan Griffin tells the story of how his chauffeur was unable to persuade the staff car to manage the ascent of Sunrising Hill, and, after several fruitless attempts, the great General was finally transported to the summit, facing backwards as the car struggled to the top in reverse gear. What a way to launch a war that would have terrible and terrifying consequences.

An emergency meeting of the County Council was convened on September 15 to decide whether teachers should volunteer to serve. It appears that Warwickshire was slow off the mark for a committee report humbly noted: "We have obtained information of what has been done in other counties." Their conclusion was " it is in the interests of the country that school teachers should be one of the last classes from whom many recruits should be drawn, it being essential that children's education should not be interfered with."

Bolton King 'at War' with Committee

War nationally was to generate conflict locally, precipitated by an unlikely trouble-maker. An editorial of the Warwick Advertiser in October 17 commented on the proceedings of the Education Committee that week (October 13) thus: "The usual calm of the County Education Committee meeting was disturbed on Tuesday last by an incident which gave rise to unnecessary asperity and which nearly led to the resignation of the Director of Education."

At the outbreak of war, the Education Committee decided to issue a leaflet to all schools entitled "Why Are We at War". Bolton King prepared and circulated a leaflet but without submitting a draft to the Education Committee for approval. The leaflet caused uproar, partly because of this breach of protocol, but mainly because of one sentence: "This, then, is a righteous war. Many of the wars we have fought have not been righteous; we have sometimes done unjust and cruel things."

The Chairman of the Education Committee took responsibility for circulating the leaflet without approval but "a bitter and lengthy discussion" ensued over the above offending sentence. Bolton King refused to alter one word, but did offer his resignation. Indeed, he arrived at the meeting with a draft letter of resignation in his pocket. He was urged to replace "many" with "some" but refused. Given his repeated assurances earlier that year to angry Bedworth parents that he could only ever act in accordance with committee instructions, this implacable refusal could be seen as ironical. But the committee eventually moved on to next business, and the leaflet was not altered or withdrawn.

The local paper's support was unequivocal: "Apart from the point of procedure - that the Education Committee as a whole had not had the opportunity of considering the leaflet … we regard the pamphlet as by far the best explanation of why we are at war yet issued to the children of this country." The leaflet was reprinted in full in the October 17 edition.

On November 13th, at the annual meeting of the Leamington Head Teachers, the new president Mr. W. E. Smith gave a talk on "Teachers and the War". "Hundreds of their members were fighting for the honour and liberties of their country and thousands were doing what they could to relieve distress and suffering at home."

The year ended with no further reference to education other than brief reports of usual school activities: concerts etc. Declaration of war and its consequent mobilisation of troops passed largely unremarked. At Churchover, on September 3, 1914: "The children lined up and gave a hearty cheer to our volunteers who left the village for Winchester and Portsmouth." But such references were rare.

School Life Continues

The curriculum was largely unchanged, except for some 'one-off' events. For example, on December 23rd 1914 the children of Abbey sang "many patriotic songs"; they forewent their Xmas tea, sending the money to a fund for distressed Belgians. On the same day at Coten End: "The French, Russian and English national anthems were sung". Queen's Road School cancelled their 1914 concert. Three years later they would resurrect this annual event to raise funds for the soldiers at Weddington Hospital.

At St. Matthew's Rugby, lessons included " ….. a weekly survey of news from the front and lessons on love of the Empire". Pupils at Ullenhall were taken to see a regiment's manoeuvres in Henley. The Head at Quinton ordered 'The Daily Sketch' "so that they may follow the present War."

At Polesworth the school started a garden with associated activities on March 22, 1915. The L.E.A. clearly took a close interest in this and similar projects, for:

"If a lesson was not held for some reason or other, Warwick was informed. By September 1915 Mr. Dunkin, the County Adviser for Horticulture, was praising the boys for their keenness, and by 1917 he felt able to report in glowing terms: "Plot kept in a perfectly clear and orderly condition. Many of the crops excellent.""

In December 1918 the school received an award and a letter of thanks from Bolton King, congratulating the boys on their efforts.

Unsurprisingly, staffing schools was a challenge, partly because of the absence of males, and partly because of lack of money. Bolton King felt impelled to write to the Pailton managers in March 1916, warning them against over-staffing. In consequence, a departing teacher was not replaced. At Long Compton, staffing shortages were even more critical: 'Through my being called to the Colours tomorrow and there being no-one here to succeed me, I have been advised from Warwick to close the school until further notice" (June 1, 1916).

An entry from Austrey suggested that the L.E.A. redistributed some of its resources, though why is unclear: "Received orders from the Director of Education to send 3 copies of 'Uncle Tom's Cabin' and 2 copies of 'Tom Brown's Schooldays' to Mr Sharley at Amington School. Also 3 copies of "Pilgrim's Progress" to Mr Ireson, Brandon School."

Official Wisdom

Early in the New Year, the head at Abbey " ..... spoke to the children this a.m. about our Naval Victory in the North Sea" (Jan 25, 1915).

This particular Head did detail a number of war-related events, unusually for the head of an elementary school. He noted receipt of letters from the Education Committee on celebrating Trafalgar Day (October 18th 1915), and on the need first to economise on, then to recycle paper (May 31, 1916 and April 1917). Less than three weeks later there was another on leave of absence for woman teachers whose husbands were home on leave. However, given that Nuneaton was a Part Three authority, these letters may have been a local initiative rather than county-wide.

Subsequent entries reveal the Head taking advantage of Empire Day celebrations to address mothers on the need for economy: "I pleaded with them not to fail our men ....." (May 23, 1917). He particularly stressed the need for economies in food, and three days later he noted that "I have already had a little chat with each class about the need of eating crusts etc." The Head of Southam Boys recorded the receipt of leaflets from the Ministry of Food including "Thirty-four Ways of Serving Potatoes."

Pupils' Health

In 1913, the Chief Medical Officer of the Board of Education had reported that of the six million children in public elementary schools in England and Wales, significant proportions had conditions which gave cause for concern. For example: 10% suffered from "a serious defect in vision"; 50% suffered from "injurious decay of their teeth"; 10% have "uncleanliness of the body".

These figures, too, prompted a demand for a national response. Soon afterwards, the war hit local school medical services; at Leamington, work was constrained by "..... unavailable shortage of staff ...... it is now necessary to confine the inspection to ailing children only".

Bolton King's Report to Committee

In 1916, the Director took stock, in a detailed report, presented by Bolton King to the Education Committee "The Schools and the War" in April 1916. This last paper took some effort to locate. Even in 1978 Browne et al reported only one surviving copy. A phone call in 1997 to great grandson Peter Bolton King eventually led to the retrieval of this copy from an old tin trunk belonging to his father (Bolton King's grandson) at his home in Dorset. It has now been copied and given to Warwickshire County Record Office.

I go on to summarise this paper before going back to detail some of the events recorded in log-books that contribute to this picture. The report was prepared based on information "sent in by the Head Teachers of all the Warwickshire Committee's Elementary Schools."

Bolton King first listed figures for the ex-elementary boys who had obtained commissions: "1 Lieutenant Colonel, 2 Majors, 10 Captains, 65 Lieutenants ...." etc. and honours so far awarded to Old Boys: "28 D.C.M.'s ... 3 Military Medals ..." etc.

According to the report, thousands of Old Boys had written from the front to their teachers and this provided much information. Many had put skills learnt in school to practical use: sketching, geography, science etc. Bolton King's pet project of a prefect system which had attracted attention and visitors from around the world was seemingly vindicated " ..... it is found that the Prefects most readily rise to N.C.O. rank".

Part two dealt with the work of the schools, principally in raising money and collecting materials, but also in knitting and stitching by "the girls (and) occasionally the boys".

A few statistics on output gave some sense of the cumulative effort: 2300 pairs of socks; 2600 pairs of mittens; 350 body belts; and 37,000 eggs collected for the National Egg Fund or local military hospitals.

Part three offered more general reflections on the war effort, for example, on how: "Rough boys are sobered into steady ways." Apparently: "Their hero worship has drifted from professional footballers to Nurse Cavell and Lieutenant Warneford". I assume that the latter name was a reference to R. A. Warneford, educated at Stratford Boys' Grammar, who in 1915 brought down a Zeppelin in London and was awarded the V.C. He concluded " ..... how immense is the debt that the country owes its teachers."

This report was sufficiently striking to attract national attention "The Spectator" noted: "This noble record of work needs little comment from us. For facts so moving few words are best."

News from the Front

In October 1915, more than a year after the outbreak of war, Sergeant Pinchbank of the Coldstream Guards gave a talk to pupils at Polesworth County. This was doubtless linked to recruitment, for conscription had not yet begun, and an ex-pupil, Private Clark, also spoke. This was just before he was due to leave for the front. Meanwhile, on the other side of the county, the Head of Newbold-on-Stour school gave a lecture on October 21 1915 to the whole school on the centenary of Trafalgar Day. However, the logbook made no explicit link with the war.

The Head may have been helped in his talk by a lecture given at the Town Hall, Leamington on the teaching of history the previous May. Some schools, for example, Hampton Lucy, closed to allow their teachers to attend and an attendance of more than 500 was reported.

Attendance

Of course, the pupils had to attend school in order to be inspired by such lectures, and attendance was once again a contentious issue. In August 1914, the then Prime Minister, Henry Asquith, had indicated that local education authorities could use their discretion to release boys aged 11-14 to help in various ways, for example, farming. However, the entry for Long Lawford on Oct 13 1915 noted receipt of a letter from Bolton King informing schools that " ..... children under twelve cannot be released." This rule was relaxed under pressure in 1916: "Six boys, eleven and twelve have got exemptions from school to work on the farm" (Cubbington C.E., March 1916).

Collections

As in the Second World War, and as reported to Committee by the Director, schools demonstrated their patriotism through collecting all manner of things. At Pailton School, children brought eggs, fruit, flowers and cigarettes for wounded soldiers at a military hospital set up in Pailton House. The girls there painted flags on postcards that could then be sold to buy wool. The second half of 1915 and onwards were particularly good times for collecting, perhaps because it had finally become clear that the war was not going to end quickly.

A few examples to illustrate the diverse efforts made:

Sept 1915	Studley: Eight dozen sand bags made by girls.
Dec 1915	Coleshill Parochial: 15 shillings to provide gifts for soldiers and sailors.
Dec 1915	Polesworth: 351 eggs
May 1916	Shrubland Street School: 160 fresh eggs
June 16 1916 -April 1919	War savings: £3430 4s 6d
Sept 1916	Dordon: 223 eggs. Wilmcote: 131 lbs of blackberries.
July 1916	Long Lawford: 245 Queen wasps
April 22 1917	Westgate: postal order for seven shillings for food for wounded horses on the front.
Sept 1917	Polesworth: a "blackberry ramble" collected 196 pounds.

Not to be outdone, Ilmington next year collected 1286 pounds of blackberries. They, like Rowington, also collected horse chestnuts destined for "The Director of Propellant Services" where they were used to make explosives. Children worked at Wootton Hall near Henley, in a temporary military hospital, where they would read to injured soldiers.

Pupils were made aware of their responsibilities in other ways. For example, Kenilworth pupils assembled in Abbey Fields in 1917 for an Empire Day address on the need for economy in food. Early cinema programmes brought the war a little closer. 161 children from Atherstone North went to the Picture House to see "Battle of the Somme" in November 1916, and: "At 9.45 the scholars who wished to went down to the Cinema to see the film 'The Empire Fighters' (St. Paul's Stockingford, April 4, 1917).

Business as Usual?

But many more log book entries indicated a "business as usual" approach. Reminiscences from pupils at Stretton-on-Dunsmore and Alcester R.C., approximately 25 miles apart, both recalled the popularity in 1915 of hopscotch and skipping. In the same year, and in spite of cutbacks, Long Itchington received its first piano. Abbey reported its annual May Day celebrations with the crowning of the May Queen.

Some sense of daily life in schools can be found in Leslie Wells' history of Lawrence Sheriff School, his account drawing on reminiscences of an ex-pupil:

"When we came back to school in September it was in a very excited mood. The hubbub at the beginning of every term as boys look round for changes and yarn about holidays was vastly more intense. The staff, of course, soon changed by the departure of some for the war, and this, combined with the sight of troop trains, for which many of us spent hours hanging over the railway bridges, made us feel that we were participators in great affairs.

Mr Hart used to drill the School in the field at 12.30 two or three days a week. There was a rumour that he himself had been a guardsman, this presumably to account for his dictatorial efficiency with the whistle and in changing us from close to open order, or putting us to the very frequent double. This drill had its brighter side. To trip someone up while the Head was dressing down another part of the line, or to recover blank composure in a flash while actually engaged in a scuffle, provided great amusement with an element of chance. Sometimes the Head would omit to give the next order in time, and the line would march chest forward against the Hillmorton Road railings to demonstrate its machine-like obedience to orders, especially after an harangue for doing something different from the word of command.

As time went on, paper became a very scarce commodity, and all sorts of devices to economise it were used. Instead of giving written answers, the class worked orally. The scheme of standing in a row with "go up one" for the correct answer was much in vogue. This was quite popular, as it was more active, with chorus of "Please Sir" and "Ooooh, Sir" (as in toothache), when everyone but the individual pitched on was prepared to give the required information. Written answers would be reduced to "yes", "no", or a date or number, all squeezed up in microscopic writing on sheets of paper about five inches by four. This shortage had the advantage of reducing the number of "I must not" this, that or the other, which the average inattentive, talkative, sweet-toothed, or rubber-faced individual had to write out. Ability to construct pens with two or three nibs was no longer so valuable, and the doubtful satisfaction of wanly amusing oneself by writing lines in fancy patterns to be filled in towards the end, ceased to be ours. No doubt it was taken out of us in other ways. I cannot say whether the wartime schoolboy was more sober and industrious than the pre- or post-war; it may well be that he was so."

Some logbooks reported incidents that aroused excitement, but their connection with the war was uncertain: "An aeroplane descended in the village today. As many children had never seen one I took all the children to see it" (Wilmcote, December 20, 1915). "A monoplane having descended near Wormleighton, registers were closed at 9 a.m. and school dismissed at 11.05 a.m. to enable the children to view the same during dinner time" (Fenny Compton, January 27, 1916).

Even as the war neared its end, male teachers were still being called up. The Head at Stockton noted such a call as late as April 1918.

Peace at Last

There are many more references to the end of the war in schools than to events during it, and also to subsequent celebrations of Empire Day and the Armistice. On November 11, 1918, for example, the rector visited children at Great Alne to tell them that the war was over. The children then stood and sang "God Save the King". At St. Paul's, Stockingford, the whole school assembled; the roll of honour was read out and the National Anthem sung. Children at Napton were taken out to see two captured German guns on Butt Hill (Dec 20, 1918). By 1919 the Napton logbook was able to record deadpan an ironic conjunction of entries: "School closed for one week's holiday being requested by H.M. the King" (Oct 31, 1919) and "Ten summonses have been issued to parents of those children who attendance was unsatisfactory" (Nov 12, 1919).

The objective, emotionless nature of logbooks seemingly precluded any real sense of the loss of life of soldiers and sailors in the war. But there are other carefully compiled sources. For example, in an analysis of the casualties in just one village, Kineton, Ashley Smith notes one family of 5 sons, two of whom were killed on successive days; another lost a lung and one was badly gassed. By a cruel irony the head of Shustoke School learned on the day the war ended that his son Captain J Richards had been killed.

More personal if somewhat stilted accounts of reflections on the war survive in an edition of "The Murrayian", the school magazine of Murray School, a boys' elementary school in Rugby. There were articles by pupils, somewhat incongruously interspersed with short essays on "My Pet" and "The Blackberry": "When the good news that the Armistice was signed came on Monday November 11th, nearly everybody was happy. The buzzers went twenty times .... flags were hung out of the windows"; "We have been very pleased to have the help of the lady teachers during the last four years and when the time comes to welcome back our men we shall feel regret that we cannot keep both ladies and men with us"; and letters to the magazine from old boys serving at the front: "The other day I made 83 not out and took 6 wickets for 15 runs. Even in war there is time for a game." At School Thanksgiving Service on November 19th the Head spoke of the World as a Big School where the nations were represented by the boys.

Fortunately, bomb damage had been virtually non-existent, though not far away, a Zeppelin dropped bombs on Bedworth and near Whitley Abbey. Boys from Lawrence Sheriff cycled over to Coventry on the following day to see the damage: " ..... namely, half a dozen cows turned inside out."

Aftermath of War

The end of war did not, of course, end wartime deprivations. In September 1918 Bolton King sent a directive to all schools: "I have also been directed to report to the Committee the names of any children ..... who are unable by reason of lack of food to take full advantage of the school curriculum."

Disillusion by and on behalf of returning soldiers soon set in. A Stockingford resident, Austin Bazeley, recalled a childhood memory of "the ex-soldiers who used to come busking along the road with their caps in their hands ..... the war had not done much for them." Teachers were little more prosperous. Bazeley continued: "You can tell how times were; even a school teacher from King Edward Grammar lived in a council house ..... most other teachers were in rented houses." To add to the woes, an influenza epidemic caused closures of varying lengths in "177 departments".

Counting the Cost

Duncan Watson, himself a local headteacher for many years, explored the stories of all those listed on the war memorial at Brailes. The stories are terse but eloquent. All were educated at the local school:

2nd Lt Walter Elliott: killed on the Somme in 1916 aged 29, buried in France.

Private Joseph Spencer: killed in Greece aged 22 (1917), 3 medals.

Private Jonathan Whing: killed in Ypres aged 20 (1917), 3 medals.

Driver Owen Bradley: educated both at Shipston Council School and Brailes. Killed at Ypres aged 21 in 1917, won 3 medals.

Private Walter Box: killed 22nd November 1917 at Ypres (no known grave)

Private William Field: killed overseas in May 1918 aged 19.

Private Arthur Spicer: killed in France, April 1919 aged 22.

Nor in this war were the sons of the wealthy spared: 686 ex-pupils of Rugby School were killed! On a smaller scale but with distressing local impact, Shipston Library has a memorial to eleven members of the Adult School killed in the war. The Honours Boards for Chilvers Coton School listed 67 deaths. A Kenilworth publication recalled "hardly a family unaffected".

What might those young lives, and so many more, have achieved? But it was now time to look forward and prepare for the future ..... with a generation of young males cruelly diminished in number, or permanently injured .... and a generation of young females of whom much more would therefore be expected, even though those under 30 years of age were still deemed unfit to have the vote. Major social changes and tranquil, traditional routines would speedily learn to co-exist.

5
Between the Wars

Accommodation

After the war, the authority struggled to provide adequate or better buildings for its pupils. It was a long, long struggle. This war had created a backlog, and injustices remained to be rectified : only 833 girls in secondary education compared with 1498 boys was just one. Often, they had to improvise. In 1932, pupils at Kingsbury were accommodated in a hall in the back of a working men's club. The aftermath of a national financial crisis in 1929 had led to an all too familiar round of cuts and restrictions. It led Morris Pryce, Head of Snitterfield School and President of the Warwickshire Association of Head Teachers, to lament the " ….. long promised improvements ….. buildings further postponed ….."

Accommodation challenges were increased by the addition to Warwickshire of some new parishes. From Gloucestershire came Clifford Chambers, Welford-on-Avon, Preston-on-Stour and Long Marston. From Worcestershire we gained Alderminster, Tidmington and Tredington.

However, the Committee made slow headway on class sizes. The percentage of pupils in classes of 50 plus gradually dropped to one percent, much better than neighbouring Coventry, though Shropshire and Staffordshire could boast none. This progress was not always acclaimed. H.M.I. E.H. Carter sent a memo observing that : "Warwickshire staffing was very generous ….. economies could be effected without serious detriment."

Competing demands for resources dogged the agendas of council meetings. Here is a subcommittee report on secondary school buildings staking its particular claim:

"Coleshill Grammar School

The conditions in this school are almost incredible, the most striking feature being the presence of shower-baths in one of the classrooms. The Headmaster's house has to afford not only provision for his family and 13 boarders, but also accommodation for the staff common room, the school library, and for some teaching of the sixth form."

Much later, more progress was made and new schools were opened in e.g. Bedworth (Ash Green) and Stratford (Hugh Clopton Girls), and Nuneaton (Higham Lane and Swinnerton). We have an account of the opening of Hugh Clopton:

"And so, the children aged eleven years and above were assembled in the Hall at the New School in Alcester Road, at the end of the Summer Holidays, in early

September 1939, to form the first classes to be held there, instead of returning to our own school in the Town, where for generations, the children had been educated from infancy until the age of fourteen years, when they left to start work. The boys and girls were to be separated, the building being duplicated within itself, although the gymnasium was shared at different periods.

The building of the huge school in Alcester Road had been a great topic of conversation for some time; at the enormous cost of £50,000 with facilities never seen before such as a gymnasium and showers, sports field, separate school for boys and girls and much more and was waited for with great anticipation.

The New Educational System had a great social effect upon the population, as I have already stated, the children had always attended the local school from infancy until leaving - this applied also to village schools. This meant that we in the town did not meet or know the village children. When they came to Stratford at the age of eleven years from Long Marston, Welford, Binton, Tredington, Alderminster, Snitterfield, Tiddington, Wilmcote, Bearley, etc. we made pals and started mixing. I still meet people my own age who came in then.

I remember on the opening day the corridors in the school were full of bicycles wrapped in brown paper. These were given to the village children to come to school on. I think the nearest to get one was Tiddington. They travelled many miles in all weathers every day, backwards and forwards with a good record of attendance. Weather conditions were generally not accepted as an excuse for not coming. We used to bike out to the villages to see them, once we had got to know them." (From "Voices of Hugh Clopton Girls and Boys 1939-59" by Hewins et al)

The Classroom

Meanwhile, other buildings continued to provide sterling service. This description of the classroom at Offchurch was typical of many: "The village school was heated by large open fires with guards around them. If you were lucky you sat near the fire, but when you got too hot it set up the itch in your chilblains. At the back you often shivered and your fingers often went numb with cold."

The classroom fire has figured prominently in the memories of ex-pupils. At Norton Lindsey, for example, if the stove smoked too much, school would be closed early. This led some of the less motivated children surreptitiously to put wet paper on to make it smoke. The stove fulfilled more purposes than mere heating of a room. It was used to dry wet boots and socks. If the resultant odours were too overpowering, the head would put orange peel on top of the stove to mask the odours. A drive, also at Norton Lindsey, took place in the 1920's to exterminate "vermin". Children were paid tuppence for each rat-tail or sparrow-head they could produce as evidence of a contribution to the drive. The "verminous" body-parts were inspected and then dropped into the stove. History does not record the comparative malodorousness of boys' socks or cremated remains.

Another example of the starring role of the fire came from Kathleen Adams of Churchover:

"The infants' room had a black stove which gave off a lot of heat when coal slack was shovelled into it. On windy days the smoke would suddenly puff into the classroom setting us all coughing. The big room, or top classroom, had two open fires. They were nice and cosy and if it was a very cold day we were allowed to come out, a few at a time, and stand in front of them to warm our hands. On damp days the condensation would run down the walls so Mrs Browning told us to move our desks nearer to the fire."

At Bearley, the fire was positively aggressive: "The stove is smoking very unpleasantly this morning. Occasionally, a flame comes out at least a foot from the opening of the fire."

Elsewhere, memories of a Coleshill education (Back Lane School) included one of the head who on cold days stood by the fire, wiped the children's noses and dropped the paper in the fire. But away from the fire, or at the start of the day when Winter was at its fiercest, the problem could be bitter cold. At Wilmcote in 1921, the Head recorded temperatures of 35 and 39 degrees Fahrenheit in two classrooms: "The children were marched about the playground until the rooms were warmer." At Leamington Hastings around the same time the head responded to temperatures of 46° thus: "We gave up ordinary lessons and took P.T. and folk dances."

Even when the fire glowed hospitably the children did not always benefit, as Ray Huckvale recalled at Binton: "Miss B - would sit on the guardrail - we couldn't see the fire or feel the heat."

The Usual Routine

Memories of school days were usually of quiet, or subdued routines, day after day. John Walling of Atherstone retains a clear memory of the "obligatory arms on desk and heads down nap in the afternoon." (This was certainly a tradition alive and well post-war, at St. Matthew's in 1945, for example, and at Baddesley Ensor in the early fifties.)

The routine at Wood Street Infants, Rugby was simple and unvaried:

"Head greets the children
Hymn …. Prayers ….. Register
Copying letters onto slate
Teacher reads to class"

Many recalled working on slates with chalk, until after the war: "It was quite an event when coloured chalks came in." At Harbury "Each afternoon we rested on small fold-up canvas beds ranged in rows, inside when cold or wet, outside when fine and sunny.

The First Labour Government Newly-elected: 1924

The newly-elected Labour Government albeit a short-lived one, never showed any sign of radical intent. Indeed, its President of the Board of Education, C. P. Trevelyan, himself an ex-Liberal, appealed for a consensus to be built round a gradual expansion in education. This 'policy' remained in force during the second Labour Government (1929-31).

Interruptions to the Routine

Routines were often interrupted by absence, more or less legitimate. At Norton Lindsey, one could concoct a seasonal list of reasons for absence on agricultural work:

Feb/March	:	bean-planting
March	:	stone-picking
July	:	hay-making
September	:	harvesting/fruit-picking
October	:	potato-picking
November	:	"beating for sportsmen"

Other logged interruptions to school attendance included the Royal Show, and fairs at Stratford and Warwick.

Tragedy could interrupt routine, occasionally with grimly ironical timing: "A very sad event occurred at Hartshill when the Head of thirty years' standing died after his chair overbalanced while he was standing on it to put curtains up for the school concert."

At Back Lane, Coleshill, Doris Harrison retained vivid memories of another fatality: a cow impaled on the railings of the school: "I went to the Post Office and I daren't go back. When I did come back it was all cleared and the railings were mended."

In the midst of life, was death. But life re-asserted itself rapidly. Births outstripped deaths, and in each home each birth triggered the age-old debate: 'What shall we call her/him?"

A Few Names

The Reverend J. Price logged popularity of local first names for boys and girls in Nether Whitacre between 1922 and 1955. The "top ten" were:

Boys		Girls	
William and James	1st	Ann	1st
John	3rd	Margaret	2nd=
Robert	4th	Mary	2nd=
Arthur	5th=	Patricia	2nd=
Frederick	5th=	Elizabeth	5th=
George	5th=	Susan	5th=
Brian	8th=	Christine	7th
Graham	8th=	Jean	8th=
Leslie	8th=	Jennifer	8th=
		Joan	8th=

At the time of writing, this would presumably mean numerous parents, uncles, aunts and grandparents with these names.

From School to Work

There was no real direction as to where one might go in quest of a career once one had left school. Aubrey Seymour related a rare example of careers guidance from a schoolteacher: "You're only fit for hoeing turnips." "I was inclined to agree", mused Aubrey ruefully. Thus began his lifelong career in agriculture.

Not much is recorded on career destinations of school-leavers from elementary schools. An exception is a philosophical summary from Norton Lindsey: "It was accepted that most village girls would go eventually into domestic service and a lot of the boys would be on the land, unless they were lucky and had parents who could afford to apprentice them."

There was often a fatalism about decisions, dictated by parental precedent or aspiration. But there were changes afoot. Girls in particular were beginning to switch to shopwork or, more ambitiously, into the growth area of clerical work. The development of "central schools" made it easier for girls to learn shorthand and typewriting.

Some pupils combined schoolwork with work at home. A then 13 year old at St. Paul's, Leamington, recalled his day: "I got up at 4.00 a.m. to help with the cows. After that, delivering milk before going to school."

Rewards and Punishments

Gardening continued to flourish, supported by L.E.A. advisory staff. Wilmcote School received this note in 1936: "The Elementary Education Committee have considered the Annual Report of the County Horticultural Advisers upon the work of the Day School Gardens. I am pleased to inform you that as a result, the Committee have decided to make a special award of £1.00 to your school."

Not far away in Haselor, former pupils recalled the converse of prizes and rewards: punishment for failure to take one's responsibilities seriously: "Each senior boy had a vegetable patch and a man came every Friday to teach them gardening. He was very stern, and if a boy did not behave would pick him up by his ears and throw him over the fence"; "If you were quite bad you were made to stand in the corner with a waste paper basket over your head. Very naughty children were banished to the dark gallery where there were no lights."

The Hadow Report

In 1926, a major report initiated at first thinking and then, slowly, action on post-eleven education for elementary school pupils. It recommended as follows:

"..... between the age of eleven and (if possible) that of fifteen, all the children of the county who do not go forward to 'secondary education' ..... should go forward nonetheless to what is in our view a form of secondary education in the broader and truer sense of the word ..... should spend the last three or four years in a well-equipped and well-staffed modern school."

Committee and its officers were about to embark on a thirty year programme to create "primary" and "modern" (later "high") schools. Some schools had already been relabelled as "junior" including those at Avon Dassett, Brandon, Frankton, Priors Hardwick and Wasperton (the last mentioned by now under threat of closure). The financial crisis of 1929-31, and the Second World War both delayed progress, and it would not be until the fifties that the last eight year olds lined up in the same playground as fifteen year olds.

Guidance From Above

The 1930's logbook entries were increasingly supplemented by references to visits of L.E.A. advisers and organisers and by references to teacher-absence at refresher courses or talks on (e.g.) "the teaching of retarded children." There is evidence of embryonic in-service training for teachers, as this 1936 logbook entry from Milverton indicated: "Mr C Blagdon, H.M.I., will give a lecture on "The Written Word" today at 4.00 p.m. at Clapham Terrace Senior School. The Director is anxious for all teachers to attend and suggests that afternoon school should commence at 1.30 p.m. and close at 3.30 p.m. to enable them to do so."

Though the fears of "payment by results" had long since gone, diocesan, H.M.I. and local authority inspector visits still continued, and acerbic observations featured: "A lesson given during the inspection in Drawing to Class Six was a poor one. The teacher of the class should make herself better acquainted with the rudiments of a subject she has to teach."

It may be that her struggles had been caused by the Warwickshire Education Committee's 1926 regulations for teachers which contained the terse injunction: "Drawing must be taught to girls as well as to boys. This subject must not be omitted from the girls' curriculum."

Another H.M.I. questioned the breadth of the curriculum at St. Austin's R.C., Kenilworth: "History and Geography lessons can have little value for children who are unable to reproduce a simple story with any fluency."

The Authority Takes Stock

Bolton King was anxious to make schools more accountable to the public and encouraged the practice of annual 'Education Weeks' in the sizeable towns. A typical example took place in Rugby in 1926. The Rugby Education Week was clearly a major event. The President of the Board of Education, Lord Eustace Percy, both wrote a foreword to the handbook and came to speak. In the same handbook, Bolton King wrote a lengthy essay in which he summarised the achievements of Warwickshire as L.E.A. since 1903, and looked forward to what he saw as the future challenges. His tone was partisan: "The new authorities took up the work with zest. Order gradually emerged from chaos." He chronicled the developing relationship with the Board thus: "The Board shed its narrowness and became more of a friend and less of a taskmaster."

The authority's pre-war achievements had included an increase of 50% in the number of adult teachers, a first list of "approved" textbooks (1910) and the introduction of the prefect system (1912). Both the war and post-war financial retrenchment interrupted progress: "The War necessarily meant some loss of ground." Although in 1919 the authority had opened twenty "central" schools and appointed its first "advisers" for infants and for physical training, shortage of money meant that: "Educational administration was driven from fruitful work to the wearisome calculation and recalculation of teachers' salaries."

Though within two years of retirement, he concluded with a manifesto for the future; the themes included one of continued growth and expansion, a raising of the leaving age to "fifteen at least" and "a great extension of central and secondary schools". He also advocated reform of training colleges and less official control, replaced by more trust in teachers. At the time of writing, this belief has not been in fashion, but there are signs of a cautious return towards trust of the profession.

School Games

In 1919 the L.E.A. had adopted the Board of Education syllabus for Physical Training. This replaced "drill" with daily exercises. There was an emphasis on teamwork and on games <u>training</u>, not just games playing.

Memories of school games seem to be more evident from the late 1920's onwards. Pupils at Coleshill remembered walking to the River Blythe for their swimming lessons. At Fenny Compton, the head liked to captain one of the cricket teams. The opposition would have a tacit understanding if he came in just before 3 p.m.: "Bowl him easy balls …. if you get a catch, just drop it." The idea was to keep the match going to avoid any further lessons back indoors.

Girls' athletics were slowly becoming more adventurous; there had been a fear of girls "overstraining" themselves in a "masculine" sport, but the First World War had raised expectations, though the 800 metres for women was not introduced into the Olympics until 1948. An associated issue was dress. Short skirts were coming into fashion, but still provoked disapproval. A 1933 L.E.A. report urged the adoption of more sensible dress to facilitate movement: "dark knickers, blouses with, as a rule, no stockings."

To Mix or Not to Mix?

Though many elementary schools and one grammar were mixed, they might just as well have been single-sex institutions. Here is a typical memory from the one mixed grammar school then and now ….. that at Alcester:

"Despite the co-educational character of the school, segregation of the sexes at all levels, and in all activities, was strict. In class, boys sat on one side of the room, girls on the other, and on the whole, teachers arranged seating so that those showing the least signs of budding interest in the opposite sex sat along the line of division. Beyond the kindergarten there were no mixed classes in gymnastics or games. Boys played football in winter and cricket in summer; girls played hockey and tennis. Only boys took part in athletic sports at the annual sports day. The girls, however, had an annual tennis tournament, competing for a gold and silver medal. For sports day the girls took part in competitions in what were designated 'arts and crafts', which included sewing, cookery, and such things as picture framing, photography and the making of 'historical models'. Some of these competitions were open to boys."

Discrimination apparently flourished there alongside segregation. The school debating society passed in 1934 the motion: "The misuse of leisure and the wrong conception of women's positions in the community are the two greatest evils facing mankind today …..", albeit by a small majority.

Technology Spreads

Technology began to pervade the life of schools in four different ways: the arrival of cinemas and educational films, the arrival of electricity, of the telephone and of the radio (or 'wireless' as it was often then called), though many schools did not even have an electricity supply till after the war.

The information is patchy and in most cases not substantiated. There is a claim, for example, that Eastlands School had electricity installed in 1913, but had to wait to 1935 to acquire a radio. The first figure has to be queried unless town schools were well ahead of the game. Few other schools received electricity until the 1930's. Leamington Hastings gained its supply in 1926, but the flurry of activity appears to have been in the next decade, e.g. 1931: Coughton; 1932: Baginton; 1935: Napton and Pailton; 1936: Clifton; 1939: Shipston.

Stretton-on-Fosse waited until 1950 for the installation of electric lighting. At Hampton Lucy a wireless set was installed for the funeral of King George V in 1936. Both children and adults listened to the service. Leek Wootton gained its first gramophone in 1927. A memory of Ash Green School in the winter in the thirties was that the only lights to be seen after school were lanterns used by the caretaker and his wife.

The tiny outlying village schools sought valiantly, sometimes with spectacular success, to keep up to date. Combroke C.E. School had a wireless installed by the B.B.C. in 1931 in recognition of their work in music. Pupils composed verses and tunes regularly broadcast by Sir Walford Davies in music lessons from Savoy Hill. Their success continued, so much so that the Director of Education Mr. Perkins visited in 1933, bringing with him a portable wireless to fill the gap while the school's permanent set was repaired.

At Southam, the arrival of the radio was vividly recalled:

"Radio was in its infancy, yet the Boss decided we must have a school wireless. He printed cards on the school duplicator and we had to find people who would give us a shilling or alternatively a penny a week for twelve weeks. The set was made by local amateurs led by Frank Rainbow. It was an imposing sight the size of a small bureau with seven brightly shining valves on top, each with a separate switch. The coils had to be taken out and changed according to whether long or medium wave was required and it was surmounted by an immense horn speaker. It was a battery set and the accumulator was charged at Kaye's cement works, Mr Dencer taking it down on his motorbike with a boy on the back holding it. Every radio then had to have a very high aerial. Two large pine trees were carried from Stoneythorpe by the two top classes. I resented not going, being in the lower class, but our turn came later, as every playtime we sat along the poles and with our penknives removed the bark and smoothed every knot. They were erected one weekend and after a little adjusting the set worked perfectly. Some Saturday afternoons the school was opened so that the people in the town could listen to the Boat race, the Derby, or similar events ....." (Rumasy and Hayward).

The "Boss" also formed a tin whistle band, broadcast on the Home Service in 1936.

Some schools mentioned the introduction of a radio but not of electricity. There is a reference to the installation of a radio at Nether Whitacre. The children would stand to attention as the 'Last Post' was played on Armistice Day. Leslie Wells described radio as having a "clandestine existence" at Lawrence Sheriff from 1925 but schools such as Nether Whitacre had to wait until 1937 and Fenny Compton till 1938. Westgate made rapid use of it for broadcasts in Geography, History and Nature Study. At Studley, on Derby Day, older pupils were brought together to listen to the race on radio. At Eastlands in September 1938, they assembled to hear a broadcast of the launching of the Queen Elizabeth.

Interest in the educational potential of wirelesses was growing. Following demonstrations by B.B.C. "officers", many schools enquired whether the Committee would offer assistance to those wishing to install receiving apparatus. The March 1934 Quarterly Circular to schools invited applications for loans but added a cautionary note: "If the school is not supplied with electricity, the cost of keeping batteries in order must be met out of school funds."

Funds for wirelesses had usually to be painstakingly collected. In Long Compton in 1936, the managers agreed to allocate £8 towards a 'Wireless Receiving Set'. Shortly afterwards, Lillington School started a subscription list for the same purpose.

The wireless generated the kind of debate all new technology triggers. Mr Duffield of the Borough School Warwick bemoaned "the inability to convey gestures and facial expressions ….." Mr Gough (Coten End) countered that it broadened "the very insular minds of the average elementary school boy or girl."

The Cinema

If children's listening was parentally censored, they could try broadening their outlook by going to the ever-increasing number of cinemas, especially those in the towns offering special programmes for children on Saturday mornings. Entry before the war was twopence or, according to some memories : two jam jars. After the war, prices rose to sixpence at "the flicks". It was easy to judge which hero was the subject of the serial that kept the children coming. The ways in which boys in particular wore their macs, or leapt on to bikes, as they exited would tell you whether they had just seen 'Batman' or a 'Western'. Whether schools approved, records do not show. Selective schools often had lessons on Saturday mornings, so term-time attendance was not an option, unless one 'skived' or truanted or 'wagged it'. Not to be left out, the head of All Saints Warwick installed a small cinematograph (1930) with five minute films on history and geography purchased at 2/6d (12½p) each. For older children an embryonic teenage culture was emerging : cinema, dance-hall, popular music or (less expensively) just "walking out".

Children's early cinema visits seem often to have been linked to health. The older pupils of Abbey School attended an illustrated lecture at the Scala on "Care of the

Teeth" in October, 1924, though they returned two weeks later to see "Across The Sahara". The notion that films could expand the children's geographical horizons was also evident elsewhere. In Shottery, in 1923: "Miss Jellyman and twenty children visited The Picture House to see "The Wonderland of Big Game.""

The Telephone

There were reports of telephones being tested in the Gaydon and Kineton area in the 1920's and a demonstration in Polesworth of the Automatic Telephone Set in 1930, but logbooks and reminiscences rarely record more than the bald fact of technological innovation. I have found almost no accounts of the uses to which these novelties were put, or the excitement they presumably would have engendered. One exception is a note that boys in the Gaydon area used to fire catapults at insulators on telegraph poles as they walked to and from school.

In many ways, and in spite of technological advance, the schools experienced a period of stability through the inter-war years. A member of Snitterfield W.I., reminiscing about her schooling reflected: "The pattern of education was substantially the same as it is today."

The Central Schools and Specialist Centres

One development to extend the curriculum of the older pupils was the development of "Central Schools" and 'Specialist Centres'. The idea was that certain schools would function as designated specialist centres and older children would travel there for tuition. Snitterfield, for example, offered courses in "housewifery" and "rural science". As part of the latter course, pupils were taken to see "manure trials" at local farms.

Pupils travelled from Gaydon and Chadshunt to Kineton for cookery and woodwork, and, similarly, from outlying villages to woodwork and cookery centres at Alcester. Other examples, recalled or logged included:

- Boys and girls walking from Long Itchington to Southam for cookery and woodwork classes.
- Older girls from Ilmington cycling to Quinton for domestic science classes.
- Girls marching from Eastlands on the edge of Rugby to the Central School's kitchen in town for cookery lessons.
- Boys walking weekly from Attleborough to the Old Mining School in Nuneaton for woodwork.
- Girls walking to Henley for cookery and laundry while boys worked on the allotment.

A variation on this idea was the 'Central School' where admission was by an exam. taken at or about the age of eleven. The idea was a school with a four year curriculum, taking pupils beyond the statutory leaving age of fourteen. Some courses at least would be vocational. By 1926, eighteen had been established. For reasons not clear, Rugby had four but (e.g.) Atherstone had none. Provision ranged from Baddesley Ensor across the county to Long Compton. It included schools no longer part of Warwickshire - Meriden and Wilnecote, for example. These developments often attracted controversy. They were seen as a threat to the survival of the small village school. Both Bolton King and Perkins attended lively meetings in villages around Southam. The W.I.: "viewed with grave concern the suggestion that children between 11 and 15 should be required to travel 2 miles to the nearest senior school on bicycles ..... in heavy traffic."

The Hon. Mabel Verney, still a sceptic where L.E.A. innovations were concerned, and where rural closures were threatened, asserted that: "Religious Education was 10,000 times more important than the gymnasium." In meetings with parents, Bolton King was adamant that the choice was between 'better staffed, better equipped schools', or 'an inferior education'. Mary Hill, remembering her years as a pupil at a new High School recalled "a wonderful school ...... coming from a church school where the teaching left much to be desired."

Travelling to School

Perhaps because little travel was by car or bus, there are many reminiscences about the journeys by foot pupils made daily in order to get to and from school. Residents in Ashow, for example, walked 3-4 miles daily to school at Stoneleigh, but the journey did give them an extra education: "We did know the names of wild flowers, birds and animals."

From the age of five, children from Lowsonford had to walk $2^1/_2$ miles up hill and across fields to school at Rowington. Pupils from Shrewley and Kingswood also faced long walks. Children from Arlescote faced a daily journey over hills of three miles to their schools at Ratley and Radway. Peggy Thornton, later to become deputy head at the Borough School in Warwick, retains memories of being kept in after school and then walking to the farm where she lived even at the age of six, and sometimes in the dark. Mollie Harrell claims that there were pupils who walked a distance of two miles each way to and from Fillongley C.E. School to get home for lunch! Provision of school dinners was variable across the county. Elsewhere in the north at Polesworth, for example, these long distance walkers could have stayed at school to enjoy stew with slices of bread, cooked in the cookery room.

Clearly, cycling even then had its risks ..... enough to cause an intervention from the Education Committee in the form of this minute: "With a view to minimising the risk of accidents to children, head teachers have been given instruction not to provide accommodation at the schools for bicycles used by children who reside less than one mile from the school they attend." These days, of course, school cycle sheds, where they exist at all, are often empty and derelict. Matching provision to need has never been easy.

Small village schools were always under scrutiny in order to assess viability. Travelling distance was just one of the arguments to fight off closure even for the tiniest : Avon Dassett (8 pupils) and Idlicote (15 pupils) were just two instances.

Village Games

Games came and went. At Baginton in the playground the children played 'The Farmer's in his Den' and 'Ring o' Roses'. Outside school, some resorted to less innocent pursuits: scrumping, and smoking hand-rolled cigarettes, for example.

At Ashorne the whip and top and hoop-bowling were continuing favourites together with five stones and hopscotch. Pupils from Wood Street, Rugby "played a game when we formed a long line with linked hands and sang, turning under the first arm until we were all linked with crossed arms. We gathered speed and the last one in the chain was in danger of flying off the end." Later, they would buy   gob-stoppers or 'dabs and suckers'.

Evelyn Lock recollected life in Leamington " ….. scrumping apples, swinging on and round the lamppost, playing football in the street ….." At Stretton-on-Dunsmore, after school, pupils rushed to the village green to make " ….. paper boats and then float them on the brook that runs through the centre of the village."

Here are some more memories:

"Childhood games and pastimes at Clifford Chambers included skipping, tops, hopscotch, "fag" cards, five stones or dids, ball games, hoops etc. The boys' hoops were iron with an iron handle hooked on for steering. The girls had wooden hoops with wooden sticks to hit them along. Boys kept a look out for men smoking cigarettes and would say, "Can I have your fag card please?"; usually they were lucky."

"At Brailes in the 1930's we played ring games such as "Drop handkerchief", "Sally go round the moon", "Around the mulberry bush", "Here we come gathering nuts in May", and "Stand and face your lover as you have done before". We also played top and whip, five stars and five stones, and bowled wooden hoops using a stick for guidance. When spring came in Tanworth in Arden, out came the wooden hoops and the whips and tops. Children played with their spinning tops in the village street, always being warned by Father to watch out for a car coming in case we were knocked down. We had races with our hoops up one side of the street, round the village green with its chestnut tree, and down the other side."

Reminiscence does not tell us exactly how these games were played. How many have survived?

The Curriculum

The curriculum remained firmly based on 'The Three R's'. Religious instruction had an anomalous status: no money to support it but daily scripture readings expected. Other subjects such as History, Geography and Literature were at the schools' discretion. Practical subjects usually separated the boys from the girls. At Harbury, girls "were taught to knit on thick, short, wooden needles. I can never remember any of us actually completing a recognisable article until much later when we progressed on to dishcloths". But at Coleshill Girls' Parochial School, pupils "made a different garment each school year. In the last year knickers were the set garment chosen."

English was the priority, but usually subdivided into parts: comprehension, spelling etc. Object lessons continued at some schools at least until the 1920's. A 1921 photograph of a class at Shustoke Infants included the cards used for object lessons: a mug, a top, a pig for example.

People who recall the anti-climax of the total eclipse of the sun in August 1999 may be a little consoled by events 72 years earlier at Abbey School: "Many scholars, accompanied by seven teachers, went to Tuttle Hill at 5.30 a.m. to witness an eclipse of the sun. Clouds till 7.15 a.m. A great disappointment to us all."

The General Strike

The General Strike of 1926 rarely featured in either logbooks or reminiscences. It did cause distress in some areas. At Bedworth, many miners' children suffered hardship and pupils at Leicester Road, for example, were given free food by local traders who supported the strike. The Head of Abbey School in nearby Nuneaton noted its seriousness: "At midnight a General Strike was declared. The country has an anxious time to face." (May 3 1926). In the nearby mining village of Arley a soup kitchen was started in the school playground. Food was provided by local farmers and well-wishers and often included rice pudding. At Atherstone, forty children attended the Salvation Army Hall each day for breakfast.

Caning

Caning remained a common but contentious policy. At Abbey School the head faced a "most abusive" mother protesting that her daughter had received one stroke on the hand for disobedience. Later, the father arrived at the school to apologise for his wife's behaviour. At Milverton, 'hooligan behaviour' earned '4 on hand', 'telling lies ….. 'a severe thrashing', and 'wilful damage' received 'slipper on bottom'.

Frances O'Shaughnessy noted the ubiquity of caning, even for girls: "Caning was administered indiscriminately, to boys and girls alike; it was the medicine to cure everything, from bad behaviour and insolence to bad writing or an unfortunate inability to do arithmetic." At Tanworth two canes were in use, the thicker one being reserved for the offence of swearing. At nearby Alcester Grammar: "Corporal punishment was a last resort, and applied only to boys. The usual beating was 'the slipper', a walloping with a plimsoll".

Last resort it might have been, but its use was not confined to misdemeanours on school premises. Audrey Dunning recalled that at Churchover she would not dare pass the head's house after 8.00 p.m. for fear of the cane next day. Teachers without canes improvised variations. A teacher at Radford Semele used to rap children over the head with a thimble, or poke them with a knitting needle, for example. Stockton managers met in 1931 to discuss parental complaints about the allegedly excessive use of the cane, but they concluded that the complaints were no more than trouble stirred by a local resident.

An early reference to the now ubiquitous graffiti was made at Wilmcote in 1930: "It was distressing to find undesirable scribbling in the offices." The punishment for this novel offence was not recorded.

Health and Diet

An increasing pre-occupation with the health of children led to experiments with nutrition. In 1932, for example, the Head at Napton decided to trial a mid-morning drink of Horlicks, for "health ..... and the washing up should be good too for the girls." Two years later, milk at break was started at Radford Semele.

Visits from school dentists were regularly recorded. Their increasing regularity might conceivably have been welcomed, given at least one alternative. The Head of St. Marie's, Rugby, Brother John Dolby reportedly " ..... gave First Aid and extracted teeth with the help of a penknife." Equally basic was the scene remembered by an ex-pupil at Wellesbourne: "Tonsillectomy for children was a very primitive affair. I had mine removed in a nursing home in 1925. We were a little late arriving and the surgeon stood at the top of the stairs with a bloodstained apron or overall, holding a knife in his hand, calling out 'Next please .....'"

Health and Fitness

Reports from the School Medical Officer showed encouraging evidence of slowly improving care. Medical inspections had first been undertaken in the county in 1908. By 1930 there were eighteen health visitors, enabling mass screening to take place when pupils reached the ages of eight and twelve. Ringworm and scabies were in decline and more than 50% of parents responded to the invitation to be present for examinations, an increase of 8% in five years.

The Officer's reports included an annual report from Mr. P. Marsh, Organiser for Physical Training. Most schools devoted at least two hours a week to "physical activities". Two and a half thousand pupils from just 34 schools were receiving swimming instruction. Nearly 300 teachers were attending evening classes across the county from Alcester to Atherstone in order to improve their teaching skills in the subject.

Days Out

Motor coaches were now seen regularly on the roads and trips for children became more common, especially to Wicksteed Park in Kettering which opened in the 1930's. Pupils at Mancetter visited Dudley Zoo, another popular venue for school visits, just before the war. These visits may now seen unambitious, but even ten years earlier a pupil at Stockingford Council School was able to assert that: "To see Nuneaton was like a foreign country". Schools at Stratford and Wolverton had more ambitiously run trips to London and to the seaside.

Indeed, pupils did not need to travel far to find excitement. A trip for Henley pupils was to catch the train to nearby Wood End. At Wolvey, children travelled just 1½ miles to Leicester Grange where: "Tables were laden with sandwiches and cake, usually slab cake. One year there was a plague of wasps and half onions were placed at intervals in case of stings."

The Abdication

National events were seldom recorded, probably because heads still obeyed the limiting regulations on what could be entered in logbooks. But the head of Hampton Lucy made an illicit and heartfelt comment on the abdication of King Edward VIII: "This is the most disappointing and saddest event in our history." Doubtless all felt better there when the school, in common with all county schools, closed for the coronation of George VI in May 1937.

Rugby Day Continuation School

One part of Warwickshire's educational provision eventually proved to be so unusual as to earn itself a sentence in A.J.P. Taylor's 'History of England 1914-45'. In writing of the 1918 Education Act, better known as the Fisher Act, he referred to Fisher's proposal that L.E.A.s should institute part-time education in "Day Continuation Schools' up to the age of 16. However, by 1921 only five actually existed, largely due to a shortage of money after the First World War. As Taylor tersely noted: "None was ever set up on a compulsory basis, except, for some unknown reason, at Rugby."

Rugby's school became unique, surviving until 1972 when the school leaving age was finally raised to 16. All employed youngsters under the age of sixteen were compelled to attend The curriculum was broad: English, Maths, Science, Handicrafts and P.T. for all, though girls did either a 'commercial' course: typing, shorthand etc. or 'housecraft': domestic science and needlework. Boys worked either in the "industrial" section: science, drawing etc... or in the "distributive" trades: commercial arithmetic book-keeping etc. The school received strong support from local companies such as the 'B.T.H.' (British Thomson-Houston Company Ltd) or the 'E.E.C.' (English Electric Company). Pupils attended one day a week at the school, situated on the site now occupied by East Warwickshire College.

One ex-pupil echoed the sentiment of many of today's students who choose to go to a sixth form or F.E. college: "I did like going to Day Continuation School ..... because they didn't treat you as a child. On the day I started they said, 'Well you're not a child now, you're a young person'." But, of course, they were still only 14 or 15.

The Office

Education Office staff continued to grow - in 1933 the Chief Clerk presided over twenty-one clerks, eight typists and four office boys. However, there is evidence of due regard to economy. Although the county now had the services of two Organisers for Physical Training, one of those spent a day a week in Coventry and both spent half a day each in Leamington. These organisers seemed to be engendering great enthusiasm as evidenced by letters of appreciation from heads: "We must have more of this; it is making such a wonderful difference to the school. The children are altogether more alive and alert ...." The P.E. Advisers also ran regular courses for teachers, and more and more children attended swimming lessons at local baths.

Educational Standards

What was happening to standards? How would they compare with today's. The 1934 Examination for "Special Places for Candidates under 12" offered some clues, albeit contradictory. In Arithmetic pupils were asked to "multiply 15.2 by 8" or "divide 48,921 by 69".

In English (why not 'General Knowledge'?) they had to name:

"a) a Prime Minister
b) a famous writer born at Stratford-on-Avon
c) the first book of the Bible" etc.

The rubric seemed somewhat peremptory: "I have made a list of nouns. I want the feminines of each. Don't copy any masculines but ....." etc.

Starting School

So, schooling moved placidly on through the decades. Children started, stayed, and learned:

"We attended the Catholic school in New Road, Studley. The headmistress was a nun, Sister Joseph-Marie, and an older nun took the six and seven year olds. The other teachers were all single women (a rule in those days - married women left teaching). Discipline was strict, but on Friday afternoons the "Baby" (Reception) class had a tea party. New starters came to this. One day when I was four, Granny took me round, just for tea. Great trays of home-made jam on buttered crusty bread were followed by hunky pieces of plain fruit cake. The 13 year old Top Class girls helped prepare and serve the meal. I loved it, except for the tea which was handed round in chipped enamel mugs. The year was 1929, I was too young to understand the hardship many families endured. My own mother was not the only one to die and leave a young family; three other girls in my class were orphans too. Three children died of TB before leaving school, and one of diphtheria."

Pregnant Schoolgirls

One category of S.E.N. provision rarely mentioned was that for pregnant schoolgirls:

"The Leamington and Warwick Girls' Shelter started before World War II in 6 Church Hill, but moved to Leam Terrace when the opportunity arose, as the house in Church Hill was too small. The Shelter took about 10 girls; these were unmarried mothers, and we only talked of this among ourselves - not to outsiders - such was the climate of opinion before and during the War. Miss Brooks ran it and both she and matron were marvellous. The Shelter took girls who were pregnant and also girls with their babies. The Coventry Diocesan Moral Welfare worked with it and found places for the girls to work and placed the babies etc." (Leamington Literary Society).

Democracy and Accountability

And finally, a brief note on an innovation which was well ahead of its time in the county, and probably nationally too: the introduction of a School Council at King's High in Warwick in 1925. Headmistress Miss Doorly enunciated the principle that: "..... no-one in school lives to herself but that each is responsible for all and all for each, that wisdom for action may be found in the very youngest and that even if it is not, it is interesting to hunt for it." Thus, delegates were elected from every form, and participated in an educational innovation way ahead of its time. It was also Eleanor Doorly who, a few years later in 1939, won the Carnegie Medal for her book "The Radium Woman", the story of Marie Curie. It was rated the best children's book of 1939.

Conclusion

So ended two decades of national turmoil but relative local tranquility ..... of technological innovation, but curricular continuity. But not even the tiniest or most isolated village would escape the horrors that another world war would bring.

6

The Second World War

Preparations

There is a temptation to recall the Britain of 1938 and 1939 as dismally unprepared for what, with hindsight, can be seen as the inevitability of war. But scrutiny of records shows evidence of much pre-war activity. There was certainly and unsurprisingly a naivety about events overseas, captured in this extract from the diary of a girl attending Alcester Grammar School: Helen Hunt, by then a sixth former: "Fraulein Lang came to school this afternoon and told us all about Austria. She is a Nazi ..... She says she thinks Hitler has done wonders for Germany and the German people. She does not hate the Jews personally .... only as a race" (June 24, 1936).

But even in 1937 the Education Committee had met with the County Air Raid Precautions Officer to approve "elementary school buildings to be used as first aid posts in the event of grave national emergency or hostilities." In September 1937 an H.M.I. visited schools such as Abbey Junior and, during his visit, discussed possible positions for air raid shelters.

During 1938 gas masks were issued in every town and village in the land. As early as January that year, the Vicar called into Cubbington C.E. School to examine the pupils' gas masks: "Several were found to be poor fitting. Vicar said he would bring replacements as soon as possible." Many childhood memories of the war are about these masks. Here are some from a former pupil of Campion Girls:

"Earliest recollections of school during the war years were of being given gas masks, trying them on, and all the children sitting in the class with them on ..... During mock air raid warnings we used to sit for half an hour at a time doing lessons whilst wearing our gas masks; they used to mist up inside and in those days most children seemed to have runny noses and it was impossible to wipe one's nose .... I leave the rest to the reader's imagination."

Another Leamington former pupil adds her memories: "These gas masks became an extension of our persons; we took them to Prayers in the morning, to the Gym and to the Games Field. They were kicked, used and hurled about." Some children claimed that they could smell gas in the masks. This was probably no more than the lingering odour of disinfectant.

The Munich events precipitated further alarm: trenches were dug and Mr Perkins informed the Elementary Education Committee that he had issued air raid precautions to all schools.

Evacuation

Plans for evacuation had also begun in 1938. A Government committee chaired by Sir John Anderson planned "Operation Pied Piper", as they met between May and July that year. It is difficult to comprehend the sheer scale of the evacuation enterprise, but nearby Birmingham provided a convenient example. In September 1939 there were evacuated: 25,241 unaccompanied children; 12,377 mothers and children; 4,260 teachers and helpers. The Chief Education Officer there also assumed the title of Chief Evacuation Officer. Even so, two thirds of Birmingham children stayed behind. At Coventry more than 8,000 children were registered but only 3,200 appeared on the day. Many of the evacuees travelled only the relatively short distance to Warwickshire.

Some of those children who did leave came to Lapworth where, like many schools receiving evacuees, shortage of space compelled a 'two shift' system. At Swinnerton shifts were arranged from 7.00 till lunch and from early afternoon till 5.00. Milverton adopted a less taxing régime: 8.45 - 12.15 and 1.15 - 4.45. Snitterfield, Cubbington and Shrubland Street had to close for several weeks to prepare for an influx from both Birmingham and Coventry. Evacuees to Shottery from Birmingham were first examined by "Nurse Shakespeare for cleanliness". Stratford Councillors heard that 21 of their first arrivals had "nits". Other examples of movement indicate the widespread repercussions of evacuation:

Children from:
- King Edward (Camp Hill) to Warwick High *
- Stoke Newington to Pailton and Churchover
- Coventry and Dagenham to Long Itchington and to Baddesley Ensor
- Ilford and Birmingham to Lapworth and to Ullenhall
- London to Ullenhall
- London to Clifton
- Coventry to Claverdon
- Coventry to Mancetter
- Coventry to Warmington
- Coventry to Kingsbury
- Barrs Hill to Atherstone *
- Coventry and Birmingham to Shrubland Street, Leamington
- Coventry to Oxhill

- Grays, Essex to Stockton
- Broad Street, Coventry to Long Compton
- Bablake to Lawrence Sheriff *
- King Henry VIII to Alcester Grammar *
- St. Osbury's R.C. Coventry to St. Austin's Kenilworth
- St. Mary's R.C. Coventry to Binton
- London and Coventry to Dunchurch and Willoughby
- West Ham to Stretton-on-Dunsmore and to Wolston

(N.B. The asterisks indicate that at secondary level there were evidently attempts to match type of school: grammar with grammar etc.)

Entries from the logbook at "far-flung" Newton Regis posed a puzzle. There were references at different points to evacuees from Birmingham, Coventry, Gravesend, Liverpool, Sheffield, Walthamstow and West Lavington. Clearly, Newton Regis had an early opportunity to trial 'multi-cultural education'! It also claimed to have had chicken pox imported by two evacuees.

Warwickshire in 1939 took 1825 pupils from Coventry and 1210 from Birmingham in total. By 1941 the increase in school rolls was estimated at just over one third. Leamington College took refugees from the Channel Islands, Gibraltar and even the children of Czech soldiers quartered nearby. A recurring image of the late thirties was of waves of children, address labels round their necks, gas masks and bags on their shoulders plus scraps of luggage, trudging on and off trains. More than 400 evacuee children arrived at Stratford station in 1939. They walked to the nearby church school where they were allocated to families. The process of being "allocated" ..... or chosen was just one traumatic memory still recalled by many. Peter Milligan, evacuated from Coventry to Studley with his sister, recalled his arrival: "We stood in a village hall on a stage and people would come and pick one. We were the only two kids left on stage .... we both cried; we wanted our mums".

Artist Frank Smith was evacuated from Birmingham to Tanworth-in-Arden. He recalled being one of the last two to be chosen in the school there. Even when taken in, evacuees often challenged authority in their unfamiliar classroom. The head of the school called him up to the front once for spilling ink: "As he raised his cane, I suddenly felt angry, and snatched at it. Mr Benson and I wrestled for it together, ending up on the floor. When we got up, Mr Benson gave me a good hiding anyway."

The impact of evacuation on the county was widespread and massive. Simply finding places to educate the evacuees tested the resourcefulness of the authority and the goodwill of local communities. Sixty six evacuees from Coventry received schooling in the Oddfellows Hall and Reading Room in Leamington. The Oddfellows Hall in Wolston was also used. St. Austin's at Kenilworth and Pailton, like many schools, introduced a double shift system. In Wellesbourne the W.I. Hut, the chapel and the Conservative Club were all drafted in to help. In Long Itchington pupils evacuated from Dagenham and Coventry found their new classroom to be in a local pub. Ullenhall used the Village Institute and an old chapel. Dunchurch rented rooms from the Methodist church. (In the First World War the rooms had functioned as a soup kitchen.) Methodist church halls proved to be a useful resource in many places e.g. Oxhill.

These improvised plans were not without their problems. At Stretton-on-Dunsmore, the village hall was appropriated, but "much damage being done to school property in the Village Hall when it is let for entertainment" (Feb 21, 1941). No that evacuation could guarantee safety. An evacuee from Coventry, placed at Newbold-on-Stour: "tore off his nail on a piece of corrugated iron." More seriously, a Coventry boy was killed in Wellesbourne when he fell between a tractor and plough. In Bidford a

London boy evacuee was killed when he was hit by a car in the main street, and some bombing was reported near Grendon, and at villages such as Brandon, Bretford and Dunchurch.

Evidently, evacuation did not always move children very far from war activity. 'John', a Coventry evacuee moved to Atherstone, recalled tanks and lorries rumbling through the main street day and night. American troops stationed at Merevale used to throw parcels to the children.

Evacuee children were required to take with them: 2 vests, 2 towels, 1 comb, 1 face flannel. plus the ubiquitous gas mask. The girls would need 2 liberty bodices while the boys took 2 shirts. At Warwick, older girls at Kings High were brought into school early to prepare for the arrival of the evacuees. They spent the morning in the cloakroom, packing 300 carrier bags, each containing: 1 tin of corned beef, 1 tin of unsweetened milk, ½ lb of milk chocolate and 1 lb of biscuits. These were to serve as iron rations to tide evacuees over their first days.

Relationships were invariably wary, as at Binton: "A large curtain was hung up across the room dividing it in half with the village children on one side and the evacuees on the other, the reason being that the evacuees were Catholic."

Expectant mothers from Coventry were evacuated to Bidford too, also as a measure of safety. They made such demands on the local shop that Peggy Griffiths, its owner, had to take on extra help, including two 14 year old girls who went straight from school to the shop each afternoon. Once it became apparent that no bombing was imminent, many evacuees drifted back. Some walked the ten miles or so from Long Itchington to Coventry. An Ash Green ex-pupil recalls her mother coming to fetch her back to Bedworth with the words: "If we die, we will all die together." Many returned home for Christmas, and stayed at home thereafter.

But the drift-back had begun long before. It continued with breaks throughout the rest of the war. Thus, the County Council relinquished its tenancy of various emergency classrooms: the village hall at Long Itchington and Amington Band Hall in 1943 and Ratley Village Hall and Brinklow Church Room early in 1944 were a few of many examples. Some lingered; 108 evacuees remained even at the end of 1945. Two at Newton Regis, for example. completed a five year stay there. At Ullenhall: "Some of the boys remained after the war and eventually married local girls."

The Declaration of War

When war was declared on Sunday 3rd September 1939 there was widespread despondency. Everyone knew that this war, unlike the last, would be fought 'at home' as well as abroad. Schools postponed their starts to the term. Heads met with L.E.A. representatives in different parts of the county such as the Rugby College. St. Marie's, for example, did not finally open till September 18th and even then only thirteen children arrived. It took several more weeks for parents to decide that there was no immediate cause for concern, although some schools had organised meetings for parents to try to allay concerns. During these opening weeks, many schools met their parents to "discuss matters pertaining to attendance at school and the children's safety."

Events were brisker at Snitterfield, as the opening logbook entries of September 1939 illustrated:

"Sept 4th : School closed till further orders.
Sept 11th : School opened plus children from Coventry and Birmingham"

Even in these turbulent times, logbooks would usually state only the bald facts.

Pupils from Nuneaton, Rugby and Cubbington all remembered schools responding to county instructions to tape or board up windows to avoid splintering glass etc. The Education Office sent adhesive tape to all schools for this purpose. A memory of this taping is one of the few school memories to be found in biographies of the world champion boxer, Randolph Turpin. Windows were blacked out. Children cycled to and from school with "shaded lamps front and rear fitted to ensure the lights tilted towards the ground. The lamps were powered by carbide and had to be lit with a match."

Deprivation flourished. Materials for woodwork and metalwork all but disappeared, as did such luxuries as bananas and chocolates. The girls were often less than thrilled with the fashionable potential of their wardrobe:

"Was there ever a garment as ugly and as uncomfortable as the liberty bodice? In the 1930's and 1940's little girls everywhere were encased in these horrors. Fortunately, the liberty bodice was only really suitable for the flat-chested figure. How thankful I was when I started to develop a bosom."

But fashion was not a priority. It was rather the era of 'make do and mend' where damaged parachutes became sought after as fabric for underwear and there was a roaring trade in unused clothes coupons.

Bombings

The opening months of the war were unnaturally quiet and, ironically, it was not until after many evacuees returned home that intensive bombing began. This is not the place to describe in any detail the destruction of the nearby City of Coventry. Much has been written already. But in the eleven hour bombardment on November 14 1940: 300 incendiaries, 500 tons of high explosive and much more were reported either tersely or with a dash of sympathy in many Warwickshire logbooks. More than 3000 people were killed or injured, many of them children. Fourteen schools were destroyed or damaged. Doreen Lowe at Bishop's Tachbrook remembers: "You could actually see the German planes passing by the moon like flies."

Clearly, sleep was interrupted for many miles around. At Cubbington, well under half of the pupils attended on the morning following, though most had returned by the afternoon. At Eastlands, attendance dropped to 45%. Even at Hampton Lucy: "Attendance was very bad today." At Wolvey the bombing brought "an influx of children to be cared for ….." The immediate aftermath was glimpsed through other logbook entries: "Mrs Conway absent all day as a result of her house being bombed during the night" (Coten End, Nov 15, 1940), and at nearby Emscote: "I have reported to the Director slight damage to the roof and of two broken windows which occurred during last night's raid over Coventry" (Nov 15, 1940). Schools such as Wolston where bomb blast had broken windows also reported much reduced attendance the following day.

Of course, bombing was not confined to Coventry. In February and in May 1941, Nuneaton was heavily bombarded, the latter attack causing damage to many schools and almost destroying King Edward VI School. Its pupils had to move temporarily to Nuneaton High, while pupils at nearby Attleborough were moved to Swinnerton. The County Council approved an allowance to the Head for accommodation "until the school house is fit for occupation." Alan Cronshaw of King Edward's recalled trying to retrieve his textbooks next day from the rubble. He was chased off by a Bomb Disposal Squad.

First Warwickshire School to be Bombed?

The Committee minutes of these early years were cautious on detail. It was important not to provide tactically useful or morale-boosting information to our enemies. They noted one school "virtually destroyed" … and "minor damage" to six more schools in 1940. The former, though not named, was probably Pailton. Even before the destruction of Coventry, bombs had fallen on the village of Pailton in June 1940, badly damaging both the school and the headmaster's house. The Director, W.H. Perkins, visited next day to assess the extent of the damage. The incident was at that stage still unusual enough to attract "thousands of sight-seers and souvenir hunters." The bombing may have been linked to nearby attempts to bomb an airfield in Ansty. Elsewhere, war damage was usually confined to broken windows, dislodged slates and damaged ceilings.

Minutes of the Diocesan Board reported an estimate of "£1650 less the cost of the drains" to restore Pailton. At the same time, the Board discussed an estimate of £25 for unspecified damage at Wootton Wawen. Soon afterwards, bigger bills would arrive : of £3000 to repair Attleborough School at Nuneaton, for example.

Children out in the villages were by no means totally safe from stray bombs or tactical incendiaries. However, their relatively safer position may have left some of them in a state of worrying naivety. Alfred Woodward recalled the morning after some bombs fell on Brailes that: "I saw schoolchildren carrying unexploded incendiary bombs in their hands, oblivious to the danger they were in."

Incendiary bombs also fell on the small village of Walcote. Pupils at Shipston reportedly took remains of incendiary bombs to school, perhaps to swop? Bombs were dropped on the hills at Great Alne, but the only loss of life was that of a goat, perhaps from shock! One bomb fell on Stratford in October 1940, not far from where Thomas Jolyffe school now stands. Boys from King Edward School helped to fill in the crater. There were reports in Birmingham in official papers of bombs falling near Lapworth. Heavy daylight raids took place at the time on nearby Redditch too.

Air Raid Warnings

Many schools reported interruptions to schooling when air raid sirens sounded. In the Autumn of 1940, Eastlands in Rugby reported sirens going off several times a day on occasions. It must sound rather exciting to today's children to imagine exiting from classrooms as rapidly as possible in order to go down the air raid shelter. Few accounts of the reality exist, but those that do all insist that the novelty and excitement waned very quickly. The shelters were generally cold, dark, unheated and cramped. Teaching methods had to switch from the written to the oral as lighting was poor and blackboards rarely available. At Newton Regis the pupils had to rely first on an A.R.P. warden and later on the Rector to be notified of an air raid warning.

The precise nature of a "shelter" is not always clear from the records: "Acting on the Director's instructions, I have purchased some butter muslin which I am having pasted on to the windows in the corridor - this is to make a shelter in case of air raids" (Stockton). Locating shelters was also problematic; children at George Street, Bedworth had to travel some distance because no suitable land for shelters was available nearer to the school.

Accounts of the experience of air raids were varied indeed. At Cubbington ".... the air raids were often a welcome interruption to the daily routine ..... there was the dash home, and then the dawdle back to school when the 'All Clear' sounded. In the playground, boys were transformed into Spitfires and Hurricanes and girls skipped to rhymes about Churchill and Hitler."

At St. Marie's: "To keep the children occupied during the time in the shelters, lessons took the form of reciting poetry and arithmetic tables and singing songs; there were also quizzes and general revision questions for older children ....."

Shrapnel collecting and swopping were popular in Bedworth and Nuneaton. One unintended effect of shelter location was a reduction in swimming instruction in any pools not close to shelters.

Elsewhere, the novelty soon palled. The sheer frequency could rapidly become tiresome. Leicester Road faced a series of air raids in October and November 1940, some lasting nearly 3 hours. At Abbey, children were in shelters on one occasion (December 1940) from 6.30 p.m. to 4.15 a.m. There were regular air raids reported, too, at Eastlands and Nathaniel Newton, but even after an early one (September 1940) the latter's Head was proudly able to record the stoic spirit of her young charges " ..... not a single case of fright or upset during the whole time the children were in the shelters."

Few places could feel safe. What with bombs dropped in error, or simply unloaded, and with rural airfields in places like Baginton, Bramcote and Honiley, detonation could happen anywhere.

Footnote

As far as I am aware, the only school that still retains an accessible shelter is that at Burton Green, though an Anderson shelter has been recreated at St. Giles, Exhall. The head purchased the shelter from a back garden in Coventry for £25 ("buyer collects"). Once a year, it is furnished in authentic style: bunk beds, fire bucket and so on and used for a history topic.

Air Raid Procedures

Instructions on procedures in the event of air raids varied from school to school. They had to; the variables were so many, for example, age of children, distance from home and the likelihood of overhead bombing. At Great Alne, the children were instructed to scatter in the fields" in the "unlikely event" of a raid. Ironically, 23 bombs were dropped on the Alne Hills in August 1940. Out in the countryside, Leek Wootton, Hampton Lucy and Grendon all found themselves near to several dropped bombs. Dunchurch received a direct hit close to the school.

At Shottery, pupils were divided into groups for dismissal, according to where they lived:

1 : dismissed immediately (children within 2 minutes)
2 : fetched by parents (children within 10 minutes)
3 : stay on premises (too far to go home)

At Cubbington, older pupils were expected to get themselves home rapidly while for their infants: "Mr Ellis's cellar has been allocated to us. 31 children can be comfortably accommodated."

Prisoner Camps

Prisoner of war camps sprouted all over the county, often out in the villages where escapees would be more visible. At Haselor, the children thought that they were "doing their bit for the war effort" when they "messed up the prisoners' camp", scrawling remarks and damaging property. There are reminiscences, too, of camps at Studley and Coleshill. At Wormleighton, one lady recalled the Italian prisoners being more popular than the Germans. Even at five years of age, she recalled learning enough German to trade insults with German Prisoners of War.

Doing One's Bit

One feature of the First World War, repeated in the second, was that of collections. Again, some examples, selected almost at random, indicate the variety and the commitment evident:

Ilmington	300 lbs of paper and 20 lbs of tinfoil
Radford Semele	3748 books for Book Drive
Shrubland Street	9176 books (40 racks) for Book Drive
Little Compton	1.5 cwt of chestnuts
Over Whitacre	900 jam jars
Stockton	2 cwt of horse chestnuts
Wolvey	£639 for Salute the Soldiers
Clifton	Knitted thousands of pairs of socks and mittens
Cubbington C.E.	14 lbs of rose hips in one day
Leek Wootton	8 cwt of waste paper and ½ cwt of cardboard.
Newton Regis	200 fresh eggs for Tamworth Hospital
Stratford Boys	£830
Stratford Girls	£668 for 'Wings For Victory'
Shottery	114 pounds of potatoes grown in school garden

Even a relatively small rural school like that at Napton could reflect with pride in 1942 on amassing:

6 tons of waste paper
5½ tons of scrap iron
1 cwt of brass
3 cwt of bones
2580 lbs of paper
1 cwt of rose hips

Pupils at Attleborough and at Leamington College recalled school fields being dug up to grow vegetables. Even the smallest children were involved. At Ryton-on-Dunsmore: "We also went rosehip picking from school. The teacher had a walking stick to pull the branches down to our height." Older children at Hampton Lucy went pea-picking.

Teachers made their own contributions to the war effort outside school time. Each night three teachers on rota from Rugby High took turns on fire watch duties. They were later reinforced by sixth form girls. There would be three shifts, with those not on duty trying to sleep: pupils on camp beds in the hall and staff on beds in the secretary's office.

Children outside school time also contributed. Chief Scout, Lord Somers, presented the sixth Nuneaton Bermuda Scout Group with the Gilt Cross Medal "in recognition of their gallantry in fighting fires and rescuing people from the ruins following an air raid on Nuneaton on 17th May 1941."

Schools were kept in touch with events by wireless and papers. Letters home also provided personal accounts. A Bedworth teacher, Francis Yallop, sent vividly illustrated letters depicting his service abroad to his daughter Frances. They have been exhibited at the Parsonage Project but are now back in the possession of Frances.

Accommodation

Sometimes, buildings were taken over at short notice for war work. This happened, for example, at Leicester Road and at Ash Green. Part of Leamington College for Girls was temporarily requisitioned by the War Office. At Leicester Road, alternative space was rapidly improvised at two Sunday schools and the Miners' Welfare Pavillion. For security reasons, council minutes did not always specify which schools had been commandeered.

Though these arrangements were only short-lived, they did add to problems of accommodation already compounded by the arrival of so many evacuees. Where new building was imminent, it was usually suspended as money and labour became in short supply. Examples included Atherstone Infants, Keresley Junior and Infants, Hillmorton Paddox Senior, and Southam Senior, suggesting that the disappointment was spread evenly around the county. One consequence was a loss of hall space which severely limited indoor physical training. However, it is not clear whether Mr Rowse, President of Warwickshire County Association of the N.U.T. spoke the literal truth when he praised " ..... good work being carried on in houses, old stables and even cowsheds."

Attendance

The Annual Report on School Attendance for 1942-3, presented by the Director, showed that war had made the usual problems worse. Perkins reported that average attendance was 5-6% below normal: "a deplorable loss". He cited various reasons:

a) working mothers: older children were kept at home to look after younger siblings.
b) difficulties in obtaining footwear.
c) Hairdressers were refusing to cut children's hair in evenings or on Saturdays.
d) Fathers on leave "made an occasion for neglect of school".

The authority did what it could. One decision of the time was to make grants available to children at (e.g.) Churchover, Mappleborough Green and Newton and Biggin to acquire cycles for travel to senior schools.

Sustenance

The war gave fresh and powerful impetus to the sporadic pre-war attempts to introduce school dinners. They began at Westgate and Lapworth in 1942, for example, though not till 1943 at Coughton and 1944 at Nathaniel Newton. Their image then was no better than it would be for most of the rest of the century. Typical fare " ..... some sort of meat in gravy, mashed potatoes and stringy dark cabbage ..... puddings ..... either semolina or tapioca, and, if we were lucky, a spoonful of jam on top."

Potatoes were a staple diet, whether baked, boiled, fried or roasted. There is a story of a teacher at Queen's School disciplined for having asked each child to bring in a potato, ostensibly for study. She then took the whole lot home.

At Bedworth in November 1940, a canteen was opened in a church to serve local schools. The local paper claimed "First School Canteen in the County Great Success of Bedworth Scheme. Two Hundred Children Fed Daily" but with what accuracy is uncertain. At Lapworth, school meals replaced: "margarine sandwiches which had formed the staple diet of so many pupils."

Memories of wartime were often of food: of chips cooked in dripping and then, as dripping became scarce, in butter. This was because at least each family had a ration of butter. Sweets, if they could be found, were often of ingenious concoction such as cocoa and dried milk. The Board of Trade issued helpful guidance to pupils on how to help the war effort. Their leaflet urged girls to use old felt hats to make slippers and instructed boys on how to darn and to clear blocked sinks.

The arrival of American forces brought occasional relief. At Lillington in 1943, the Head noted: "The Director called on Friday to bring 170 bars of chocolate given to the school by the Optimistic Clubs of Canada and the U.S.A." Occasionally, pupils would have the luck to get an unexpected treat. A Chilvers Coton scholar remembered American soldiers throwing sticks of pink bubble gum as they drove by.

Life Goes On

Meanwhile, heads and teachers strove (mainly) womanfully rather than manfully to preserve some normality to aid learning. Though there was little paper and a general shortage of foodstuffs (cookery lessons were severely limited), life at home went on. There were some gains: Aston Cantlow gained its electricity supply in 1943. Even in the dark days of 1940, the Committee felt able to authorise the installation of a new cooking range at Burton Dassett and the resurfacing of the playground at Curdworth.

Normality itself was not always unalloyed relief: "School continues more or less normally ….. Scarlet Fever epidemic" (Eastlands, October 1940). Molly Kenning of Wilmcote was taken by the vicar to Stratford Hospital with a " …. bead up her right nostril."

Older pupils were frequently commandeered to help with agricultural produce, especially in the Autumn: potato picking at Bubbenhall was one of many examples. At Leamington College: "Staff and boys were working almost one hundred garden plots on the school field" and in Atherstone: "In Maths on fine days we would garden as part of "Dig for Victory".

Schools often had to co-exist with others and goodwill could be strained: "The Master's desk appears to have been damaged by acid on the previous evening when the premises were being used by the Home Guard" (Priors Marston, November 18, 1943).

Entertainment and Leisure Activities

The cinemas were popular, and Pathé, Movietone and Gaumont British newsreels kept audiences in touch with morale-boosting news. "Children's Hour" entertained children at tea-time with Uncle Mac, and adventures from Toytown. Some children's authors wrote specifically about the war. Richmal Crompton's William tried to help the war effort in all sorts of ways: "William and the A.R.P." etc. Captain Biggles was also up there fighting for the country. But the highly popular Enid Blyton stories seldom if ever acknowledged the existence of the war at Mallory Towers, or in the idyllic adventures of the Famous Five or The Secret Seven.

A. Green of Rugby contrasted the scarcity of toys with the ready availability of boys' comics: 'Lion' 'Tiger' 'Wizard' 'Film Fun' 'Beano' 'Dandy' and 'Eagle' were examples.

Looking Forward

For much of the war, R.A. (Rab) Butler had been preparing legislation on education to follow the war. Churchill took little interest and expressed surprise that Butler wished to devote time to such matters: an indication that education was not the political priority that it is now. Churchill reportedly dismissed education as "smacking children's bottoms and wiping their noses". Thus, Butler was able to capitalise on the free rein given to him and on a mood of post-war consensus. Early in 1944 a draft Bill's proposal was discussed in detail. The Head of Nathaniel Newton noted in February 1944 attendance at a conference on "The New Education Bill". It proposed to replace the word 'elementary' with 'primary' and had a slogan: "Secondary education for all".

In January 1944, Perkins spoke vehemently at a meeting of the "Stratford

Wranglers" on the need to reform the pre-war system, which he described as " ..... a disgrace ..... too many people were getting too little." He spoke of " ..... a marked inequality of opportunity caused by poverty or wealth ....." ('Warwick Advertiser', Jan 21, 1944).

On 16th February 1944, the Chairman of the Education Committee made a statement welcoming "the general changes" and explaining the provisions. The final paragraph of the statement acknowledged the unreality of planning for such extensive changes when present conditions were "almost desperate" but he pledged "every effort to maintain the reputation of the County Education Service." The Act was to lead to the production of a major county Development Plan designed to implement its proposals.

It was not the 1944 Act that initiated the tripartite system but the Norwood Report that preceded it in 1943. The Norwood Committee, chaired by a former headmaster of Harrow, asserted without apparent evidence that pupils could be categorised into three "types of mind":

a) those capable of learning for its own sake.
b) those who needed knowledge and skills to be applied.
c) those who dealt more easily with concrete matters than with ideas.

Once again, a major Education Act followed a war (The 1902 Act followed the Boer War and The Fisher Act followed the First World War in 1918). One small consequence of the 1944 Education Act was that as from April 1945 the term "County Education Officer" replaced "Director of Education".

The End of the War

Even in February 1945, life had not become completely safe. That year a U.S.A. aircraft loaded with bombs crashed near Temple Grafton. Windows in the school were blown out and the roof damaged. Fortunately, no child was harmed: "The children took shelter under their desks and no-one was injured. When it was felt to be safe, they were taken away from the scene of the explosion. They had a picnic in the fields and were taken home."

The end of the war was greeted in true logbook style with the minimum of fuss. Hampton Lucy provided two examples: "Beginning of two days' holiday to celebrate the cease-fire in Europe. Flags flown" (8.5.95)" and "V. J. Day End of war in Japan and the end of World War II (15.8.45) Wilmcote's entry was a little more fulsome: "The school closed at 4.00 p.m. today; during the evening a public announcement was made that the following day V.E. day was to be a general holiday and Wednesday 9th inst also .... 'God Save the King'."

A General Election occurred in July, and Winston Churchill visited Leamington to speak on behalf of local M.P. Anthony Eden. Shrubland Street School closed for the afternoon: "To allow anyone who wished to see and hear the Prime Minister speak at the Pump Room Gardens."

All kinds of shortages remained, as this reminiscence from Baddesley Ensor shows: "I remember helping George Poole (caretaker) to tear up the newspapers into squares for the toilets. If there was a lesson that Ann and I didn't like we went and asked him if we could help so we could avoid it."

Christmas that year was the start of a slow return to normal. But as the Rugby Advertiser reported, it was a restrained affair:

"The war may be over but schools will still not be able to give the pupils a really good meal at Christmas, although most of them made the best of a bad job and produced something for the breaking-up parties. In all the schools the children had made their own Xmas decorations and arranged them. Carol concerts and plays had been arranged in some cases and at several schools the children received gifts from Xmas trees."

Schools began to turn to problems that would bedevil their lives for most of the rest of the century such as space and staffing. Bearley School, with a proper eye to the main chance, temporarily alleviated its shortage of space by occupying vacated Air Force huts.

An entry in the Stockton logbook in November 1945 exemplified the move of Forces personnel into teaching: "Mr Edwin Collins commenced duties as a temporary teacher. He is an ex R.A.F. Warrant Officer and is attending for teaching practice before entering college."

The County Development Plan

Submitted in 1947, and revised in 1953, its recommendations were a mixture of those that lasted and those overtaken by subsequent events. It envisaged several schools for rebuilding that have long since gone: Honington, Warmington, Alderminster, Brandon, Bickenhill and Wolfhampcote etc. One was threatened with closure but has survived to tell a tale: Mappleborough Green. Less fortunate were those threatened with a closure that would soon engulf them. The roll call of honour included Burmington, Idlicote, Lighthorne, Shotteswell, Wormleighton, Binton and Upper and Lower Shuckburgh. The intention was "to provide at least a three teacher school."

More creatively, new schools were planned for the growth of secondary education: at Shipston, Kineton, Keresley, Southam, Bedworth and Rugby. The Plan also envisaged special schools, perhaps in co-operation with Coventry and Birmingham, for a range of categories: the "delicate" the "sub-normal", and "maladjusted boys", adding tersely: "The need for boys' schools is greater than that for girls."

It declined to contemplate an end to selection: "It would be dangerous to tamper with the existing grammar schools." That decision would be revisited often in future decades.

Emergency teacher-training institutions were rapidly set up, for example at what is now Exhall Grange School but what had then been a munition workers' hostel. In the same year (1948) the City of Coventry Training College was established, also in a war workers' hostel. The students were mainly trained for older pupils. All came straight from the forces. The College was the birth of what would eventually become the Warwick University Institute of Education.

And if local novelist Ursula Bloom was correct in her reflections on life in Alderminster at the end of the war " ….. most families had one baby every 18 months, many (mothers) valiantly suckled their children until they were two years old in the wild hope that it would stop another coming," ….. then it would be no surprise to learn that two issues the LEA would have to tackle in years to come were those of a growth in pupil numbers, and sex education.

Short term measures were inevitable, and some of those measures echoed the war-time resourcefulness that had been used to accommodate evacuees, especially when the school leaving age was raised to fifteen in 1947. Church halls were enlisted in Kingsbury and Leamington, and: "The classroom I taught in was converted from a bicycle shed" noted Mrs. Cooke of her postwar years at Attleborough.

The ubiquity of television at homes and in schools was some way off. A pre-requisite was still for many schools to have a connection to an electricity supply. Fenny Compton was an early beneficiary, in 1945. With such a supply, much more could follow. Many schools had telephones installed. Radford Semele had first a wireless set (1948) and then an electric gramophone (1950).

Heads began to seek a brighter environment. The head of Alveston was reported by the local press to be longing to see the end of "the pea green walls and dark brown and black doors era."

As male teachers returned, so leisure-time activities were galvanised into action. Rugby opened a new amateur theatre in 1948, and the opening production, a home-grown musical, starred several local teachers. Elsewhere, amateur groups and concert parties would utilise the rudimentary facilities of the 'Co-op Hall', found across the county from Bidford to Nuneaton. Basic the facilities might have been, but many youngsters (and young teachers) would begin a lifelong interest there, now that their evenings were restored to them, and properly lit.

In retrospect, the post-war years are often recalled as austere years of unremitting hardship, worsened by a prolonged bitter winter in 1947. Surprisingly, there seem to be few recorded instances of schools closing in spite of deep snow, though children in outlying villages often failed to get in. Sweets were still rationed; events such as Bonfire Night were often no more than a bonfire and some paraffin in the back garden. Cars were a luxury and in schools, cycle sheds were essential, while car-parking space was a low priority.

A New Decade

The fifties were to be a decade of increasing prosperity for most. When was the turning point? Some would see the election of a Conservative Government in 1951. Others might cite the "last fling" of a tired Labour Government: the Festival of Britain in the summer before the election. The latter certainly precipitated travel, with schools from Coughton to Lawrence Sheriff decamping en masse. Either way, optimism was in the air. We had won the war. After five years of post-war austerity, we could begin at last to try to win the peace.

7

Postwar Decades

The 1950's were seen as a more exciting, even decadent period, but only by comparison with the austerity of post-war years. They were as nothing compared with the decade that would follow. But it was actually becoming possible to find somewhere to go out of an evening to other than a pub for a coffee or snack. In towns such as Rugby a converted shop became a "milk-bar" where young men would make a tea or coffee last an hour while they worked their way through the repertoire of the mechanical record-player. Or one could always stop at home and watch the current police and pop programmes: 'Dixon of Dock Green' and '6.5 Special', then seen as positively controversial. A few intrepid souls made the evening journey from Rugby and Nuneaton to the post-war glamour of the Locarno Ballroom at Coventry, but decorum remained a restraint: "For some reason you were not considered to be very ladylike if you jived," said Maureen Kindon. She recalled more staid, genteel pastimes " ….. going for walks or bike rides and calling in at the British Restaurant for a cup of coffee and listening to the jukebox."

Where did one play? Whether the nearest 'rec.' was near or not, you still could not beat " ….. a bomb site, wild long grass, trees, a small pond, lots of tins, bricks ….." This was a description of a part of New Bilton, Rugby, near the Cement Works known as 'Happy Valley'!

Part of the excitement of childhood then was the staged ending of rationing. A sweet ration of a couple of ounces weekly did much for healthy eating but little for morale. The announcement of unlimited sweets, pocket money permitting, was understandably a memorable event: "I distinctly remember the assembly where Mr Hinde the Headmaster announced that sweets were off the ration …… Stebbings the corner shop was jam-packed from then on" (Shirley Wallbank : then at the Paddox School).

It was a time when deference and staid conformity were being challenged by subversive forces. The perceived bastions of respectability were caricatured: the B.B.C. as "Auntie" and the typical, easily shocked theatregoer as Aunt Edna. The first 'Teddy Boys' appeared : young males with greased back hair, thick-soled shoes and long jackets.

The first transistor radios allowed youngsters to escape from the parental restrictions and choose more adventurously. "The Goons" and "Hancock's Half Hour" were preferred to "A Life of Bliss" and "Meet the Huggetts". They could even seek out the forbidden charms of Radio Luxembourg's "Journey into Space". Indeed, science fiction films and books became much more popular as, imaginatively at least, youngsters sought to escape from post-war parochialism.

Sexual boundaries were extended, or at least the explicitness of the media in discussing them. Denis Norden, co-creator of 'Ron and Eth', once described courting in the fifties as " ….. like driving with one foot on the accelerator and one on the brake, simultaneously."

There would be less braking in the sixties. Young singers embarking on their careers were incurring the wrath of horrified parents and the fervent support of excited youngsters : singers like Cliff Richard and Tommy Steele! With hindsight we can see that Bill Haley's "Rock Around the Clock" was a more reliable harbinger of the direction pop music was to take. Or Elvis Presley : "I just glower and wiggle my jeans and the women scream out loud." A few years later, a little-known group played the Co-op Dance Hall at Nuneaton ….. a group with the name of The Beatles.

Cinemas became very popular, with many providing Saturday morning programmes for the children. But inflation ensured that the pre-war 'Tuppeny Rush' had become the 'Saturday Flicks' at sixpence a seat. But for the moment the radio programme 'Children's Favourites' reflected the last of a more innocent age. It was still getting requests for 'The Runaway Train' 'Sparkie's Magic Piano' and 'How Much is that Doggie in the Window?' And as for dancing ….. on wet games days, many pupils learned (in single sex schools) those dances deemed necessary to prepare oneself for adult life : the waltz, the quickstep or the Gay Gordons.

Technology Advances

At least one writer, Arnold Evans, writing in the Times Educational Supplement I.C.T. supplement, has noted that the most sophisticated technology encountered by most people in the early fifties was "the ingenious little key that mysteriously opened the tin of Spam."

After the war, few homes had a television. The Coronation in 1953 provided the incentive for many families to make their first purchase ….. or rental. Nearly half of the population saw the Coronation on 2,700,000 sets. Clearly, there were some very crowded living rooms or (occasionally) halls that day. But even in 1955, the wireless still led the way : the audience for 'The Archers' outnumbered televisions viewers by two to one. By 1966 however, the proportion of households with television licences had risen to nearly 80%.

Two major royal events stimulated great enthusiasm for television, not least in schools. Children from Over Whitacre were taken to watch the funeral of George VI on television. The venue is unclear. The following year a television was installed at Fenny Compton School so that children could watch the coronation of Queen Elizabeth II. Again, it is unclear whether the installation was temporary or permanent. Installation of televisions was not always recorded, but many schools waited for nearly twenty years to have their own: Long Compton and St. Anthony's finally received a set in 1968. Meanwhile, the 'wireless' continued to support learning. Generations of children such as those at Eastlands and Harbury sat round the wireless for their music lessons, joining in to the upbeat entreaties of William Appleby in 'Singing Together'.

Though technology continued to help to widen horizons, it was never without its limitations: 'T.V. delivered. Can only be used in Hall and two rooms as will not go up hall steps. Over one third of hall time given over to viewing. Applied for second set' (Bishop's Itchington, 1971). Yorke-Lodge chided schools such as Quinton for over-use of the telephone to contact the office at Warwick. He urged a return to letter-writing. It was cheaper!

Technology began now to insinuate its way into the life of schools in a variety of forms: piped water for Lapworth and flush toilets for Clifton (1951) ..... an 'electric gramophone' for Radford Semele (1950), and reminiscences of an adventurous teacher at Baddesley Ensor who taped his class's play readings early in the decade. Pupils from All Saints and Oken at Warwick listened to a tape sent to them by pupils from Queensland, Australia.

Not all technological innovation was welcomed, as Josie Commander, former secretary at Baddesley Ensor recalled:

"One of my worst nightmares was the duplicating machine. This should have been in a museum 10 to 20 years before I started work at the school. To use this machine you had to type out what you wanted onto a 'skin', then fix it to the machine, make sure it was 'inked' with duplicating fluid and then switch It on. If you were lucky, it worked, but nine times out of ten it had to be done manually. This was really messy, and there used to be blobs of ink all over the paper, especially the first few run off. These 'skins' used to be kept in case they were needed again. They were hung on the back of the door in my office; was I glad to see the back of them when the machine eventually was disposed of! I am really grateful for photocopiers!"

Early 'Primary' Education

A report belonging to Anna Hunter is instructive. It came from Rokeby Primary in 1957, and was part of a Jubilee exhibition in Rugby Library in 2002. One comment could sum up the frustrations of educating children over hundreds of years: "Anna tends to forget old work when some new work is informed."

On the report the subjects R.I., Handicrafts, Geography and Nature Study had no comment. Art and History had been deleted and 'Tables' and 'Mental Arithmetic' substituted. Plus ça change? The priorities seem familiar, and the debate on the merits and the distractions of a broad curriculum was still at an early stage. Reports on many younger children were confined to five entries under the headings: Reading, Writing, Number, Activities and Remarks (the head's summary).

Catch a Falling Standard?

For those who believe that education's decline and fall began in the wicked decade of the 1960's, they should note that decadence and falling standards were thriving long before. A major conference for teachers was held in Leamington in 1952. Nearly one thousand delegates heard the Vice Principal of Saltley Training College denounce "the appalling ignorance of trainee teachers in simple arithmetical calculations." The cause? Apparently, a lack of commitment to "the basics". According to one inspector: "The three Rs have been ousted." He added: "What I miss as I go about schools is real teaching."

Clearly, a Numeracy Strategy was needed.

Sanctions

Throughout the fifties and sixties there were campaigns to abolish corporal and capital punishment. Most who supported one, supported the other. Some even confused the two. In two different schools in which I taught I requested topics for debates. One answer that came back on both occasions was 'abolition of capital punishment in schools'.

Caning outlived hanging by many years. Schools continued to use it untrammelled generally by either parental or public concern. Apart from the occasional letter asking that it be administered on the hand only, few documentary records survive. Though every school using caning would have been required to maintain a record : a 'punishment book', few appear to have been preserved anywhere. One exception is that of Dunsmore Boys' School, Rugby where 43 pages of a Warwickshire Education Committee exercise book diverted to this purpose recorded three years of offences. They ranged mostly from stark one word offences: 'disobedience' ….. 'impertinence' ….. 'insolence' ….. 'discourtesy' and the enigmatic 'indecency' through the elaborated versions: 'deliberate disobedience' ….. 'open insolence' ….. 'gross impertinence' and the less obvious 'indecorous behaviour' to the 'two-for-the-price-of-one offers': 'yawning and laughing' ….. 'stealing and lying' ….. 'insolence and disobedience'. A particular favourite of mine, suggesting that children don't change that much, was: 'Hurling words of abuse through open window at visiting cricket team'.

Another book retained on site is that at King Edward College, Nuneaton, where one offence was reported enigmatically thus: "Inappropriate use of a poker." Lesser caneworthy offences were: "Slackness in note bringing" and that now dated umbrella term: "Horseplay". Cross-curricular initiatives were seemingly discouraged, the cane being used for such offences as: "Doing Maths in History lesson" and "Singing in the classroom." Another entry, reflecting unacceptable behaviour in school but in harmony with some early popular feeling outside, came a little later: "calling the metric system b …… lousy."

One departure from the expected standards much harder to deal with was that of the lad at the Borough School in Warwick who often came to school smelling unpleasantly. The head finally, and with trepidation, wrote to his mother. She responded tartly: "I send him to school for you to learn him, not to sniff him."

Sins of Youth

There were competing versions of the worst evils to beset young people. The head of Rowington School offered his nomination: "The increasing number (of children) who went to bed late." Local Councillor Keith Judge, reflecting on his wartime schooldays at Long Lawford, ruefully noted: "These days everyone appears to be obsessed by sex. It was certainly not mentioned when I was at school."

The Development of 'Secondary' Schools

The long slow process, begun by the Hadow Report, of turning elementary schools into either primary or secondary according to local need, continued well into the 1950's. In 1955, Polesworth Central became Polesworth Secondary. Soon afterwards the Eastlands schools reverted to primary while the eleven plus pupils moved to the newly opened Dunsmore Schools a mile away. Some ex-pupils still recall walking to the new school carrying items that would be needed there.

But even in 1958 Richard Hoggart, about to take up an appointment at the newly-created University of Leicester, was able to write: "Most (pupils) were educated at what ought now to be called a secondary modern school but is still popularly known as an elementary school."

One debate that dominated the educational agenda both locally and nationally was that between those who favoured selection at eleven plus, or at an age close to eleven, and those who favoured comprehensive schools: ones which catered for children of all abilities. A Fabian pamphlet in 1941 had suggested multi-lateral schools: ones which housed pupils of all abilities but who had been divided into "streams": grammar, technical and modern, by a test at eleven.

Moves towards comprehensive schooling were slow. Brian Simon who, for many years, taught at nearby Leicester University, set out in the Spring of 1954 to visit every functioning comprehensive school in England and Wales. It did not take long; he found only thirteen, eight of which were on Anglesey and the Isle of Man. The nearest to Warwickshire was in Walsall. Soon afterwards, the first two opened in Coventry, including Binley Park, very close to the Warwickshire schools in Binley village. Coventry's distinctive contribution was the establishment of the house system as a physical entity. The first comprehensive school opened in Birmingham was at Great Barr in 1956. A local indicator of the debate was a book called "The Child of Eleven" by Dennis Skeet, French teacher at Lawrence Sheriff School, and published in the late 1950's. It received national coverage in the press.

By 1964 a Labour Government had been elected for the first time since 1951. It was committed to promoting comprehensive schooling and one year later the number stood at 262 comprehensive schools educating 8.5% of pupils in the maintained sector. That percentage had risen to 32% by 1970 when a Conservative Government returned to power. After four years of Ted Heath's government it had rocketed to nearly 70%. Who presided over education in these eventful four years? The Secretary of State was one Margaret Thatcher who approved more comprehensive schemes than anyone before or since. She has never been allowed to forget this although, in truth, she came into office when an L.E.A.-driven irresistible acceleration was under way. But what was happening in Warwickshire during these momentous years?

The 'High School' Experiment

While Warwickshire was slow off the mark with comprehensive schools, Committee in 1956 began to initiate the 'High School' project, as this report cautiously tells:

"It would accord with these lines of thought if the terms "Secondary Technical" and "Secondary Modern" were not used to describe any secondary school in the county, and if schools of these kinds were known in future as "High Schools". The suggestion that there should be increased specialisation means that the schools would progressively require to be staffed and supplied for the wider range of courses they would be providing.

In present economic circumstances, the development of the scheme must of necessity be slow, and we take the view that the best approach will be to start with the equipment of a few schools in the coming year. Accordingly we have instructed the County Education Officer to work out, in consultation with the heads, the application of the Warwickshire High School principle to the existing Secondary Modern Schools, so that the requirements may be considered at our meeting next quarter."

A leaflet to parents in 1965 explained the system thus:

Going to a Secondary School

"Next July, some 7,000 Warwickshire children will leave their primary schools, and after the summer holidays will start the second stage of their education, in secondary schools. That will be an important point in their lives. Their parents will want to know about the secondary schools which their children will go to, and these notes answer some of the questions they will wish to ask.

In most parts of the County, there are two kinds of secondary schools - High Schools and Grammar Schools. Most children will go to High Schools, and some to Grammar Schools. What is the difference?

Grammar Schools and High Schools

High Schools are for all children except those who, by the age of 11, have already shown that they can learn a good deal faster and more easily than most children can. Because these children - about one in four or five - learn so much faster and more easily, they go to a Grammar School where the pace is quicker, and more exacting demands are made on them, than most children can manage.

In High Schools, children can leave when they are 15, but more and more are staying on for one, two or even three years longer, with great advantage to themselves. In the Grammar School, every child is expected to stay at least until 16, and normally until 17 or 18."

To this day, Warwickshire's non selective schools in the East and South of the county are designated 'High' Schools : Studley High, Bilton High etc. This dates from a time in 1959 when Committee finally decided to redesignate all of its so-called secondary modern schools and encouraged them to develop into 11-16 schools, following trials at Bidford and Polesworth, with examination courses. This change in nomenclature was reported thus in the Birmingham Post: "All 53 secondary modern schools in Warwickshire have now been converted to high schools and are in academic orbit."

Kineton: A Typical Warwickshire High School?

Kineton has provided a fine example of how the 'High School' initiative brought long overdue opportunities to all parts of the county. There had been talk of a senior school in the village at least as far back as 1937. The honourable Mabel Verney, still active in local education, advocated the case with characteristic energy almost literally till the day she died. But the war, and post-war stringencies, delayed action. Kineton High School opened to pupils in September 1957, a striking example of an early purpose-built school. Built at a cost of approximately £61,000, it opened with 262 pupils from an area which stretched from Ettington to Fenny Compton. A brief calendar takes the story on:

1959 : Sixth form started
1961 : First students to College of Education
1965 : First student to university
1968 : First student graduated

When the school opened, its intended maximum was 560. But the growth of sixth form numbers and its popularity produced a roll of 740 by 1969. In a letter to Lord Willoughby de Broke, the chief guest at the formal opening of the school, the County Education Officer, Yorke-Lodge had written: "Warwickshire is making a determined effort to take secondary education forward a whole generation in a few months."

But Kineton was just one of many new schools, both secondary and primary, to open in the next few years. In Alcester, three opened in three years : St. Benedict's R.C. High (1963), St. Faith's C.E. Junior (1964) and Greville High (1966).

The First Comprehensive School

Warwickshire's first comprehensive school, like many claims to be first, is subject to some debate about exact terminology. But a powerful case must be accorded to Nicholas Chamberlaine School.

Back in 1919 representatives of the local churches, the council schools and the Miners' Union unanimously urged the building of a County Secondary School, using funds from the Nicholas Chamberlaine Trust. But the church and the county council failed to agree on funding. Eventually the Trust lost interest and it was not until the late forties that a model of a new school was displayed in the window of a local department store. It opened in September 1952 with the full ability range of pupils. Thus, it had a comprehensive intake, the first county secondary school to do so. But it was not truly comprehensive, for the eleven plus test remained, and its intake arrived labelled according to their results in that test : 'grammar' 'technical' or 'modern'. They were streamed and taught separately, mixing only in games. The stream a pupil was in determined what was taught, learnt and by whom. School historian Thomas Anney observed: "It was always the 'modern' girls who sorted laundry and served the staff with their tea."

Pupils took annual exams in December, and on those results it was possible to move from one stream to another. But the streams remained quite distinct. Thus the school then was a 'multilateral' or three stream intake school, similar to some large schools in London, precursors of the comprehensive, but not truly so because the eleven plus still dictated the label that pupils brought to school. According to Anney: "It was not until 1957 that the county agreed to the name 'comprehensive' ..... the school was then one of only 26 comprehensives in the country ..... In 1969 it was still the only comprehensive in Warwickshire."

Purists would argue that even in 1969, given that four of its twelve forms of entry were selective, it was still not truly comprehensive. The Dunsmore Schools in Rugby, organised on similar lines, continued to be designated "bilateral". But given that supporters of Eton have contended that it is a comprehensive school, there will always be scope for debate.

In October 1962, the Committee received a report that: "Warwickshire was leading the country in its high school system." A year later they learned of an eight fold increase in the number of G.C.S.E. passes obtained by high school pupils since the system had begun.

But once again, the county managed to insert a maverick into its system: Rugby High School, within a mile of Bilton and Harris High Schools, was in fact a selective girls' high school. No wonder that initially there was local annoyance at the use of the same label to describe very different kinds of school.

The Education Committee learned in September 1962 that staying on rates beyond the then leaving age of fifteen were increasing rapidly. Before High Schools replaced their 'secondary modern' predecessors, the numbers were 506 (1958). By 1962, they stood at 3,338. The increase was attributed chiefly to opportunities to take external examinations. Numbers of G.C.E. 'passes' had risen dramatically over the same period. Another consequence of the 'High School' system was a drop in the number of pupils seeking transfer to grammar schools at thirteen plus.

The development of the system was not without its troubles or its sceptics. Many schools found it difficult to staff examination courses with suitably qualified teachers. The Head of Shipston High, reporting to his governors in 1959, noted ruefully: "It is most unsettling and worrying to feel that I might lose staff. The fact is that they are being implored to go and work elsewhere." Nor did the G.C.E. seem the ideal examination for many of the pupils now opting to remain in school an extra year. The same head, noting relatively low pass rates in 1965, informed his governors that: "We have had serious and professional doubts about the narrow and cramming methods that have to be used."

By now there was a powerful impetus to improve the educational lot of the so-called 'average' and 'less able', or the 'lesser abler' as one Warwickshire head used to call them. An enquiry into their education, especially the 13-16 year olds, led to the publication of the Newsom Report in 1963. Entitled persuasively 'Half Our Future', it examined the education of the youngsters still almost entirely in the country's nearly 4,000 secondary modern schools. It recommended the raising of the school leaving age by 1969. It happened eventually, after postponement, in 1972, and for a while ROSLA was an oft-mentioned acronym in relation to buildings and courses.

The Certificate of Secondary Education

The late sixties saw a much-welcomed introduction of a new 16 plus examination : the C.S.E. or Certificate of Secondary Education. In shorthand it was seen by most as the examination that took over where G.C.E. success tailed off. Its advocates, however, insisted that it was a quite different examination and not directly comparable to the G.C.E. Notwithstanding this disclaimer, a C.S.E. Grade 1 was deemed officially to be the equivalent of a G.C.E. pass, though some employers locally took time to accept this. The Committee learned in 1967 that there were 8,652 entries across the county, including some from grammar schools.

More New Buildings

The 1960's led to another and essential acceleration in an already ambitious building programme. It was hardly surprising: the school population was to increase by 50% over the next ten years. Sometimes this was prompted by rapid growth in housing : in Chelmsley Wood, Keresley and Weddington, for example, where new primary and secondary schools were built. Elsewhere, as at Newbold, existing schools were significantly expanded. Often, the buildings were to replace existing schools and to provide pupils with brighter, more modern facilities. At one end of Rugby, Westlands High School for Girls was rebuilt alongside Herbert Kay High School for Boys. The two would soon merge to form Bilton High School, although to this day its dual origins are evident - in two sizeable halls, for example. At the other end of town, two schools prepared to move to new premises with cautious optimism. The Head of Murray School, in a Christmas edition of "The Murrayian" mused thus:

"Within the next four years, our boys will be based ..... in a modern building. It will be good, too, to have our sister school, St. Andrew's Benn with us. In the past, the social training of the odd party or dancing lesson, though a step in the right direction, was never really adequate."

Thus was anticipated Fareham High School (which itself would in the 1980's be absorbed into Ashlawn School).

Meanwhile, never wasteful of precious resources, the Education Committee put the vacated schools into other uses: Westlands became St. Matthew's, while St. Andrew's Benn retained its name but became a primary school. Murray School was demolished and the site is now used for old people's flats. Elsewhere, schools were opened to serve new housing developments: Sydenham, Brookhurst and Budbrooke were just three examples within a few miles of one another.

Out with the Old - In With the New?

Continuing Changes

Notwithstanding the widespread and energetic activity in opening new schools, Committee had in April 1965 drawn up plans to close some seventy small schools. While most were to go sooner or later, some under threat have survived to this day: Newbold-on-Stour, Gaydon, Stockton, Temple Grafton, Dunnington, Salford Priors, Haselor, Lapworth, Newton Regis, Mappleborough Green, Burton Green and Leek Wootton form a roll of honour. Others such as Bubbenhall escaped the axe then, but just missed the twenty first century.

Ironically, it was the sheer number of small and scattered rural primary schools in South Warwickshire that would exempt the area from the 1970's re-organisation into middle schools, and therefore from the 1990's re-reorganisation.

Each proposed village school closure caused protracted opposition. Many proposals were rejected by the Government, at least in the short-term. For example, Maxstoke School was reprieved by Education Minister Ted Short.

"If these children are swept away to receive their early education in Shustoke, it will amount to murdering the community spirit," was the assertion of a local alderman. Similar statements were invariably made whenever closure proposals were announced. In an attempt to head off opposition, George Hoopell, Assistant County Education Officer, assured critics that the Education Committee had wished to keep every village school open, but they had now changed that policy because of: a) a shortage of teachers and b) developments in primary education that needed more specialised education.

This latter point presumably referred to early thoughts of a re-organisation of primary education into 8-12 middle schools where specialist teaching would be needed for the older pupils, not least as part of a deal to placate the wrath of secondary schools who were to talk of the "lost year". The wrath was not always confined to secondary schools, although middle schools also had fervent and cogent advocates.

Openings and closings continued throughout the 1960's and 1970's, with closures of small primary schools. A few examples across the county:

1966 : Wolverton
1967 : Preston Bagot, Withybrook
1968 : Wolfhampcote, Flecknoe
1969 : Brandon
1970 : Shotteswell/Warmington

Shotteswell had dropped to fifteen on roll, and Warmington to 20.

In 1972 three coach loads of parents from Ryton travelled to Rugby to protest against proposals to make the village school a first school. An independent school was set up in the Village Hall for a while.

Visiting some of these villages now, one finds it hard to imagine that there were ever enough pupils to justify a school. But opponents of these and other closures would and did argue that the closing of the school itself often discouraged growth and encouraged people to move elsewhere. Each closure generated meetings, angry correspondence and heated altercations, but it was only in a few cases, for example at Warmington in 1970, that protests succeeded in forcing the authority to postpone closure.

Villages that lost their schools often included those close to busy thoroughfares:

Halford and Hunningham (the Fosse Way)
Ufton (Leamington to Southam road)
Marton (Coventry to Banbury road)
Brandon (Coventry to Rugby road)
Warmington (Warwick to Banbury road)
Burton Hastings (Watling Street)
Great Wolford (Shipston to Woodstock road)
Clifford Chambers (Stratford to Mickleton road)

Other villages would merit a special journey to find them. One is unlikely to be 'passing through' Preston-on-Stour, or Grandborough, unless on a country drive.

Some villages had their own schools while not being deemed large enough to be recorded either in Arthur Mee's guide to Warwickshire or, fifty years later, the 'Warwickshire Village Book' published by the Warwickshire Federation of Women's Institutes; in a lifetime of criss-crossing Warwickshire, I have yet to visit Flecknoe or Stretton-on-Fosse. Yet each one had a thriving school with generations of pupils, memorable headteachers and countless stories to tell.

A project at Fenny Compton School enabled pupils to compile a complete record of the local parish as it was in 1947. A further twenty years later, enabled some comparisons between the forties and the sixties. Though with three fewer pupils in 1967 (it had lost those pupils aged over eleven) it had one more classroom, five more sinks, seven more washbasins, hot water, central heating and a playing field. By 1967 the average ten year old spent 3 hours watching television on a weekday, and 4 hours at the weekend. Bucket toilets had almost disappeared. Growth occupations among parents included lorry drivers, electricians and office workers. In decline were those working on farms and railways.

Ufton School was another to respond to an invitation by the Warwickshire Rural Community Council to contribute to a village survey project. It included an item on the leisure time of a ten year old in the sixties:

	Weekday	Weekend
Average T.V.	4 hrs	5 hrs
Average reading	1 hr	1/2 hr
Average playtime	1 hr	4 hrs

But Ufton School disappeared, along with many more. Often, their passing was signalled only briefly in the final logbook entry: "No songs, no concerts, no ceremony beyond the presenting of two cheques" (Aston Cantlow, 1965). "It is a sad day for Maxstoke as the school has closed for the last time" (1968).

The Opening of New Schools

In the midst of death was yet more life. Many fell; many more new schools opened. To take just one instance, between 1956 and 1970, four new schools opened in Whitnash. In chronological order, they were Whitnash Primary, St. Margaret's C.E., St. Joseph's R.C. and Briar Hill C.E. Of course, opening did not always mean ready. Whitnash Primary waited four days after its opening for paper towels and a month for typewriters. When Nicholas Chamberlaine School opened in the early nineteen fifties, the Head noted an audit of what the school had "no traditions, a staff of strangers, no telephone, no playing fields, an unfinished building …. but with the bright-eyed faith of a venture into the unknown."

One effect of the sixties building programmes was to move schools out of town. This was most evident in Rugby, where schools such as Elborow, Wood Street, Benn, Chapel Street, St. Matthew's and Murray all disappeared to be replaced by new schools on the edge of town. Now, only Northlands and Lawrence Sheriff remain "in town". The same was true, though to a lesser extent, in Atherstone, Nuneaton and Warwick. One admittedly fallible way of testing this dispersal from the town centres was to see how many schools remained within a reasonable walking distance of their town library. In the larger towns it is usually only the older schools such as Etone in Nuneaton, St. Peter's in Leamington and St. Matthew's Bloxam in Rugby. New schools had to search for land out of town, for that was where the new housing estates were …… estates that were producing a school population growing at twice the rate of the national average for England and Wales.

Rugby illustrated well the post-war acceleration in the building of new schools. Between the wars just three had been built : Rugby High, Paddox and Northlands. Between 1945 and 1971, thirty new schools were opened.

Most postwar new primary schools were built on the 'open plan' rather than the traditional 'closed classroom' system to encourage more flexible and integrated ways of working. Staff were not always convinced either of the value of the methods being promoted, or the real motive. "The Philosophy was money" observed a retired teacher who worked at Woodloes First School. The staff and managers at St. Francis R.C. Bedworth were, in 1970 "unanimous in asking that this part of the school should not be in the open plan system."

Meanwhile, the demand for secondary places seemed almost insatiable : 450 at Newbold Grange, 150 at Keresley Newland High etc. (Yet within 25 years one would be threatened with closure, and Keresley would indeed close.)

New school buildings, like all new buildings, generated heated debate. In committee, Alderman Tickle described the new schools as "hideous" and Councillor Harris (who gave his name to the Harris School) complained of too much glass. Yorke-Lodge pleaded post-war government regulations on areas of light in mitigation.

As early as 1952, the House of Commons Select Committee had expressed concern about the proportion of glass in school buildings. It could cause hot classrooms in summer, for example, and problems with glare. But it was cheap ... or cheaper. And with a mounting school population, the building went on.

Politics and Education

The 1950's and 1960's had been characterised by optimism and a consensus about much that was educational policy. The major challenge had been how best to cope with larger numbers of children. The breakdown of the consensus began soon after the Plowden Report in 1967. Symptomatic of this breakdown was the publication of the "Black Papers", the first in 1969. They could be loosely termed "right-wing", attracting writers such as Kingsley Amis and Rhodes Boyson. They ranged from the polemical to more thoughtful critiques. They opened with attacks on the increasing numbers of university students, but soon moved to attack recent developments in primary and comprehensive school developments. Writers such as H.J. Eysenck and Cyril Burt all supported selection, setting etc. and cited in support a paper by Arthur Jensen arguing that racial and social class differences in intelligence were genetically determined; at least 80% of the variance was due to heredity.

While much of the debate was about schools in London, one did not have to look far to see examples of the polarisation of issues. The education department at nearby Leicester University contained Professor Brian Simon of the left and G.H. Bantock, regular Black Paper contributor. Within fifteen miles of Warwickshire's grammar schools and of Rugby School was Countesthorpe College, arguably the most "progressive" state school in England, where most policies were settled by vote of the pupils and staff combined.

Circular 10/65

In 1965, the recently elected Labour Government, albeit with a tiny majority, issued a circular (10/65) in which it required local authorities to prepare and to submit schemes for re-organising their secondary schools on comprehensive lines. Secretary of State Anthony Crosland recalled that he seldom had to take education matters to the Cabinet, but Circular 10/65 was a rare exception. The Government saw this as a major part of its policy.

The Education Committee's response to Circular 10/65 was to consult, prepare a complex and comprehensive draft plan and then consult again. Their proposals were for 11-18 comprehensives where possible. To respond to the particular size and distribution of schools in the Alcester, Bidford and Studley areas the proposal was for 5-9, 9-13 and 13-18 schools. Though this scheme never really left the drawing board, it was adopted in parts of neighbouring Worcestershire.

Correspondence exists to show how the County worked with the church authorities to keep them informed and co-operative by giving them advance details. Just as well, given a prolonged debate, characterised variously by passion, principle and politics. For the next ten years at least, plans, consultations and heated debate were rarely far from the headlines. The Coventry Evening Telegraph retains carefully compiled files which chronicled such movement as there was:

'Schools - Future Again Unsettled'
'Committee Stays Silent on the Future of Education'
'Re-organisation Hits Snag'
'Shire Hall Asked to Think Again on School Plans'

All kinds of people felt impelled to offer a view. ' "Preserve Choice of Schools" says Actress' (Wendy Craig)

As early as November 1967, the Evening Telegraph was asking whether the battle for comprehensive schools was almost over: 'County's last 11 Plus?' it asked, rhetorically. Yet the County still has its eleven-plus in two parts of the county to this day. What went wrong - or right?

In short, the combination of Conservative-led county councils and a series of Conservative Governments, countered sporadically by minority Labour Governments, meant that there was rarely prolonged and concerted political will. In Stratford in particular, proponents of the comprehensive cause were faced with strong, even hostile opposition, and buildings not easily adapted. Some used the oft-claimed success of the 'high' schools to question the need for change. Others wondered why there could not be an extension of the bilateral school idea.

Bilateral schools were 'two stream' schools. Examples included the Dunsmore Schools at Rugby, and the Hugh Clopton Girls' School at Stratford. The latter had been designated bilateral after the war in the absence of any grammar school provision for girls in Stratford. Each admitted both eleven plus 'passes' and 'failures', though the words 'pass' and 'fail' were studiously avoided. The intake comprised a comprehensive range of ability, but children arrived at their schools with a label and their ability intake was skewed towards the more able. A true comprehensive would have the equivalent of 20% of grammar school successes. Bilateral schools admitted up to 50% (then, but not now).

The Dunsmore Schools were envisaged when opened as "Technical Schools", a kind of school anticipated in the 1944 Act. In the mid fifties there were more than 300 in the country. After that, they declined in number, largely because of no clear conception of quite what these schools were meant to be. With more vision, they could perhaps have become 'City Technology Colleges.' But they were popular with the parents; the story was that in Rugby, estate agents had the Dunsmore catchment area boundaries on their maps.

The issue of the future of these schools was resolved in Stratford by the opening in 1958 of its first grammar school for girls at Shottery. When Lieutenant Colonel Fordham Flower moved out of Shottery Manor, the Council purchased the property, rapidly added a complex of buildings and opened the school still often referred to as "Shottery". Hugh Clopton thus lost its grammar intake to its neighbour across the field and instead combined with the boys' school next door to make Stratford High a non-selective mixed school.

Meanwhile, the comprehensive debate continued to flicker and flare elsewhere. The somewhat unexpected election of a Conservative Government in 1970 led to the withdrawal of circular 10/65 at the instigation of the new Secretary of State, Margaret Thatcher. Proposals to turn Lawrence Sheriff into a sixth form college with remaining schools as 12-16 comprehensives attracted some support from teachers, notably at Harris, Fareham and Herbert Kay, but considerable hostility elsewhere. But the strongest opposition to the abolition of grammar schools was in Stratford.

Eventually, after a plethora of meetings, documents and heated correspondence, two areas of the county 'went comprehensive'. Nuneaton developed a sixth form college. Leamington and Kenilworth developed large 'federation' comprehensives, on split sites. North Leamington and Kenilworth developed sixth form centres some distance from the rest of the school. Just one quotation to illustrate the powerful feelings generated on both sides of the debate came from the history of Leamington College for Girls. The history of the school began: "This is the story of the birth, growth and premature death of a county grammar school."

Many of the decisions made stemmed from the need to have schools large enough to generate economic sixth forms, while not so large as to fuel the fears of those who thought comprehensive schools were too large. And whatever plan emerged had to take account of the existing buildings and, rightly or wrongly. the historical status of and the powerful lobby for the grammar schools.

The Introduction of First and Middle Schools

There is so much more that could have been written about the decade leading up to the opening of Warwickshire's new comprehensive schools. But this was not the only re-organisation debate to occupy the minds of councillors and teachers. Committee responded to the influential 1967 'Plowden Report' by deciding to re-organise the county's primary schools. The key idea was the development of 8-12 middle schools. Thus, the age of transfer from primary to secondary was to change from eleven to twelve.

Although prompted by the Plowden Report, this policy initiative was seen by some as a convenient way to pre-empt the classic anti-comprehensive accusation: that they were too large and therefore impersonal. By removing year seven, the embryonic comprehensive schools could remain large enough to generate an economically workable sixth form, while not becoming too large in numbers overall. Nationally, the growth of middle schools accelerated: 15 in 1969, but 1,650 in 1978.

This re-organisation had its own attendant round of consultations, proposals etc. One logbook entry could have been replicated many times. From Long Lawford School:

"Mr Ruscoe, the Divisional Educational Officer, visited the school to interview all the staff individually so that he could explain how the 1973 re-organisation might affect teachers and so that he could make himself aware of individual preference."

Meetings with parents were at best anxious and searching, at worst cynical and hostile: "The Deputy C.E.O. outlined the scheme for first, middle and senior schools; he left the unfortunate impression that consultation with parents was largely eyewash"

Such meetings would have taken place in most of the county's 300 or so primary schools, each striving to reconcile concern for the individual with a countywide strategy.

In the event, Long Lawford would have a 5-12 combined school, as did the less sizeable villages such as Harbury, Hurley and Wolvey. Most primary schools became either 'first' (5-8) or 'middle' (8-12). Committee strove to provide extra funding for combined and middle schools in order to provide more specialised teaching and accommodation for "the extra year". The Southern Area remained unchanged. Its scattered and numerous small village schools defeated planners.

Local Government Reorganisation

And then there was the mere matter of local government re-organisation. The Heath Government reforms of the 1970's created new administrative areas such as Avon and Humberside. Locally, it effected significant changes, turning Warwickshire from one of the largest to the sixth smallest county in England. It reduced the county's population almost by a third by removing Solihull and Sutton Coldfield. There was much regret but a little relief; at least county had no longer to worry about provision of school places for the rapidly burgeoning estate of Chelmsley Wood on the edge of Birmingham. (In the event some pupils then, as now, continued to attend Warwickshire schools, chiefly in Coleshill.)

Whatever the upheaval in the council offices at Sutton Coldfield and Solihull, the change appeared to leave the schools relatively unruffled, provided that the salary cheques continued to arrive. At Chapelfields, once a Warwickshire primary, now part of the Solihull family, the hand-over received no mention at all in the logbook. The only clues were in the names of some of the L.E.A. visitors before and after. This school, like most, had long been used to dealing mainly with a local office at Solihull anyway.

A New Minister

An early adviser to the new Secretary of State, Margaret Thatcher, was one Dr Rhodes Boyson, head of Highbury Grove School in London. In an article in The Spectator in July 1970 he urged her to slow down comprehensivation, introduce student loans instead of grants and restructure teachers' salaries to ensure that better teachers were paid more. But comprehensivation proceeded faster than ever in her period of office, though she intervened to modify some schemes, for example in Birmingham. Margaret Thatcher replaced Sir Edward Boyle, M.P. for Handsworth in Birmingham and seen as the personification of "the educational consensus" which had promoted comprehensive schools and 'progressive' teaching methods.

Mrs Thatcher paid an early visit to the county. Her day in Warwickshire was typically long, energetic and eventful. She was met at Coventry Station early in the morning and taken to several schools in Chelmsley Wood and Sutton Coldfield. Her day was to end with a prize giving at Leamington College where she faced a student demonstration. In order to spare her too much hostility she was taken out afterwards by a side-door and driven to Rugby Station to pre-empt further demonstrations at Coventry Station. Perhaps this was one of her reasons for eventually avoiding all train travel.

In an early statement as shadow spokesman she denied opposition to comprehensive schooling but merely to the kind of development in her own constituency where there was "a botched up scheme" ..... a grammar school and a secondary modern amalgamated, one mile apart and separated by main roads, for example. Clearly, she would not have been enthusiastic about the formation of "federation" schools such as Trinity (two schools almost half a mile apart) and Kenilworth (three schools ..... two side by side and a third : Castle, a mile or so away.)

A New Prime Minister

Though challenges to the educational initiatives of the 1960's came initially from the right, the Labour Government was not slow to join in. Many date the policies of the 1980's and 1990's from a speech by newly-appointed Prime Minister, James Callaghan in 1976. Speaking as that rarity among premiers, one who himself left school at sixteen, he challenged head-on the view that the curriculum should be left to the professionals:

"I take it that no-one claims exclusive rights in this field .... Parents, teachers, learned and professional bodies, representatives of higher education and both sides of industry, together with the government, all have an important part to play in formulating and expressing the purpose of education and the standards we need."

It is hard to recall any equivalent public involvement in debate about education by a Prime Minister since Balfour in 1902. Churchill had taken no interest in Butler's work on the seminal 1944 Act. Callaghan's speech was to trigger a series of events, starting with the relatively innocuous "D.E.S. Enquiry into L.E.A. arrangements for the School Curriculum" (Circular 14/77) and culminating twelve years later in the imposition of a highly detailed 'National Curriculum' and its associated programme of testing and the publication of results. The 'buzz' words were 'Accountability' 'Standards' and 'Entitlement', with 'Quality' close behind.

The Curriculum

Before the 1980's, there had been a continuing and unanswered question on the curriculum: "Who decides what?" Curriculum planning, if planning was the word, was often an eclectic mix of published schemes, television or radio series, an initiative from a national body such as Nuffield Science or Schools Council History, and a teacher's own "thing". Secondary schools added to this "the exam syllabus" for years ten onwards. The uncertainty had several consequences: it was easy to disclaim responsibility if under attack, and only the child ever knew, or at any rate experienced the curriculum in toto. This led Michael Marland, speaking to teachers in Rugby early in the 1980's on 'Language Across the Curriculum to say:

"I came to realise that the reason schools had such difficulty in developing a language policy across the curriculum was that they had no real curriculum across which to put a policy."

The D.E.S. Enquiry would unearth curricula with much in common, but also with characteristics of a lottery.

Innovation

The more liberated nature of the 1960's encouraged curricular and organisational experiments in schools. Committee were told in 1967 of: "a fundamental and systematic rethinking of objectives, methods and curriculum" in its schools.

Mixed-ability teaching began to replace streamed classes and therefore was initially called 'unstreaming'. A cautious note from Aylesford School reflected on early tentative initiatives: "The experimental scheme of first year unstreaming has, as far as can be ascertained, been successful."

Different methods of teaching children to read came into and out of fashion. One, barely remembered now but influential in its time, was I.T.A. (Initial Teaching Alphabet), an alphabet based on the sounds of letters. It was in nearly 40 schools for some of the sixties and much of the seventies across the county from Polesworth to Studley. It was cautiously endorsed by the Bullock Report 'A Language for Life' of 1976, but disappeared from the last Warwickshire school with the retirement of the head of St. Mary's R.C., Studley, early in the eighties.

Some sixty schools had introduced teaching of French; many more trialled 'Nuffield Maths'. Proposals to raise the school leaving age to 16 led to working parties to develop more "relevant" courses for those not then entered for public examinations.

Meetings!

In spite of the many topics to be aired, and calls on expenditure, the Committee was often able to dispatch its business with impressive speed. The Coventry Evening Telegraph of 18th October, 1965, reported that:

"Business at today's meeting at Shire Hall was completed in twelve minutes, making it one of the shortest on record. A total of twenty recommendations submitted by eight sub-committees were passed without comment. These included a recommendation that the C.E.O. be instructed to prepare a draft plan on the re-organisation of secondary education in the county on comprehensive lines."

Likewise, governors' meetings were untroubled by today's demands. A typical six point agenda from St. Anthony's R.C. included uniform, school fund, transport and the inevitable 'A.O.B.' Bishop's Itchington had similar agendas, a sample six point one being correspondence, staff changes, visitors, school fund, meals and cleaning. Meetings at Marton were often concluded in less than forty minutes. Compare any agenda today and you will see how the topics have changed and increased in number.

The area officers were a very influential, accessible, well-known presence. Norman Turrell recalled that he and Mr Ruscoe, Divisional Education Officer in Rugby, used to clerk all the governors' meetings they attended in an advisory capacity only. This clerking tradition survived for many years, although as demands on governors grew, and paperwork engulfed them, increasing the number of meetings, this service became an intolerable pressure on evenings. Those who now sit regularly through meetings lasting two, three, occasionally three and a half hours, may envy the meetings of their predecessors where Norman Turrell could expect to clerk three in an evening, moving from (e.g.) Marton to Leamington Hastings and then Bourton-on-Dunsmore.

Top of the Form

Warwickshire won national fame briefly when both Rugby High School and, later Leamington College for Girls won the B.B.C. "Top of the Form" quiz series. The successful Leamington team received fan mail from as far away as Scotland and the Isle of Man. They were even stopped and asked for their autographs.

Education of "Immigrant" Children

Another challenge for the whole of the sixties and seventies was summarised in this report to Committee:

"In Leamington, Rugby and Nuneaton, there are a number of immigrant children in both primary and secondary schools. The recent legislation restricting immigrants has resulted in fewer children entering schools directly from overseas. More are coming in at the infant stage and pursuing the whole of their educational career in Warwickshire schools. However, a language problem persists because many of the Indian children admitted at five come from homes in which little or no English is spoken. Good work is being done in the infant schools to overcome this problem and it is hoped that the additional class which is planned for Clapham Terrace School, to which children can be admitted before their 5th birthday, will further help to develop linguistic skills."

A New Local University

On October 5th, 1965, Warwick University welcomed its first students : 339 undergraduates in all. There had been much debate about its name and, at different times 'University of Coventry' and 'University of Mid Warwickshire' had been canvassed, but Warwick was the outcome. The name was and is misleading; Warwick Station has a sign unhelpfully informing would-be students that they have dismounted at the wrong place. The university is tantalisingly situated on either side of the Coventry/Warwickshire boundary, and close to Kenilworth.

Warwickshire was involved in the detailed stages of planning, with Mr Yorke-Lodge and the Chairman of the Education Committee attending key meetings from 1960 onwards.

Since then, the University has educated many Warwickshire-born students. The Institute of Education, formerly the City of Coventry Training College, has worked in partnership with Warwickshire schools to provide teacher-training placements for B.A. and for P.G.C.E. students. The Institute Director at the time of writing, Chris Husbands, was himself educated in the county : at Camp Hill Schools and King Edward College, Nuneaton.

The World Outside

Two logbook entries indicated contemporary challenges : one still with us, one long since gone. The first came from Aylesford School in May 1971: "Talk on Young People and Drugs - 200 attended."

Notwithstanding current feverish debate about the euro, schools managed the introduction of decimalisation with typical sang-froid, as this entry from Wilmcote shows: "Decimal Day! All payments made and books balanced without any fuss."

Another event whose impact was slower to permeate minds was recorded soon afterwards at Shustoke: 'Thursday of last week M.P. voted for this country to join the E.E.C. ….. Here in school it perhaps gives a sense of purpose to our study of metric measures.'

Often, schools could not escape the consequences of national incidents. Miners' strikes in the early seventies led to power cuts, cold dinners etc. across the county and left many schools uncertain as to whether their evening productions would finish unscathed. One example of many: "School was organised today on a part-time basis due to the state of emergency caused by the miners' strike" (Nathaniel Newton, 14th February, 1972).

But from now on there would be a plethora of national policies and Acts of Parliament on education that would ensure something akin to a total ban on local discretion.

8

Reform Rules: The Eighties and Nineties

Finally, we move to what Alan Bennett has called: 'That remotest of periods, the recent past."

It has been said that history is written by the 'winners'. Very difficult to say therefore who should be recounting events of recent decades!

'All Change'

It is hard to grasp the extent of the revolution in the running of English education in the late eighties and early nineties. Even as recently as 1987, local education authorities ran half of the country's higher education institutions (mostly polytechnics) and nearly all its further education colleges. All the money for schools, except for the purchase of books, equipment and stationery was spent by town and county halls. They were also largely responsible for deciding which child went to which school. Warwickshire could also have chosen to influence the curriculum in schools much more than it did.

Professor Michael Barber described the L.E.A. post-war as "the engine room of the post-war education system". It was LEAs (though not Warwickshire) that started moves towards comprehensive education. Yet, ironically, the 1944 Act had given to the government in its very first clause "control and discretion" over them. But it was not till the late 1980's that government decided to exercise such control, at first tentatively, but eventually almost contemptuously.

The last quarter of the twentieth century was thus to be one of unprecedented change. Even with a little hindsight, it is not easy to stand back and assess the relative impact of a succession of changes on standards, attitudes, workloads or working practices. It is incontestable to assert that the running of English education was revolutionised. At the risk of simply listing titles and dates, let us recall at least some of what happened.

For the first time since the war the Committee faced the extra problems of managing falling numbers of children within its boundaries. By 1985, 500 teaching posts had been lost, as humanely as possible. Committee worked closely with the unions to avoid any compulsory redundancies. Bidford High School amalgamated with the Greville School on the latter's site at Alcester. Keresley School, still in relatively new buildings, amalgamated with Ash Green on the latter's site. No trace of Keresley or Bidford School now remains; housing estates have taken their place. North Leamington School lost one of its halls. It was now becoming possible for people in their early forties to have lived long enough to see a new school built, opened, closed and destroyed within their lifetimes.

Partly for financial reasons, but given educational credibility by the 1981 Act, more special school children were moved into mainstream schools. Associated with this was a decision to rely less on residential care and more on day schools and community care. These initiatives often attracted hostility, as would the re-organisation of primary schools in the 1990's. The favourite charge was that change was being introduced for economic, not educational reasons. It was a curious way to polarise the argument, since schools could only benefit from wise economic policies, so why not indeed try to save money where possible?

Parental rights were strengthened, and appeal panels of councillors, governors and teachers began to meet more frequently.

Our five colleges of further education were removed from local authority control and made self-managing institutions. They had contributed substantially to the work of schools in many and diverse ways, for example by providing resources, facilities and training for teenagers, teachers and adult classes. They still do, but informal, relaxed arrangements have been replaced by tightly costed, contractually detailed procedures which have removed casualness and haphazardness but have deterred much worthwhile activity too.

If we add to this list the introduction of the General Certificate of Secondary Education (it replaced the erstwhile G.C.E. and C.S.E.) with all of its associated in-service training, followed soon afterwards by T.V.E.I. (The Technical and Vocational Educational Initiative), those who lived through it all will recall a plethora of meetings, papers, appointments etc., often encapsulated in a meeting in the school hall where a succession of themselves only recently-trained 'experts' would give 'en masse' briefings at speed.

The Technical Vocational Education Initiative (T.V.E.I.)

At least T.V.E.I. brought with it money, first to the Central Area Secondary Schools that piloted it, then to all secondary schools and, as a pilot project, to Exhall Grange Special School. Its history could and probably should be written. It is available in countless evaluation reports in dusty box files. Enormous amounts of time were invested in it, often in evenings and at weekends. While it lasted, T.V.E.I. dominated much of secondary school life. But, as ministers came and went, government enthusiasm for a costly project waned and then disappeared. The many T.V.E.I. co-ordinators returned to schools in and out of the county, usually in senior management positions, for they had acquired valuable skills in curriculum development and budget management. The project also had a lasting impact on the curriculum, funding subjects then new but later to be very popular such as Media Studies. It also encouraged teachers to extend their repertoire of teaching skills. Such developments largely survived the gradual withdrawal of funds.

Technology Moves In and On

Computers now began to feature more regularly in school life, at least at secondary level. Thomas Anney recalled the first computer at Nicholas Chamberlaine School:

"The first computer in the school was known as a Research Machine 180Z. It …. looked like a massive thirty pound black box with a disc-drive and an on-off switch. It was very noisy and sounded like the old teleprinter that used to bring the football results on Saturday T.V. ….. The second 380Z arrived a year later ….. It was to revolutionise constructing the timetable. In the early seventies six senior staff were taken off teaching for six weeks. By the eighties it was the responsibility of three Heads of Faculty … for a week."

Computers were expensive and fashionable. They thus both generated excitement and attracted unwelcome attention. High Meadow School lost much of its recently-acquired equipment in a break-in in 1987, an early example of a long-running worry. Computers were to transform both teaching and learning. However, in the latter case they did not magically free staff from basic tasks, as this 1991 Claverdon logbook entry recalls: "During the Easter holidays, the Headteacher laid carpet tiles in the new secretary's office in preparation for the arrival of the L.M.S. computer package."

Early use of technology in the office produced some rapid learning, regular cursing and a few lighter moments. The office weekly circular recorded that the Word for Windows spell-checker was unimpressed by many school names and suggested its own versions:

Austrey	became	Austere
Canon Maggs	became	Canon Magus
Feldon (now Long Itchington)	became	Felon
Rokeby	became	Rookery
Shilton and Ansty	became	Shilton and Nasty
Whitnash County	became	Whatnot
Woodloes	became	Woollies

More primary schools such as St. Joseph's R.C. Nuneaton began to acquire their first computers. At this particular school I arrived on the same day as the computer. It was still in its wrapping in the entrance hall. I asked the head what his plans were for its use. He replied:

"It's already been useful. We had two girls who kept leaving the taps running and the plugs in the washbasins till they flooded the toilets. We knew who was doing it but we couldn't get them to admit it. Today I said in desperation 'Well, we shall put the facts into the computer and the computer will tell us who is doing this', whereupon the girls owned up at once."

Reprographics

It has been asserted that the recent pace and volume of educational change would not have been possible without the development of sophisticated photocopiers. The thought of all those voluminous documents coming via a Banda defies belief. Paddy Wex described the revolution as it spread across one school:

"The introduction of photocopiers radically changed many teachers' approach to teaching during the last 20 years. In the early 1980s, neither the teaching staff nor the secretaries had access to a plain paper photocopier. The Headmaster had a 'wet' photocopier, on which single (and expensive) copies on light-sensitive paper were sometimes made but it was unsuitable and too costly for general use. The school office produced multiple copies of letters and exam papers using a Gestetner machine. For each page, a separate stencil had to be typed, with the typewriter ribbon removed so that the keys cut the letter shapes into the stencil. Errors had to be painstakingly corrected using a pink fluid not unlike nail varnish, and great care had to be taken not to crease the stencils.

The staff could make copies of documents on a spirit-based Banda machine that had possibly represented the cutting edge (albeit a rather blunt one) of reprographic technology in the 1950s. Master copies were handwritten or typed on a double sheet of paper with a thick, inky coating on the surface of the second sheet. The two sheets were peeled apart so that the top one, with its reversed image, could be fitted onto the Banda's print roller. The machine was then primed with 'Banda Fluid', spirit that dampened the roller and enabled it to transfer the text from the Banda master onto plain paper. The machine was hand-cranked. Each master sheet was good for about 100 copies and every copy smelt of Banda fluid for a few hours afterwards. When you gave them out in class, everyone used to sniff them!

Photocopiers transformed the teaching approaches of a number of departments. They shifted the emphasis away from using books to documents that a student could store alongside his work. Among the first benefits was the opportunity they provided to produce large numbers of original and up-to-date worksheets, instruction sheets, model answers and internal exam papers. In English, for example, instead of relying on old and battered text-books for language work, teachers could devise and print materials that were focused on the particular needs of the classes they were teaching at the time. Photocopiers enabled subjects dependent on current and constantly changing information, such as Business Studies and Media Studies, to come into being."

Visitations

The 1980's saw a flurry of ministerial visits to the county, beginning with that rarity: a prime ministerial visit. Margaret Thatcher visited Tyntesfield School in 1980 to open the residential wing. Even her critics acknowledged that she developed a rapport with the pupils.

Soon after his arrival at Exhall Grange, the head Richard Bignell was invited along with five others to go to the Department of Education and Science at London to meet the then Secretary of State for Education and Science, Sir Keith Joseph. The meeting took place on May 10th, 1983. Richard, never one to fail to follow up such an occasion, wrote on 25th July 1983 to invite Sir Keith to visit the school: " ..... the largest special school in the country .... with a national catchment area." Once he returned from holiday, Sir Keith confirmed his willingness to visit. After some correspondence between the minister's private office and the head, a date was fixed: March 9th 1984.

Sir Keith's visit lasted nearly four hours. Preparations were meticulous, even down to the Minister's preferences for lunch: "Any meat or fish in paté or mousse form" etc. On his arrival, Sir Keith made straight for pupils, sweeping past lines of official guests. Head Richard Bignell wrote in a letter of thanks: "They (the pupils) were thrilled ..... they certainly gained the impression you came to see them."

Other Secretaries of State gave time to visits to Warwickshire. Both Ian McGregor and Kenneth Baker visited Rugby, the latter promising local grammar schools a safe future with a Conservative Government on an election visit in May, 1987. Prime Minister John Major paid a brief visit to Loxley School during the 1997 General Election. The head, Sarah Davies, persuaded him to call in after his stop for a pub lunch in the village.

Miners' Strike

I have discovered little in print on the distress and the ill-feeling generated on all sides by the miners' strikes of the seventies and eighties except in contemporary newspapers. There is a book on how the miners' strike affected the village of Keresley, near Bedworth. It tells of the impact on children ..... of how Lee (age not given) saw events as "a war against the pickets and the miners." It relates how mothers in particular faced the summer holidays of 1984: "6 weeks of heartbreak ..... no holidays, no ice creams and no day trips." The following Christmas an English teacher (name not given) agreed to produce "Cinderella" with a cast largely comprising striking miners for the children of the village.

School Closures Continue

Closure of small village schools was never attempted lightly. A County Council working party made this point somewhat ruefully: "We soon learned that the closure of a village school is not to be attempted lightly, and is a shattering experience."

A former officer with the Authority, Glyn Essex, produced a case-study comparing successful attempts to close Whichford School with unsuccessful attempts to close Butlers Marston. Whichford was down to nine pupils and was eventually to drop to six. (I recall the Head phoning me to tell me that she was taking "the whole of the junior school" to the nearby paperback warehouse 'Books for Students'. Yes, all four of them ..... in her car!) Even so, a petition against the closure was signed by 158 residents.

Not far away, and untypically, there was just one letter of objection to the closure of Stourton and Cherington School, signed by thirteen residents. This letter included one objection that hinted at the tensions in the community. The letter cited as a cause for a decline in numbers: "A self perpetuating body of Managers and Governors, at least one of whom actively canvassed parents to move their children to another school."

Small village schools had long since faced threats of closure. The National Curriculum and all that went with it added to the pressures. It was argued that they simply could not be expected to manage the demands now being made upon them.

Never slow to respond, nor lacking in ideas to counter attacks, many decided that strength in numbers could disarm their opponents. Thus developed "clustering": groups of village schools which regularly met and worked together to maximise resources, keep abreast of developments and enrich the children's learning. Some examples illustrated work being done at the end of the eighties:

Haselor) Great Alne) Dunnington) Mappleborough Green)	A shared production by a visiting drama group with activity groups to follow:
Grendon) Newton Regis) Austrey) Warton)	Known colloquially as "GNAW" - they worked on shared science topics and shared visits e.g. to Birmingham Science Museum.
High Meadow First) Curdworth First) Coleshill First)	Joint in-service training on a variety of topics.

Butlers Marston	)
Fenny Compton	)
Long Compton	)
Moreton Morrell	) Joint performance of a musical, composed by one of the staff.
Tredington	) Also, a shared 'American Day' of poetry, dance, art and games.
Temple Herdewyke	)
Farnborough	)
Little Compton	)
Loxley	)
Northend	)
Newbold-on-Stour	)
Bubbenhall	)
Knightlow	)
Princethorpe	) Joint mathematics workshops, involving parents, governors and staff.
Church Lawford	)
Leamington Hastings	)
Ryton	)

Of course, such ventures involved much out of school work: planning meetings etc. It also ran counter to the culture that was being sedulously fostered: a culture of competition, where co-operating schools also had to consider their league table rankings.

Education Reform Act: 1988

Much of the innovation of the nineties was initiated by ERA: The Education Reform Act of 1988. This was a most important and far-reaching piece of educational law-making. It altered the power structure of the education system, strengthening the powers of the Secretary of State for Education while limiting the functions of L.E.A.'s, by giving greater autonomy to schools and governing bodies. There was thus a tension between central prescription (in, for example, a curriculum more minutely prescribed than anywhere else in the world) and greater freedom at the periphery, e.g. in budget management. Mr Baker, the then Secretary of State, has since declared unambiguously that one objective was to see L.E.A.'s "wither on the vine". Part of the unsettled climate was Mrs. Thatcher's appointment of nine different Ministers for Local Government in eleven years.

Ironically, the L.E.A. moved into a period of unparalleled pressure of work as it sought to implement the proposals. Michael Ridger, the outgoing C.E.O., was invited by the Chief Executive to comment informally on the suitability of his relatively new deputy, Margaret Maden, an applicant for Michael Ridger's job. With characteristic modesty, he disclaimed any wish to influence the appointment of his successor, before going on to praise in her: "an unusual capacity for innovation" and "her vigorous and determined response to the challenge of ERA".

She, her officers and her committee were to need, and to find, massive reserves of vigour, determination and integrity as they sought to implement unprecedented change. In typical Warwickshire fashion, they moved forward to extensive consultation with that blend of principle and humanity that had characterised the work of their predecessors.

Following the Act, the authority gave priority to developing closer links with parents. An Inspector for Home/School Liaison was appointed. Good practice was developed and shared through working groups. Home visiting, always a sporadic part of practice, was strengthened and encouraged The children had their own views on all this: those visited by the reception teacher from Newbold Glebe First observed variously: "I thought she was nice - my mummy said she was nice" but "I was scared and I hid."

Withstanding the Impact

Following the election of the Conservative Government, in 1979, there had been an Education Act almost annually. Some indication of the impact of the legislation can be gleaned from the log-books meticulously kept up through most of the decade by Lesley King, then head of Aylesford School. Here are just two entries to represent so many more that were or could have been made: Sept 1 1987 "The new school year began with a Teachers' Day under the new Baker-imposed conditions of service" and June 21 1989 "I attended a National Curriculum Briefing Day for heads."

Amid the anxiety and stress that was to dog teachers' lives, schools sought to retain their sanity as best they could. It was in 1989 that schools such as Shottery recorded their "First Red Nose Day". With hindsight, a 1986 entry in the Snitterfield logbook can be seen as both prescient and understated: "The role of government is changing rapidly." By 1991, the head was writing: "It has been a busy term. Even frenzied at times."

Roger Hillman, head of Knightlow (then) Middle, in a series of terse statements, gave some sense of the blizzard of initiatives that began to engulf schools: "Teachers' Day. The teachers spent the day reading - attempting to catch up on the mass of material pouring in on us." This was rapidly followed in the early nineties by a succession of training events. A few examples:

1991 : L.M.S. Training
SIMS Training
National Curriculum Training
Development Plan Training
Appraisal Training

Many heads noted with philosophical resignation that "training" had become "delivery". Just as it had become commonplace to talk of "delivering" the National Curriculum, so training was "delivered" by trainers with files containing their scripts. The scripts were carefully timed, so much so that trainers were not always allowed the time to answer questions. The trainers had no choice; they had their orders.

Seamus Crowe, Head of St. Francis R.C. Primary School in Bedworth summed up the closing years of the eighties in four ways:

a) Technology (its impact on school)
b) The National Curriculum
c) Re-organisation
d) "Hands-on"

The first three speak for themselves. The last was the memory of a time when primary education emphasised much more teacher-initiative and first hand experience for pupils. Rather than an externally imposed locally 'delivered' curriculum, teachers had more freedom to plan units of work based on the local environment. The work was more open-ended; some outcomes were predetermined, but others depended on where pupil curiosity led. Not all teachers wanted this freedom of course, and turned to published schemes for more structure.

He and other heads did not fight hard for the retention of first and middles when re-organisation returned. There was a mix of reasons:

a) the middle schools had never had the extra staffing that middle schools in authorities such as Ealing had funded (three extra teachers, not just one).

b) covering the curriculum, especially a modern foreign language, had not been easy.

c) the authority had never demonstrated an unequivocal commitment to 8-12 middle schools, having at one time considered 9-13 schools, philosophically a very different concept.

d) The trend back to 7-11 was accelerating all over the country : some 630 middle schools in the mid seventies, but less than a quarter of that number by the end of the century.

One Step Forward...?

Innovation often trotted in harness with budget stringency. Falling rolls had moved through schools in the seventies and eighties. However there had been the opening of a new school: Temple Herdewyke. This served the Army camp near Gaydon. It soon had to support its pupils through unsettled times, as the Falklands War disrupted camp life. The Head reported: " ..... many social problems .... undesirable undercurrents ....." But the school's 'traditional' annual 'Conker Competition' went ahead as usual.

As the fall in rolls moved on and away, it was replaced by Government cutbacks which turned Warwickshire into one of the most poorly funded LEAs in the country.

It was a malevolent irony which gave schools through L.M.S. (Local Management of Schools) more power to manage their own budgets at a time when in practice this meant managing retrenchment. That Warwickshire was at the forefront in financially-induced dismay was reflected in the national publicity it attracted: "Newsnight here to film effects of the budget cuts on the school" (Aylesford, March 24, 1995). Little wonder that fund-raising assumed more public and diverse forms: "P.T.A. ran mulled wine and mince pie stall at (Warwick) Victorian Fair. Young Enterprise group had stall" (Aylesford, Christmas, 1995).

Whatever one's political views about levels of government spending and taxation, it should be recorded that Warwickshire's case for a better deal was supported by all parties in the council chamber, and, with varying degrees of enthusiasm, by its Members of Parliament, including the then four Conservative members. Almost uniquely in the country it managed twice, on appeal, to achieve some relaxation on the rules governing how much it could spend.

In this and in much else, the county gained valuable support, and sometimes advice, from the newly-created and innovative Warwickshire Governors' Forum, introduced by Margaret Maden. It was rapidly to become a powerful ally, but also, intermittently, a sharply critical pressure group.

Lighter Moments

Amidst the trend towards national conformity, individual initiative continued to flicker, even to flourish defiantly. At Higham Lane School, John Terry, Head of the Rural Studies Department, or the 'Digging Department', as it was known to some, had returned to his old school to start a school farm. The results of that initiative have led to three books by John : "Ducks in Detention" etc. (see Bibliography) prize-winning entries in the Royal Show, and even a visit from H.M. the Queen. Sadly, John's health, and pressures from the government towards a more conformist curriculum, led to the closure of the farm. Prize-winning pigs don't appear in many league tables. But how many other ventures would bring pupils in voluntarily to work on every day during the Christmas and summer holidays?

In 1988 there was a notable 'first' when Jim Shera was made Rugby's first Asian Mayor. He had striven hard in Pakistan to achieve his academic qualifications and worked at G.E.C. Rugby and British Rail before becoming a teacher at Newbold Middle School in 1977. In 1982 he became an early (the first?) black councillor in the Midlands. At the time of writing he heads the county's Intercultural Curriculum Support Service.

Another event to celebrate for many pupils, staff, and some dedicated fans among headteachers, was Coventry City's F.A. Cup win against Spurs ..... 3-2 after extra time. Lighter moments in a major event happened when the Pope celebrated Mass at Baginton Airport. One of the schools contributing to a celebratory pageant was English Martyrs of Rugby. They planned an item on how St. Augustine brought Christianity to England. One of their characters was wearing a mitre for his role. He was approached by Cardinal Basil Hume, seeking to borrow the mitre, as he had neglected to remember his own. Of course, English Martyrs was proud to oblige, and later received a signed letter of thanks …. and the mitre.

Amusing only with hindsight is this graphic account of events in 1987 at Alveston: "Boiler not heating the pool. Mr Hopkins and I attempted to rectify. BANG! FLASH! All power gone."

Further examples of little local difficulties, all part of the Head's life, came in these two stories, one from St. Anthony's, Leamington, the other from Glendale, Nuneaton:

"The rabbits who had young during the holidays are all gnawing away at the supports where they are housed. They will have to be stopped or otherwise the greenhouse will collapse."

"We were reaching closing time around 2.30 pm, with 412 children in school when the Police drove two horses onto the school grounds and shut the gates. They explained that they had been chasing them up and down the by-pass most of the day and it was now time for them to go 'off duty'. The horses looked OK and had settled, so they would go. I was left with two horses grazing on the grass and 412 children to get out of school. The police advised me not to touch them as they would bite! My secretary and I collected skipping ropes from the hall, informed the teachers what was happening and then tied the horses to a tree. We held them calmly while the teachers got the children into their coats and walked them quietly to the gates for parents to collect ….. all in 20 minutes."

Local Re-organisation

There was yet one more major re-organisation of our schools in the early 1990's. This was to revert to an age of transfer at eleven, and to eliminate surplus places.

The files of papers generated by the rounds of proposals and consultations occupy some twenty shelves in the basement of Shire Hall. Even small schools such as Corley, Grendon and Napton have a box file each. The boxes for Corley and Fillongley, for example, include petitions to save the schools, counter proposals from the Joint Governing Bodies, notes on meetings and numerous letters. These voluminous collections of documents serve to remind us of the work involved as Eric Wood and his team, together with county councillors, toured the school halls of the county, once, twice, sometimes thrice to hear views, present a case and to alter proposals when strength of feeling was underpinned by strong evidence. Here is one example of literally more than one hundred such occasions.

"At 5.15 a meeting was held by L.E.A. Officers Eric Wood and Brian Barnett to discuss the proposals for re-organisation with staff and governors ..... In the evening at 7.15 the same officers held a meeting in the hall for parents and other interested parties."

(Shustoke, 22.2.93)

The entry gives no sense of strong feelings or heated altercations, but then, Shustoke's future was not in doubt.

The re-organisation led to the loss of familiar school names. When the school at Corley closed and its pupils transferred to Fillongley, the decision was made to rename the school to avoid any impression of one school having outsmarted another. Thus, the Corley and Fillongley schools were replaced by Bournebrook C.E. Primary. Other examples:

- Long Compton and Little Compton formed the Compton District Primary School
- Wroxall and Hatton formed the Ferncumbe C.E. Primary School
- St. Margaret's, Bedworth and Red Deeps formed the Griff School on two sites
- Ryton and Bubbenhall formed Provost Williams C.E. School
- Attleborough and Swinnerton formed Wembrook Primary School in Nuneaton
- Grove Farm and Robinson's End, became Park Lane.
  (Cue for a county schools' Monopoly board?)

Strong feelings deriving from local loyalties inevitably surfaced. Little Compton, for example, unsuccessfully sought grant-maintained status. But the two heads of Little and Long Compton then worked patiently for the creation of the new school which they jointly opened in 1997.

A special amalgamation was that which replaced Harborough Magna, Brinklow and the two Monks Kirby Schools: St. Joseph's R.C. and Brockhurst C.E. with the Revel C.E. which retained sites in Brinklow (annexe) and Monks Kirby (main site). There were also some re-naming of schools. Gaydon became Lighthorne Heath, which certainly helped searchers to locate it. The Polesworth County Schools combined to form Birchwood, and the Baddesley Ensors acknowledged their pleasant location by taking the name Woodside. Weston-in-Arden also favoured an arboreal theme by taking the name of Arden Forest.

Closures, whether terminal or as part of the amalgamation of schools, stimulated events high in emotion: "Tears instead of laughter much in evidence. The staff will join me next week in the sad task of packing up" (Nether Whitacre, July, 1987) and "Today is the last day of this school's existence. It is a happy school and we are sad to be leaving. Everyone has worked hard .... to pack away the belongings of 74 years" (Leicester Road, July, 1987). Nether Whitacre closed for ever. Leicester Road re-opened as Race Leys First.

The final rites of a closure can be abrupt to the point of callousness. I sat with the head of Wolston High as furniture was moved out around him. A group of girls, still being taught, came to complain that while they were out at morning break, the lab. stools they had been using had been taken away. At Mancetter, the head returned from the final school assembly in the local church at the end of the term to find builders already boarding up the windows of the school.

Each closure generated prolonged, sometimes furious activity, not least in Shire Hall where decisions on the future of schools such as Baddesley Clinton were settled by as little as one vote. When it was over, Warwickshire's approach was commended as a model of good practice by the Audit Commission in a report on school places. The Committee, its officers and its schools will surely reflect with pride on managing this onslaught of change while still seeing an annual steady improvement in its results at G.C.S.E. and A level and, more recently, in its SATs results.

The OFSTED Inspection of Warwickshire

The pre-occupations remain much the same as those of Bolton King and his committee: high standards underpinned by good relationships and integrity. How gratifying for the Committee to end the century and its own life with an inspection report from the Office for Standards in Education that referred to Warwickshire as: "an effective L.E.A. which is well managed, with many strengths and much good practice"... "the LEA enjoys enviable relationships with its schools" but "it does not shirk from taking tough decisions." The inspectors' description of a well led authority was that it was "principled, fair and honourable."

9

The Next One Hundred Years ...... ?

At the time of writing this final section the pace of change and its associated promise of re-organisation show little sign of slowing. This final chapter canters speedily around a few of the many developments that accompany the move into the new millennium.

Following consultation, the authority closed separate M.L.D. and S.L.D. schools in the east and the south of the county and opened a single 'broad spectrum' special school. In Rugby, the school retains the name 'Brooke School' and its secondary provision is on the Tyntesfield School site. A similar arrangement exists at Stratford but here there is a change of name. Out go 'Lambert School' and 'Marie Corelli School' and in comes 'Welcombe Hills School', again on two sites. Similar arrangements are envisaged for the Central Area with the Ridgeway School site retained but pupils of secondary age moving to Castle Hall, Kenilworth School. Plans for Nuneaton and Bedworth are still uncertain.

While governments have emphasised competition as the way to raise standards, schools have continued to renew existing alliances and to search for new ones. In 2001, Campion School and Warwickshire College announced a 'Concordat': partnership at post-sixteen to ensure shared experience and coherent provision for the South Leamington community. Warwickshire College and Rugby College plan to merge, the latter on a new site.

The 'Warwickshire School Organisation Plan 2001-2006' seeks to cater for a projected fall of 7.9% in primary school numbers while secondary school numbers rise by 2.4%. Predictions are bedevilled not just by housing development, and the propensity or otherwise of new residents to breed, or to have bred, but also by the 'Greenwich Judgement'. An appeal court in the 1980's allowed families living outside the authority to have equal consideration for school places with those living in the area. This has had a particular impact on the grammar schools in Rugby and Alcester, given their proximity to county boundaries. Schools in North Warwickshire close to Birmingham and to Solihull have also been particularly affected.

The Labour Government (1997 - ?)

The Blair Government came to power with education at the top of its agenda. The new Secretary of State, David Blunkett, who had shadowed the post for three years, immediately embarked on a whirlwind of activity. Within a week of his taking office a new Standards and Effectiveness Unit was established and, within two, ambitious targets for the literacy and numeracy of eleven-year-olds had been declared.

Tony Blair's three priorities were memorably asserted: "Education, education and education." It was followed, though not immediately, by annual increases on expenditure in real terms. Though welcome in Warwickshire, these increases were still based on a formula that left Warwickshire annually amongst the poorest funded of any L.E.A. in the country. As this book went to print, there had been some recognition of this by the government in its announcement of a significant increase in funding for the county. It followed a prolonged, well-publicised campaign, culminating in the presentation to government of a Warwickshire petition with 200,000 signatures, and all-party support.

For this money the government has demanded, and continues to demand commitment to rising standards, designed to meet ambitious targets. Among the methods introduced are:

i)   detailed data analysis of performance in exams and national tests.
ii) benchmark data annually for each school.
iii) comparisons with similar schools.
iv) statutory target-setting.
v)   universal professional development in national priorities (e.g. numeracy)

In order to ensure that teachers receive maximum support in facing the challenges imposed upon them, we have seen the introduction of the daily literacy hour and maths lesson with their tightly prescribed methodology. These, though not mandatory, have been universally introduced into county primary schools though they have subsequently been modified in the light of experience. Of course, nearly all schools always did have their daily English and Maths lesson, usually in the morning, and often scheme or course-book based, but, typically, more individualised.

Based on evidence of success at primary level, the government is now introducing a Key Stage Three strategy to take forward its standards-based agenda.

The School Standards and Framework Act 1998 has placed on local authorities a new duty to improve standards in their schools, making them the key agents of delivery for the government's strategies.

Change, But No Change?

What is remarkable about all the apparent change is how little much of it differed at root from the policies of the previous Conservative Government. Many of the education reforms which the Conservatives had introduced from 1988 onwards, and which were bitterly attacked by the Labour opposition of the time, now became the backbone of the Blair programme. The National Curriculum, tests and league tables, financial delegation to schools, and a 'beefed-up' inspection service were all enthusiastically embraced by New Labour.

An Eventful Weekend

We did have a visit from Estelle Morris, Secretary of State for Education in the Autumn of 2002. She was no stranger to the area, having been a Leamington councillor. Doubtless, she looked nostalgically out of the car window as she approached Manor Hall to address a primary heads' conference on technology in schools. That was on a Friday. To the surprise of most and the sadness of many, she resigned after the weekend, citing personal inadequacies as the main reason.

Other Distinguished Visitors

Lawrence Sheriff School hosted a visit by Sir Gary Sobers in 2002, generally rated as the world's greatest all-round cricketer ever, and destined to be remembered for despatching Malcolm Nash for six successive sixes at Swansea. It is typical of his modesty that, when asked: "Who do you think is the second greatest cricket all-rounder ever?", had to have the question repeated twice, not grasping its implicit meaning.

Citizenship Education

'What goes around, comes around' could sum up much of educational history. Citizenship lessons are now a compulsory part of the curriculum, as from September 2002. These lessons are to promote social and moral responsibility, community involvement and political literacy. In 1905, the L.E.A. was responding to edicts and advice from the Board of Education on how children were to be taught to become "upright and useful members of the community". By 1906, the Board asserted that "lessons on Citizenship may be given with advantage in the higher classes."

Beacon Schools

Warwickshire's first designated 'Beacon School' was Exhall Grange. John Dunkerton reported on the school's first year:

"In our first year nearly 500 teachers, students or classroom assistants have either visited the school, attended our courses or benefited from outreach support. All visits and courses have been evaluated, using a standard form where the delegates are asked to use a 5-point scale to compare their perceptions of delivery with the aims of objectives set for the course. On this scale, 5 is 'excellent' and 1 is 'poor'; the delegates are also asked to list any improvements or extra follow-up that might be needed, together with any other comments. Overall, the scores have ranged from 4 to 5 for all components with no individual delegate rating a course or visit less than 3. This is backed up by comments such as 'inspirational'; 'by far the most useful course I have attended so far'; 'at last we now feel that we understand how to use the programmes!'; and 'wonderful – it has given me a lot to think about!" Other Beacon schools in Warwickshire have been Stockingford Infants, St. Benedict's High, Whitnash Nursery, Brownsover Community, Ridgeway, Myton and St. Augustine's.

Specialist Schools

The move towards more specialist provision, making for example North Leamington an Arts College and Alcester High a Technology College, is ensuring that, specialist schools are becoming more widespread across the county.

Looking Forward

A new school is to open at Cawston near Rugby in September 2003, built by the developers of the new housing estate there. The announcement came at the the final meeting of the The Education Committee, in 1999. That meeting also hosted a presentation by pupils to illustrate the award-winning work of the Careers Service. New committee structures were introduced, with Councillor Richard Grant responsible for the Education portfolio on The Executive Committee. Members are now advised by Policy Advisory Groups on aspects of education, and their work is monitored by a Scrutiny and Review Committee on Learning Skills and Culture.

In November 2002, the first new secondary school buildings to be opened for more than thirty years came into being. This was the new Stratford High, financed by the sale of some school land. It replaced a school created in 1939 from two schools side by side: one for boys, one for girls. For many years it had the unenviable record of hosting the largest number of huts in the county. Now, it is the first school opened in the new millennium, with computer networking a priority.

The 14-19 Curriculum

Initiatives to develop the 14-19 curriculum have arrived with speed almost annually. They have usually had uppermost the aim of more vocational courses with the intent of extending education beyond sixteen. Once again, just as a century ago, we were exhorted to strive to match the achievements of Germany. By 2002, they had 95% of their seventeen year olds in education and training. Britain had just 70%.

Schools' Forum

The inception of the Warwickshire Schools' Forum, now imminent, will continue the tradition begun by Bolton King of the authority working closely with its partners to perpetuate consultation and shared decision-making.

The Education Offices at Northgate Street, Warwick. At the far end of the street is St. Mary's Church where Warwickshire's first school: Warwick, originated.

(Drawing by John Higlett)

Bishop's Tachbrook School in the 1900's.
(Warwickshire County Record Office, ref. PH 357/52)

Bourton on Dunsmore 1936. The photograph included
Miss Hales who was a pupil, a teacher and a manager at the school.
(Warwickshire County Record Office, ref. CR 1529/24)

Atherstone School staff, pictured in 1905.
(Warwickshire County Record Office, ref. PH 352/14/32)

*The Atherstone, Hinckley and Nuneaton Teachers' Association outing
– all the way to Monks Kirby – in 1904.*
Photograph by Baxter's photo series.
(Warwickshire County Record Office, ref. PH 352/105/34)

A bygone age? Temple Grafton School in the early twentieth century.
Photograph by W. A. Smith of Stratford-upon-Avon.
(Warwickshire County Record Office, ref. PH 239/119)

Post-war outings become more ambitious:
the Arley School outing to Cheddar Gorge in 1951.
(Warwickshire County Record Office, ref. CR 1479/8/2)

The Rt. Hon. Enoch Powell, then Minister of Health, at the opening of Ridgeway School, then a training Centre, in 1962.

Maxstoke School children in playground: 1960.
Photograph by E. G. Miller of Coleshill. (Warwickshire County Record Office, ref. PH 90/28)

The School House Preston-on-Stour.
Photograph by Ernest J. Bryan.
(Warwickshire County Record Office, ref. PH 352/146/4)

The author (second row from back, third from left), pictured with his class at Eastlands Junior School, 1950. Copyright: Crown

*H.M. the Queen visits the school farm at Higham Lane School, Nuneaton in 1994.
To the Queen's left is teacher John Terry who started the farm.*
(Copyright Ted Cottrell)

*Prime Minister Margaret Thatcher visits Rugby early in her period of
office to open a new wing at Tynterfield School.*
Photography by: Ashley Smith

*The following colour photos are of pupils and their work
on the occasion of visits by Nash Maghji of the County Music Service.
The workshops combined art and music.*

Examples of children and their work from Chilvers Coton School, Nuneaton.
(Photographs by Nash Meghji)

Examples of artwork by children from Wootton Wawen School.
(Photographs by Nash Meghji)

Pupils at work at the Griff School, Nuneaton.

Pupils at St. Marie's R.C. School, Rugby.
(Photographs by Nash Meghji)

Postscript

Indicators of how far education has changed are everywhere. One that caught my eye recently was the Adult Education Programme for Shipston High School for the Autumn of 2002. It included:

Aerobics for All
Line Dancing
Meditation
Kung Fu
The Internet

What would Bolton King have made of it all?

But the future lies with the young. The history is over, as Alanna Viles of Henley High School observed in her poem:

"One thousand years behind us
Time been and gone
A new millennium
All our hopes pinned on that single second."

Here's to the next thousand.

10

Special Occasions

However drab and remorseless much of the schooling of the late nineteenth and early twentieth century might have been, headteachers and managers were not averse to permitting breaks in the routine for all kinds of occasions. Here, for example, is a list of half holidays granted at Harbury in just one year: 1892:

April 8th
Broke up Wednesday night - Easter holiday (cold snowy day)
May 2nd
Holiday all day
June 3rd
Week holiday - Whitsuntide
June 24th
Friday afternoon holiday for Royal Show (N.B. one source suggests that pupils at Norton Lindsey had a week's holiday for The Royal Show)
July 2nd
Holiday all day Wednesday
July 12th
Holiday all day electioneering
August 2nd
Holiday on Monday for Harbury Flower Show
August 16th
Holiday all day Monday for the Choir Trip
August 25th
Holiday Monday afternoon - school treat. Broke up today for Harvest holiday (5 weeks).
October 17th
Holiday all day - Southam Mop
November 17th
School dismissed at 11 o'clock on account of the hounds meeting here
December 23rd
Broke up for Christmas holiday

At Stockingford, the annual list of full 'Holydays' (sic) was:
    6 weeks Harvest
    2 Xmas
    2 Whitsun

Elsewhere, occasions for celebration, if not so regular, were equally diverse. Some examples:

August 11 1883
Holiday : Godiva Procession (Burton Green)

July 24 1885
Holiday for Cottage Garden Show (Radford Semele)
1890's
Annual half days for the visit of the Barnum and Bailey Show to Rugby Races, and for The Foresters' Grand Fête Day (St. Marie's R.C.)
July 1893
Half day holiday : Humphris Street Band of Hope treat in Castle Park (Coten End)
July 19 1900
Holiday granted on occasion of opening 'Victoria' and 'Helena' wards at the new wing of Warneford Hospital (Shrubland Street)

Schools in Alvecote and Shuttington took half days for Fairs in Fazeley, Tamworth and Polesworth and the annual meet of Atherstone Hounds.

The Jubilee celebrations, arranged to commemorate sixty years of Queen Victoria's reign in 1897 were of particular importance. Pupils at Shrubland Street school were given a week's holiday, but not before they had been taught the words of "God Save the Queen" and "Rule Britannia" ..... and had processed with other schools to Victoria Park, Leamington. Not far away, pupils at St. Austin's R.C. Kenilworth apparently needed the holiday to recover from the celebrations. "School was closed today under compulsion. The children were too tired to return to work after Jubilee celebrations. Hence, school is closed till June 28th."

Special Occasions (National)

Pupils at Kingsbury Council, Lapworth C.E. and Emscote C.E. schools both received two half day holidays within close proximity.

March 2 : 1900 :   For the relief of Ladysmith
May 21 : 1900 :   For the relief of Mafeking

Clearly, military victories by the British produced "relief" in more ways than one; meanwhile, the Emscote children were out early on April 29th 1901 to greet some of the soldiers returning from South Africa.

Special Occasions (Local)

Some events were particular to one school only and were of questionable nature: "Most unusually, up to 1965, the school was still taking a day's holiday to celebrate the anniversary of Simon de Montfort's Parliament and the Magna Carta" (Combroke). "Two days' holiday to enable the Conservative Association to prepare for the Annual Dinner and to clear away" (St. Paul's C.E. Elementary Boys, Stockingford).

May Day

At Pillerton Priors, children processed though the village prior to hurling the maypole into the sheepwash (apparently a pagan ritual). May Day provided an excuse for levity, fun and frolics. Here is an account from Stockton, paradoxically on June 1 1910.

"The Schools closed for the day for the May Day celebrations which had been postponed owing to the death of the late King. The celebrations were carried out on an even more elaborate scale than last year. Under a very able committee arrangements for the festivities were made and admirably carried out. Vehicles to the number of 17 were kindly lent by different people and tastefully decorated by various helpers. The children assembled at 10.30 in Rectory Field and after taking their places in the conveyances the procession started towards the Green, where May songs were sung. The Queen (Doris Todd) was then crowned by her consort (Horace Guntrup) and 16 girls from the upper school danced the Country Dance; this was followed by the Maypole dance by 24 Infants, which was loudly cheered by a crowd of spectators. After the procession sports were indulged in and all did justice to a good tea. The Maypole dance was then given again in the presence of an enormous crowd, after which the Long Itchington Band headed the procession round the village. Dancing was afterwards enjoyed by many and the singing of the National Anthem brought a very successful day to a close."

Some sense of the excitement of a break from eventless routine comes from memories of Oxhill School by Evelyn Colyer: "Inside the cloakroom, all was bustle and confusion. The two hand-basins were overflowing with may-narcissi and other flowers while small boys sloshed happily backwards and forwards with buckets and cans from the pump outside." One month later there was another event: "School closed this afternoon for the Guild of Courtesy outing to Shuckburgh. Fifty members of the Guild and school staff journeyed by brake and traps to the Park, and an enjoyable time was spent. Tea was served in picnic style and time was spent in various games being indulged in."

Empire Day

This was a date taken very seriously. Back in 1908, Lord Leigh persuaded the County Council to give all children a half holiday to honour the event. Many accounts of the subsequent annual celebration of Empire Day have survived:

"1924 May 23, Empire Day celebrations were held today in accordance with the instructions of the Education Committee. A floral Union Jack was made and flowers were placed upon the village memorial. During the preparations, the pole of the Giant's Stride fell when Mr Spicer was fixing the school flag. Mr Spicer's arm was dislocated and he was badly bruised and shaken .... I took Mr Spicer to the bone-setter Mr Mathew Bennett, who attended to the injury" (Cubbington).

"In my first class at a Rugby school, just after the First World War, we sat on little wooden stools at tables. On Empire Day, 24th May, we sang a patriotic song which began: 'We have come to school this morning, 'tis the 24th of May, and we join in celebrating what is called our Empire Day.' Then we saluted a large Union Jack which always seemed to stand in a corner of the classroom. On the wall was a large picture of the battle of Spion Kop in the Boer War."

"Empire Day was always celebrated at Willoughby Village School in the 1920's. We all stood round the flagpole and the Union Jack was raised with great ceremony as we sang "Britons never, never, never shall be slaves" with great gusto."

"On Empire Day at Ashorne, the children would line up outside the school while the Union Jack was raised on the flagpole and the National Anthem was sung. Each child was then given a penny and a half day's holiday from school. The penny was duly deposited at the local sweet shop. This went on for several years, and then the penny was gradually stopped. Up until the middle 1930s a gentleman in the village used to come up to the school on Empire Day and present the children with a medal and a year after they would get a box to add to it with the date on."

"As Empire Day this year came on Sunday, it was celebrated at the Budbrooke Council Schools on Friday last week. During the morning the children were given lessons on Empire Day and the growth of the British Empire. After that they sang patriotic songs, viz, "A Song for England", "The Bay of Biscay", "The Minstrel Boy", "Rule Britannia", and lastly "God Save the King", when the boys saluted the Union Jack. In the afternoon all the school turned out into a field kindly lent by Mr Pettle. Games, consisting of football, cricket and rounders were indulged in. After the games were finished each child was given buns, an orange, and a bottle of lemonade. These refreshments were kindly provided by Mrs G. O. Everard. After the refreshments were disposed of the children again got together and sang the National Anthem."

The occasion had assumed particular significance during the First World War, when expectations of good behaviour would gain a patriotic tinge:

"The whole school drawn up on the playground. The Master addressed them on:

a) the Empire and the Union Jack.

b) the importance of economy.

c) the necessity of children going to bed early."

(Kineton C.E.)

Royal Occasions

Great royal occasions always provided interruptions to the school routine. "Owing to the death of the King (Edward VII), singing has been abandoned. The 'Dead March' was played to the children and "God Save the King" sang, kneeling" (Shottery C.E. School, May 5, 1910); "The Headteacher and the boys of Standards V and VI left the school at 9.10 a.m. and went to Nuneaton Market Place where at 10.15 a.m. a Proclamation of King George V took place (Abbey, May 10, 1910)

and later: "Instead of the ordinary needlework lesson, the girls were allowed to make their own paper bonnets to wear on Coronation Day" (ibid, June 16, 1911).

Such events, especially royal celebrations, continued to break into school terms throughout most of the twentieth century. A Shilton resident in 1924 recalled: "Our schoolmaster took us down to see the Royal car (Duke of York's) pass through. Just to see the car was in itself an event in those days."

In 1935 the Silver Jubilee at Hurley was marked by sports such as apple-ducking and a huge bonfire. Schools in Leamington celebrated with a pageant in Victoria Park. Pupils were dressed in white : white dresses or white skirts and shorts. Each school marched to the park with a leader carrying the Union Jack. Even in 1957, pupils at Lawrence Sheriff were allowed out of lessons to see Princess Margaret pass through the town. Patriotism was tempered in the cases of those whose G.C.E. French orals were interrupted, as the examiner questioned them about the royal visit when they returned. This was not a topic they had prepared.

A Royal Visit

As far as I am aware, the visit of the Queen and Duke of Edinburgh to Higham Lane was a first-ever for Warwickshire schools. Kings and Queens have visited Rugby School, but not an L.E.A. school. Prince Charles and Princess Diana visited Atherstone North and Racemeadow briefly in 1985. But otherwise such visits are rare indeed. The announcement of a visit for December 1994 therefore precipitated frenzied activity, recorded in a chapter of "Rabbits on Report" by John Terry, creator of the school farm. Paving slabs were relaid, walls painted, ponds cleared and a pile of manure removed 'out of smell's way'.

On the big day, a helicopter, television crews and photographers were there to ensure the security and the record of the visit. The Queen and the Duke of Edinburgh visited classrooms and heard school musicians before touring the farm. They were particularly interested to see the progress of Windsor Grand Good News, a heifer that had come from the royal farm at Windsor. They were very complimentary about the high standards of care on the farm.

Treats

But special events did not have to be regal. Numerous memories survive of treats such as that enjoyed by pupils at the catholic school in Alcester in the 1920's " ..... a charabanc to a field near Alcester ..... races ...... paste sandwiches, buns and mugs of tea...... rare treat".

As the year moved to its end, the causes for celebration continued, as at Wood Street Infants, Rugby:

"Much was made of "Special" days throughout those early years. Harvest Festival came first. Produce from the allotments was brought and later taken to the workhouse in Lower Hillmorton Road and to one of the orphanages. Class work was geared for several weeks to this event, as it was for all the other special days. We loved making the pictures, learning the hymns and songs. Halloween caused much excitement - we made witches' hats, cut out cats, spiders, cauldrons, brooms etc. Guy Fawkes again created much noisy excitement. I remember that first year, the teacher brought sparklers and we each held one. The boys got naughty and tried to frighten us girls by waving the sparklers close to our hair. What wonderful bonfire parties we had!

Preparations for Christmas started then, to make gifts for Mum and Dad. The ones I remember making were of wallpaper. For Mum a needlecase, two pieces of flannel stitched to the crease, knitting wool made into plaits and glued either side of the opening, a needle, a pin and a safety pin stuck into the flannel. A masterpiece! My mother used it for years. Dad's was also useful. A pad of tissue papers stuck to wallpaper with a loop of wool to hang it up. This was to wipe his razor whilst shaving. Paper chains were made by the yard, also stiff paper lanterns. The latter we coloured in patterns, then cut and glued, they looked wonderful."

Towards the end of the 1920's, a few schools began to hold 'Open Days' to allow parents to see the work of the school. Here is a sample timetable from St. Paul's Central, Coleshill:

3.00: P.T. Demo (Senior Boys)
3.20: Dancing (Girls)
3.50: Danish Rounders (Junior Boys)
4.10: A short French play "A Deaf Judge" (Girls)

Bonfire Night

Of course, Bonfire Night was celebrated, often with little more than a garden bonfire and half a can of paraffin. But many villages held big bonfire events. As with much else, boys could not resist injecting a note of competition into the occasion: "We always had a bigger bonfire than Upper Brailes." (Lower Brailes)

Thus, daily routine was enlivened by all kinds of festive interludes, some that are still with us and others that now seem archaic, or an unlikely excuse for a "day off". These days, the occasional day off for the children usually triggers a message to parents about the much more solemn 'training day', where fun and excitement are at best optional extras, for the teachers, at any rate.

Celebrating Christmas

Reading logbook entries for the days leading up to Christmas suggests that even from the earliest days there were modest celebrations, though often combined with business as usual: "After tests in Scripture, Mental Arithmetic and Reading, the infants were all given nuts; greater number given to those who did best" (Long Compton, Dec 24, 1868). Sometimes, celebrations took a back seat: "H.M. Inspector visited the school to examine the children" (Birdingbury, Dec 22, 1882); "Lessons on 'The Labourer' and 'The Tiger' have been given. School closed today for the Christmas holidays" (Shipston, Dec 18, 1885), and "I have tested the children during the week as far as is possible and think they are progressing slowly" (Frankton, Dec 23, 1898).

Heads then were determined not to let Christmas encroach too far into the final weeks of term: "Continued ordinary work of school with no variation of timetable. Nothing else to record" (Henley Junior, Dec 14, 1900). Many schools closed the term on Christmas Eve with the distribution of prizes, usually by the Vicar, for good work, behaviour and attendance. At one such event at Stockton in 1876, a recipient was one Fanny Adams. History does not record whether she was sweet! The extent to which any celebrating at all occurred could depend on the munificence of local benefactors: "The Vicar and Mrs Phelps gave a Christmas Tree and tea for the children, also fireworks" (Long Compton, Dec 22, 1873).

Even the temptations of seasonal excitement could not tempt all of the children into school. Absence reared its familiar head: "Only a few children assembled for afternoon school so did not open" (Leek Wootton, Dec 22, 1896); "Several boys away today owing to their parents killing the Christmas pigs" (Atherstone Boys, Dec 12, 1870) and "F Mayo away with face ache" (Chilvers Coton, Dec 1, 1897).

St. Austin's marked the festival with a parish sale, starting in the evening. You could buy gifts from a 'useful stall' or from 'glass' or 'various'. The children entertained customers with songs, and the evening ended at 10.00 p.m. with the National Anthem. Even when the children did leave school clutching something, it might not have generated unqualified excitement: "At 4.10 p.m. school broke up for Xmas holidays. Each scholar took home: a) a cyclostyled copy of the class position list, and, b) an envelope to receive gifts for the Blinded Soldiers' Children's Fund" (St. Paul's Stockingford, Dec 19, 1907).

Clearly, the newly-created Education Office was active until the end of term: "The Director of Education, G. Fitzmaurice Esq. visited the school during the dinner hour.

He made a minute inspection of the premises and made many enquiries of the master respecting the condition and suitability of the school" (Stockton, 22 Dec, 1903).

Perhaps the office feared too much premature laxity, such as that reported at Ullenhall: "A free and easy afternoon was indulged in from 2 o'clock when recitations and a scene from Dickens' 'Christmas Carol' was given by the Senior Scholars."

The typical end of term tidying could reveal unwelcome news: "Have had to spend hours and hours over registers and summary. Registers had scarcely been touched and were full of mistakes" (Austrey, Dec 21, 1906).

Christmas in the First World War and After

War inevitably hampered arrangements or diverted resources: "The Christmas tea and presents were not given this year so that the money could be sent to the Fund for Distressed Belgians and Princess Mary's Sailors' and Soldiers' Fund (Abbey School, Dec 23, 1914). One response to shortages was that of self-help: "Children had cards, biscuits, sweets and toys made by themselves distributed" (Shipston, Dec 23, 1914).

Between the wars little seemed to change. Money was never plentiful, and the occasional departures from class routines were sometimes caused by events more climatic than seasonal: "The stove refused to burn this a.m. and the temperature was 46º. We gave up ordinary lessons and took P.T. and Folk Dances" (Leamington Hastings, Dec 16, 1926).

A popular close to the term was a prizegiving: "School closed for Xmas holidays. At 3.00 pm the whole school assembled for the distribution of prizes. The ceremony was performed by the Rt. Hon. Monsignor Hudson who also addressed the school on the necessity of using more "will in the prosecution of their studies" (St. Paul's Central, Dec 19, 1929).

Attempts were made to ameliorate hardship and to ensure that all children could participate in at least one festive event: "At the end of the afternoon, I distributed six dozen 'Poor Children Xmas Dinner' tickets to the most deserving cases" (Abbey School,1920's). Once again, local benefactors rallied to the cause: "Before closing, 112 children out of 132 were given a book each, the money for the books was given by resident gentry" (Kineton, Dec 21, 1929).

The magic of the Festival was evident in many reminiscences such as this from a pupil from Exhall C.E. School: "At Christmas, the screen which separated the two classes was drawn back and an Xmas tree brought in and decorated. It was a magical time. Each child had a present and something from the tree. I always hoped I would get a sugar mouse."

The spirit of Christmas sometimes travelled from one school to another: "I am very proud to enter a note of a most gracious thing that has happened. Miss John, Headmistress of Heath End Infant School, arranged for part of her Christmas Handwork, for all her children to make and give with their love a toy for each of the 159 children in this school. Such kindness has given us all personal pleasure" (All Saints', Nuneaton, Dec 19, 1937). Hospitality was extended to schoolchildren by diverse people in diverse places: "This afternoon, all the children were entertained by Lord and Lady Willoughby de Broke at the Women's Institute from 4.30 to 7.00 p.m" (Gaydon, Dec 22, 1937).

The Second World War

The Second World War inevitably restricted celebrations. Money was short. Food was rationed. The "blackout" discouraged ostentatious lighting. Nevertheless, the first Christmas saw festivities little changed: "The afternoon was spent by the children dramatising stories and recitations and singing games followed by distribution of cakes, sweets, oranges and apples ...." (Hampton Lucy, Dec 21, 1939). Subsequent parties sometimes involved new faces: "Closed school this p.m. with party to which evacuees were invited" (Ibid Dec 19, 1940).

The war once gain received a 'make do and mend' spirit, supplemented this time by transatlantic goodwill: "Rubbers, given by Women of America, were distributed to long distance children who greatly appreciated the gifts. Village children were rather disappointed" (Middleton, Dec 20, 1944). Some just relied on self-help: "We collected egg shells, washed them out, threaded cotton through each half then painted them as decorations" (Haselor and Walcote). Those teenagers not at work were recruited to help Christmas on its way: "Fifth and sixth formers were recruited to help with the Christmas Post. The first step was to swear the Official Secrets Act" (Alan Cronshaw, King Edward College, Nuneaton).

As the pace of post-war change accelerated, office staff from the top downwards would travel out to the villages to offer a combination of seasonal goodwill and long-term reassurance: "Among visitors was Mr Yorke-Lodge (C.E.O.) who stayed about ten minutes, stated: "We are not worried about Stockton" and went his way" (Stockton, Dec 20, 1957).

Coming Up To Date

Since then, Christmas has developed its own momentum, often propelled by other festivals such as Diwali. A selection of more recent logbook entries give a flavour:

"Christmas 1964 brought Xmas parties for 1st and 6th year. Jelly and sandwiches, mince pies and cake, cream buns and lemonade per pupil for 1st and 2nd years. A slightly more advanced buffet for 3rd years. Sit down four course evening meal for 4th, 5th and 6th years. 4th year leavers had a party to themselves."

(Henley High School, Christmas 1964)

"Last day, hectic as always. Many old scholars came to wish us Happy Christmas. I provided mince pies and chocolates."

(Alveston Primary, December 19, 1975)

"Mrs B …… absent, raging toothache. Took dinner money to bank. Took sick children home. Children in 1st and 2nd years watched their Christmas film, 'Tag and Wily Fox'.

(Polesworth County First, December 19, 1983)

"Father Christmas visited the school, an event that coincided with the temporary absence of the Headteacher."

(Alcester High, 1980's)

By the end of the century one could discern a range of practice from those schools that began Christmas production rehearsals immediately after the Autumn half-term to the principal of a Leamington school who informed me in a tone that brooked no Yuletide spirit of compromise: "Christmas in this school begins at 3.30 p.m. on the last afternoon of term and not a moment before." Doubtless his pupils made up for lost time.

11

The Growth of 'Special' Education

The history of special education in Warwickshire is a book in itself. I have tried to deal with parts of that story in a history of Exhall Grange School (see bibliography). It was not until the Education Act 1944 that most local authorities considered anything but ad hoc provision for children with a range of kinds of disabilities. But the Act compelled them to make proper provision. It engendered alarm as well as enthusiasm. In 1944, before the Act had even become law, the Chairman of the Education Committee gave dark hints of trouble in store: "I will not trouble the council with the problems that will arise from the new legislation regarding the provision of ...... special schools for afflicted children."

If we take the education of blind or deaf children as an example, we find that until the Act, the authority paid for pupils to be educated in out-of-county special schools. Even back in 1908, the authority paid for twelve blind and twenty one deaf children to be so educated, at an annual cost of £722 2s 10d. Parents would typically be expected to contribute two shillings (10p) a week. By 1943, annual boarding costs had risen to £115, with pupils being educated as far away as Exeter and Chorleywood. Most, however, were educated in the Midlands at schools in Birmingham and in Stoke on Trent.

Early in 1947, the Committee acknowledged a case for children "in need of special educational treatment" to be included in the County Development Plan, but at that stage they did not anticipate a need for new county residential schools. There was mention of "joint arrangements with other authorities in the West Midlands area under a proposed regional scheme." However, the Development Plan did say: "It is probable that the effect of consultations will be the provision by the Warwickshire Authority of one or two residential schools on a regional basis for about 100 children for one of the following categories : blind, partly sighted, deaf, partially deaf, epileptic, physically handicapped".

From 1948, there were regular references in Education Committee minutes to hopes and setbacks for new special schools. In January 1948, for example, the Committee learned that early plans had been delayed: "The opening of the Special Schools has not materialised as was expected when the estimates for 1947-8 were drafted."

A major development came in January 1951, when Exhall Grange School was opened. This school was to attain national recognition. Opened for blind, for partially sighted and for physically handicapped children, it was for many years a national boarding school catering for 300 pupils. Some pupils still board there today.

Another category of need clamouring for attention was that category of children then designated as "educationally sub-normal". The Report of the School Medical Officer in 1948 alerted committee to the problems of providing properly for the 347 boys and 197 girls already identified but being educated in mainstream schools:

"There has been for some years great difficulty experienced in obtaining vacancies for these children at Special Schools. The duty to provide such Special Schools is now statutory but in view of present day circumstances it is difficult to visualise how long it will be before it is possible to .... establish one in the administrative area of this county."

A hostel existed at Meriden for "difficult boys". This was replaced by River House School in Henley in 1953.

In October 1949 Tyntesfield School had "crept into existence, it was never officially opened". Those were the words of its first head, although it had begun to take boarders in September that year. From then on, slowly in the 1950's but more rapidly in the 1960's, schools were opened throughout the county. The Mental Health Act of 1959 required authorities to provide facilities for the training of mentally sub-normal children. It replaced the previously degrading language of words like 'idiot' and 'imbecile' with designations such as 'severely sub-normal'. The first purpose-built centre, known then as a 'Junior Training Centre', was the Ridgeway Centre, opened in 1962. The centre was at that time under the auspices of the Health Authority and it was officially opened by the then Minister of Health, Enoch Powell. He was accompanied by the Chairman of the Health Committee and the Chief Medical Officer of Health. The opening of the centre had attracted criticism and some hostility from local residents and Powell characteristically met this opposition 'head-on' in his opening speech: "Centres such as these must be located in the heart of the community they serve."

The centre was seen as a model of its kind and featured in some detail in the 'Architects' Journal' the following year. Other schools opened round the county built similarly: Blythe at Coleshill, Leyland at Nuneaton, Lambert at Stratford and Brooke at Rugby.

A distinction was made between pupils with "moderate" and pupils with "severe" learning problems. The schools opened for the former were:

Central Area	Gresham
	St Michael's (replaced Warwick Priory)
Eastern	Tyntesfield (already opened)
Northern	Sparrowdale
Nuneaton/Bedworth	Red Deeps
Southern	Marie Corelli

From 1948, with no county provision, the Principal School Medical Officer was able to report in 1969, just over twenty years later that 1302 "educationally sub-normal" children were now educated in in-county special schools, 791 boys and 511 girls. Boys always outnumbered girls in these schools, and the county responded to the need to provide a school for "maladjusted senior girls", Millbrook Grange in Kenilworth, long after the opening of River House.

As is often the case, improved provision led to growing numbers of cases. The development of a Speech Therapy Service after the War corresponded to, or caused through better diagnosis and increased expectation, a rapid growth in those receiving specialist help:

1951: 35
1953: 191
1960: 654

A welcome decline was in the number of so-called "ineducable" children: from 60 in 1952 to 31 in 1954 for example. Numbers dwindled further in subsequent years.

The Warnock Report (1981) urged impetus towards more integration. From the 1980's onwards, re-organisation of special education in general and special schools in particular was never off the agenda. Whereas primary teachers had at least a "lull" of some fifteen years between being re-organised into and then out of first and middle schools, special schools were to be constantly scrutinised. At the time of writing, the futures of Ridgeway School, Warwick and Round Oak, Leamington seem to be settled, following prolonged debate. Arguably, special education has changed and developed as much in the last fifty years as 'mainstream' has in the last hundred. The biggest indicator of that volume of change is the number of children now in mainstream schools who were once educated in special schools.

12

School Inspections, Advisory Support and In-Service Training

School inspections started in 1839, but their origins lie with the decision of the Government in 1833 to offer grants from the Treasury to those who strove to promote elementary schools. There were few conditions attached to these grants and no checks on how the money was used. Government funding of state education began in a small way with a grant of £20,000. In April 1839, the Committee of the Privy Council for Education was established. The Committee began to formulate regulations setting out conditions for the payment of grants. One regulation contained the words: "right of inspection will be required by the committee in all cases."

This regulation led to the establishment of Her Majesty's Inspectorate. There was a precedent for this : The Home Office at the instigation of the Home Secretary and Tamworth M.P., Sir Robert Peel, had appointed five Inspectors of Prisons in 1835, some four years before the first two schools' inspectors were appointed. In 1840, the Committee published "Instructions for the Inspectors of Schools". Given all that has happened since, it is instructive to note the restrained nature of the wording:

"It is of the utmost consequence you should bear in mind that this inspection is not intended as a means of exercising control, but of affording assistance; that is not to be regarded as operating for the restraint of local efforts but for their encouragement ..... the Inspector not being instructed to offer any advice or information excepting where it is invited."

One of the first H.M.I. was Matthew Arnold, son of Dr Thomas Arnold of Rugby, about whom there is more in Chapter 15.

A significant event for both schools and inspectors was the introduction of the Revised Code of 1862. The main function of H.M.I., that of giving advice and encouragement, was changed to one of control and examining. The Code, better known as 'Payment by Results', ensured that schools' income was determined by the results the pupils achieved in annual examinations. This in turn helped to determine teachers' salaries. Only results in the 'three Rs', and needlework for girls, were taken into account.

It would be difficult to find a better or earlier account of the anxiety engendered by this annual visitation than that of the visits to Tysoe School found in the biography of Joseph Ashby:

"Two inspectors came once a year and carried out a dramatic examination. The schoolmaster came into school in his best suit; all the pupils and teachers would be listening till at ten o'clock a dog-cart would be heard on the road, even though it was eighty yards away. In would come two gentlemen with a deportment of high authority, with rich voices. Each would sit at a desk and children would be called in turn to one or other. The master hovered round, calling children out as they were needed. The children could see him start with vexation as a good pupil stuck at a word in the reading book he had been using all the year, or sat motionless with his sum in front of him. The master's anxiety was deep, for his earnings depended on the children's work."

Preparations for the visit of inspectors bore a striking resemblance to those today, as this testy note shows:

"The first hour entirely wasted this morning. I was with the teachers last evening numbering the specimens of work till 5 o'clock. I gave orders that after 5 o'clock tea they, with the help of the person who cleans the school, were to dust walls, pictures, cupboard etc. and leave things ready this morning for H.M. Inspector."

(Vicarage Street, Nuneaton 1883)

Exams were based on so-called Standards, an extract from which appears below:

	Standard I	Standard II	Standard III
Reading	Narrative in monosyllables.	One of the narratives next in order after monosyllables in elementary reading book used in the school.	A short paragraph from an elementary reading book used in the school.
Writing	Form on blackboard or slate, from dictation, letters, capital and small manuscript.	Copy in manuscript character a line of print.	A sentence from the same paragraph, slowly read once, and then dictated in single words.
Arithmetic	Form on blackboard or slate, from dictation, figures up to 20; name at sight figures up to 20; add and subtract figures up to 10 orally.	A sum in simple addition or subtraction, and the multiplication table.	A sum in any simple rule as far as short division (inclusive).

It will not have escaped the attention of anyone working in education in recent years that all this is strikingly similar to our current system of tests, published results and the like with unsuccessful schools losing pupils and, thus, capitation. How and why did The Code end? One of the sternest critics was Matthew Arnold. It was he who spotted the inevitable consequence that teachers would teach to the tests. It was an unimaginative game that teachers would ultimately win " ..... a game of mechanical contrivance (they) will and must more and more learn how to beat us."

Regulations were gradually relaxed and 'Payment by Results' ended in 1895, though only after more than thirty years of its fostering a narrow curriculum. Annual inspections continued long after, as Elizabeth Meaton noted at St. Austin's, Kenilworth: "These inspections were not just annual visits. Sometimes the inspectors took it into their heads to visit twice a year, and if they found conditions unsatisfactory, they would return more often ...." Visitations that will be familiar today to those schools designated as "requiring special measures".

Reports did not pull punches. Here is one on Birdingbury in 1883: "The infants are backward and have evidently not received sufficient attention at the hands of the mistress" and one on Henley in January 1889: "I am sorry to say that I have nothing good to report. My lords will be compelled to reduce the next grant unless much improvement is observable." Clearly, H.M.I. views were not easily mollified. In a follow-up visit to Henley in December that year, the report remained bleak: "The school is in no better state than last year." even though a Diocesan Report three months later was positively euphoric: "The school is in excellent order ....."

H.M.I. were clearly moving towards the contentious concept of 'child-centred' education, as this quotation from Studley historians illustrated: "The centre of our education system is no longer the State, the Department, the Inspector or the Teacher. It is the child."

Reports could be, unwittingly, what we would now see as both patronising and sexist in tone: "The latter is an extremely bright little chap and must have been a pride to his mother." (Beausale, Dec. 1905). The reports were usually brief with an almost staccato style: "The playground needs attention." (Gaydon, 1909) although there were lapses into circumlocution " ..... impossible to avoid the conclusion that in many ways the work of the school might reasonably be expected to reach a higher standard."

An unusually long report on Stretton on Dunsmore followed a two day visit in 1910. One recommendation sounds familiar: "Care should be taken that the girls in the top division do not allow the boys to answer for them."

H.M.I. were unimpressed by progress at Wilmcote:-

"In H.M. Inspector's last report the Managers were urged to improve the existing building, and attention was directed to the lighting, the flooring, the deficiency of the Classroom in respect of size, lighting and ventilation, the poorness of the offices, and the worn out condition of the furniture, apparatus and desks. Beyond the addition of the skylights in the roof, none of these necessary improvements have been carried out and I may be unable to recommend the continued recognition of the School as a Public Elementary School unless the points above named are at once attended to."

At Norton Lindsey a pupil absent from school was excused by his parents thus:

" ….. kept away from school during inspection because not treated well at last inspection."

L.E.A. Inspections

I have described earlier how Warwickshire came to have its own inspector in 1905, Gerald Fitzmaurice. Some of his reports survive, and many more have survived from his successor: R. W. Bateman-Brown. A few quotations give some sense both of the difficult prevailing conditions, and of a terse, unequivocal style: "The school is very much understaffed" (Arley, 1908); "Considering that 138 boys are being taught in one room, and that three teachers and two students are at work in it, the discipline is very good" (Atherstone Boys, 1909); "There is a marked improvement in the condition of the lavatories since my last visit …." (Kingsbury Council, 1909); and "All the teachers seemed to me to be hard-working and painstaking but a little slow. The lessons did not "go", but I think the children are themselves largely to blame for this" (Kingsbury Dosthill, 1909).

In 1910 Bateman-Brown investigated the unexpected resignation of the head of Withybrook School. He attributed the resignation to "friction with the caretaker." His recommendation was simple and stark: "In my opinion the caretaker should be dismissed forthwith."

His commitment to a broad curriculum and to the value of first-hand experience were evident in the same report: "In both History and Geography the habit of acquiring knowledge at first hand should be developed." This commitment was to be a key principle in advice offered by advisers and inspectors from that day to this:

Bateman-Brown would also investigate the disciplinary treatment of children: "Miss P's manner with the children is harsh and unpleasant" (Mancetter, 1910). At Hunningham School, he investigated a parental complaint of "excessive punishment". He found that caning was deployed for " ..... lying, laziness, carelessness, untidiness, indecency, copying, putting out tongue at the teacher, not attending in class, swearing in playground ..... " This list would not appear to have left much need for any other sanctions.

Sometimes, he was more circumspect: "The new headmistress <u>appears</u> to have entered into her duties with energy. The children <u>appeared</u> to be interested in their work." (Binton C.E., 1909) and "<u>As far as I can judge</u>, some improvement <u>appears</u> to have taken place ..... the children <u>appear</u> to work hard, but the teacher <u>seems</u> somewhat deficient in "grip" (Bulkington C.E. Infants, 1909).

H.M.I. Inspections After 'The Revised Code'

H.M.I. might recommend, and the L.E.A. usually responded, but not invariably. In response to criticism of cloakroom accommodation at Beausale, Bolton King replied: "My committee have carefully considered the matter and do not think it necessary ..... to provide extra accommodation" (1912).

As education moved further away from the Revised Code, H.M.I. welcomed more experimental approaches and were particularly impressed by postwar innovation by the head of Stretton on Dunsmore when he returned from active service. A few sample comments illustrate H.M.I.'s excitement. He spoke of a school of "unique interest and value", the head had broken away from formal routines, espousing practical activities which ensured that: "the children are as busy and methodical as bees." Their work in handicrafts also incorporated drawing, the use of balance sheets, of reference books etc. The consequence? "There are no dull children. Each finds his right sphere of interest."

At nearby Wolston, H.M.I. remarked on more outdated methods, though with recognition of practical problems: "The methods of teaching adopted in the infant school can hardly be described as modern, but the class is very large, and there is some justification for mass methods of teaching" (March 1925).

Though H.M.I. had moved away from the dreaded visit and its fearful consequences, they continued to be blunt: "The haphazard system by which some children pass on to Henley School and some remain to finish their education at Ullenhall is to be deplored. It has tended to leave behind the less alert of the children." But where the inspector was satisfied with the school, annual visits helped to cement cordial relations. H.M.I. Wilson in a farewell letter to Lillington School, prior to his appointment as 'Chief Inspector of Schools', wrote of " .... the excellent tone, good manners and friendly feeling of the school." Apart from his official visits, he would also attend events such as the end of term Christmas concert.

Amid the sporadic H.M.I. visits were those experienced more regularly by the church schools : the visit of the Diocesan Inspector. There is a full record of a 1949 Diocesan visit to Alveston in which the Inspector recorded the to and fro of debate of an eternal issue : the pros and cons of "learning by heart". The Inspector concluded with relief that the teachers' views coincided with his own: "No-one wants to get back to parrot repetition, but it is good that a child should know a certain number of things by heart: The Creed, The Lord's Prayer and The Ten Commandments."

Home Education

Then as now, parents could choose to educate their children at home. Then as now, the authorities were supposed to assure themselves that children not in school were receiving an adequate education. One day, early in the century, an inspector (we do not know whether by accident or design or whether an H.M.I. or L.E.A. inspector) found Mary Robertson and her sisters looking at the river in Eathorpe. He challenged them and, on hearing their story, took them home and examined both their work and the teaching methods in use. Presumably he was satisfied (or bluffing), for the children were not obliged to join the nearest school.

H.M.I. annual visits continued throughout the century. Reports were painstakingly copied into logbooks and can thus be studied with ease. For example, a report reproduced in Snitterfield School of six pages in length can be found in 1953.

Inspectorate Surveys

In the seventies H.M.I. began to publish national surveys of educational provision. These led to major county-wide weekend conferences for headteachers at which H.M.I. would be key speakers. The 1978 nationwide survey of primary education was less bleak than many had expected, and some had hoped. It endorsed the bedrock importance of the basic skills, but suggested that they were best learned as part of a broad curriculum rather than in isolation. But successive Conservative governments became impatient with the generalised and circumspect tone of these reports. Her Majesty's Inspectorate would soon face drastic cuts in both number and independence.

L.E.A. Advice and Inspection

The antecedents of the advisory and inspectorial team lay in a small group of organisers for practical subjects only and the small team of the early sixties included organisers for horticulture and bee-keeping. Earlier chapters have drawn on the annual reports of the Organisers For Physical Education. They had no pastoral responsibilities. By the 1970's there was a team of general inspectors as well as the now labelled 'advisers'. They began to take on a pastoral group for schools and to assume more general responsibilities. Before that time, an adviser's job was confined to subject work. Barbara Gibson had a contract bound in ribbon which she retains to this day, given on her appointment in 1963. It had just two requirements:

"1) To work as the Organiser of Physical Education under the direction of the County Education Officer.

2) To advise the County Education Officer on all Physical Training matters in schools and institutions for which responsible and to help teachers in the organisation of physical education."

Warwickshire's first music adviser was appointed in 1965. His role was to provide advice, to organise courses for teachers and to establish a team of qualified instrumental teachers with the mission of harnessing musical talent through music centres and through county units such as the County Youth Orchestra, Wind Band and Youth Chorale. Organising such ambitious ventures took much time, and assumed that most or all of an adviser's working week could be devoted to his or her subject.

Expansion of L.E.A. Services

To accompany the growth in numbers of pupils, the Education Committee now began a programme of expansion of its inspectors and advisers. (The distinction between the two was more hierarchical than task-related. Both inspectors and advisers inspected .... and advised). Not that schools worried too much about the job titles of their visitors, or about whence they came: "Mr Restorick (H.M.I.) called at 2.40 p.m. Discovered this should be Mr Raistrick, General Inspector" (Long Itchington Primary, March, 1968).

The views of advisers and organisers on their visit were seldom recorded. When they were, they were clearly not always accorded total respect, even when being complimentary: "A visit by Miss Scotney, Needlework Organiser. She expressed surprise at the high standard of plain sewing and suggested much of the work ought to be done in the secondary school. This is arrant rubbish. Surely children ought to work to their limits" (Stockton, 3rd October, 1958).

In 1967 also, Committee appointed the first two teachers to its newly established peripatetic remedial service. Its original purpose was to help teachers to meet the needs of 'remedial' children in 'normal' schools. During its history the service has grown and regularly changed its functions, its name and its bases. Many teachers will best remember it in its days during the 1970's and 1980's, when it was known as the Reading Advisory Service. While maintaining its peripatetic role, it also ran courses and tutored pupils at the centre. The centre was next to Milverton School, and established in what had been a magistrates' court. Courses were held in the old courtroom, and the cells, still with peepholes in the door, served as storerooms. From certain back windows, it was possible to see the old exercise yard, a high-walled courtyard around which prisoners used to try to exercise. The centre now houses a Pupil Reintegration Unit.

Teachers' Centres

Another significant development in advice and support was the gradual opening of a number of Teachers' Centres. On October 2 1968, Alderman Doughty spoke thus at the opening of the new centre at Long Lawford: "The purpose of this centre is to provide a place where teachers can meet in organised or informal groups to discuss their work, exchange ideas and examine and develop new approaches and techniques."

And, more or less, chiefly more, that is what the centres went on to do.

The 1960's also saw the establishment of teachers' centres in other parts of the county. The four best-remembered will be those at Leamington, Nuneaton, Rugby and Stratford. These too collected various homes. Rugby's began in the old Long Lawford school buildings but moved to premises on the East Warwickshire College site. Leamington's was on the top floor of what had once been school premises. The centre shared its upstairs premises with the Art department of Mid Warwickshire College, while on the ground floor was the library. Once Manor Hall opened it became economical to move it to part of the new centre there. Nuneaton's centre was behind the fire station, and Stratford occupied a hut, somewhat anachronistically plonked behind the centuries old building housing Stratford Library, and as next door neighbour to Shakespeare's birthplace. All four eventually moved and in the moves many of the centre records were destroyed. They live on largely in the memories of the thousands of teachers who attended courses and conferences there, usually in the "twilight" period after school. Each had its warden, secretary, library and resource collection. Each was a base for advising teachers. Each had its management committee of teachers, ensuring a regular supply of practical courses. Attendance was voluntary and so many teachers seldom if ever visited. Others came several times a week. Historians will find little documentary record and will hear contested versions of why they eventually closed. Most will settle for a combination of financial stringency and moves towards more school-based in-service training.

Mid Warwickshire Teachers' Centre

The Mid Warwickshire Teachers' Centre booking diaries survive from 1980-1990. These show the continued growth of INSET activity over the decade, particularly after the 1988 Education Act and the introduction of the National Curriculum.

For a typical week in January 1981 entries were:

Monday	4.30	Centre Committee
Tuesday	4.30	Fletcher Maths
	7.00	Reading Group
Wednesday	7.00	NAS/UWT
	7.00	Road Safety

| Thursday | 4.30 | Communication Skills 7-13 |
| Friday | | No recorded bookings |

The intervening years saw a growth in the development of all sorts of common interest groups, for example:

Deputy Heads in Primary Schools
Art Teachers
Central Area under 5's group
Combined School Heads
Classroom Assistants

Sadly, another centre for INSET, St. Paul's College at Newbold Revel, closed in 1978. The head of Long Lawford spoke for many: "The world of education in general and this area in particular will lose one of the few colleges where 'all that is of good report' is valued." As a sign of the times, the college was reopened as a Prison Officers' Training Centre in 1986 by the Rt. Hon. Douglas Hurd.

When the Teachers' Centres closed, their documentation was transferred to Manor Hall. In various internal office moves, much of it was unfortunately though understandably destroyed. What survives is largely financial : cheque book stubs, accounts, copies of invoices etc., though in some cases dating back to 1972 (e.g. South Warwickshire Teachers' Centre Stock Book). The Stock Book gives a hint of the variety of resources on offer to support teachers' work. A list jotted down more or less at random includes:

Phillips Tape Recorder
4 bevelled chisels
4 Stanley knives
Film strips (Captain Scott... British Wild Animals..Your Body... King Alfred etc.)
2 Thermometers
85 teaspoons
2 Aquaria

The gradual move towards the centre: 'downsized' area offices and teachers' centres etc. did help to justify the opening of a new resource: the Educational Development Centre at Manor Hall on the edge of Leamington. The building had once been part of North Leamington School and, with a nice irony, one of the official guests at the opening of the centre was Councillor Bill Boxley, formerly head of that very hall. As he moved along the red carpet to the front door, mayoral chain gleaming brightly, he was greeted by C.E.O. Margaret Maden. In characteristic Geordie-style, his opening words were: "You didn't have bloody carpets all over the place when I was here!" The centre was opened on June 14th, 1990 by Professor John Tomlinson, former C.E.O. for Cheshire and then Director of the Institute of Education at Warwick University.

The centre immediately buzzed with life: conferences, courses, concerts, workshops, morning, noon and night. Occasionally even pupils were allowed in. Reportedly, some groups of pupils were disappointed to find out what Manor Hall looked like because they had assumed they were going to an Elizabethan mansion. In one sense, Manor Hall <u>was</u> an Elizabethan mansion, but not in their sense! Many secondary heads shared the regret of John Hancock (Campion) that their meetings would now lose the peace and intimacy of Honiley Hall.

Warwickshire's advisory and inspection service continued to grow in the seventies and eighties. The hierarchy was Senior Inspector, Area Inspectors and Advisers. Though heads and teachers speculated on the difference between an 'inspector' and an 'adviser', the distinction was all about extent of responsibility rather than the job itself. Inspectors advised, and advisers inspected, though not necessarily formally. My own response to questions about the different nomenclature was to borrow a sentence from, I think, former H.M.I. Robin Tanner: "I inspect in order to advise."

More facetiously, I once wrote a short poem for a journal:

"After a talk from the adviser
Is anyone the wiser?
Would an inspector
be corrector?"

Inspections by L.E.A. teams did occur, though they were not always acclaimed: "The staff suggested (in response to a two day inspection) that they would prefer more frequent visits by the individual advisers" (Polesworth County First, Feb 17, 1976). However, once elected members, desperately searching for savings, began to ask questions about the utility of 'advisers' Warwickshire, like many LEAs, adopted 'inspector' as the umbrella term for all.

Recruitment of advisory teachers also grew, often funded by finite government-funded initiatives. They might be for subject, or inspired by grand, albeit short-lived government projects such as the Technical and Vocational Education Initiative (T.V.E.I.). The responsibilities of inspectors and advisory teachers gradually shifted from L.E.A. initiatives to response to government directives : matters such as the implementation of a National Curriculum or, latterly, government initiated strategies for Literacy and Numeracy.

Even the more far-flung schools received regular visits from "the office", but whether the visitors were deliberately enigmatic, or simply tentative, they often left the school somewhat bemused, as these logbook entries at Newbold-on-Stour revealed early in 1972: "This afternoon we had a visit from Mr .... of the County Inspectorate. As far as one can judge, he appeared to be satisfied with what he saw", and "Staffing allocations were received ..... there was a <u>pretty broad hint</u> that if Mrs. S were to resign she would not be replaced."

In-Service Training

A particular feature of Warwickshire in the seventies, eighties and early nineties and a key responsibility of advisers was the weekend course. Financial cutbacks and delegated budgets stopped them thereafter. Though by no means unique, they were unusual; authorities such as Coventry had no equivalent events. It seems hard to believe now that teachers would work hard all week, leave school promptly on Friday afternoon (passing parents at the gate who were doubtless convinced that they simply wanted an early getaway for the weekend) and set off for some centre or other. Favourite venues were Courtaulds in Kenilworth, the Manor House Hotel in Leamington, the Management Centre at Dunchurch and the Herbert Gray College at Rugby. Other venues were occasionally tried, including the Police Headquarters at Leek Wootton. However, the predominantly female teaching clientele were not enamoured of a police diet including fish and chips and bread and butter, and the courses soon moved off elsewhere. When T.V.E.I. began in the late 1980's with its more profligate budgets, more expensive venues in Warwick, Coventry, Stratford, Churchover and Crick all hosted Warwickshire weekends. Programmes would usually start at 5.00 p.m. on Friday evening and the initial event would be interrupted by the arrival of late and flustered teachers muttering darkly about traffic. They would run until 9.00 p.m. on Saturdays and then run through till Sunday lunchtime. Teachers would be allowed the luxury of Sunday afternoon and evening off (just time to prepare some lessons) before returning to school on Monday morning. The programme would typically be a mix of talks : H.M.I., heads, artists, writers, teachers, professors etc. and discussion or working groups. The compensation for this hard work, if compensation it be, was to eat breakfast, a buffet lunch, dinner, and have biscuits with morning coffee and afternoon tea, all at the county's expense. They were great occasions for networking. Two recurring clichés from these weekends were: "The best part was the chance to talk to other teachers." The other, in my experience, was in relation to early jousts with technology such as the overhead projector: "I can't understand it. It was working perfectly this morning."

These weekends are still recalled with great affection by many. They were invariably oversubscribed, sometimes heavily so. The self-help bar at Courtaulds is recalled with particular warmth, though most memories are hazy on, or totally devoid of detail! Teachers had perhaps their one and only experience of using a cash register and would triumphantly ring up £470 for a £4.70 bill. Fortunately, the Centre Manager confined his checks to the amount of bottles that went each evening.

Among the numerous stories from these weekends I select just one. Eric Wood arrived at Dunchurch one Friday evening to talk to recently-appointed heads. At dinner he enquired of a demure, polite young waitress whether he could borrow a potato from the kitchen. He assured her that it would be returned at the end of the evening. He wanted to use it to illustrate an analogy between schools and compost heaps: how very similar conditions could be conducive to growth or destruction, I think. The waitress returned from the kitchen with a potato and handed it to Eric with the words: "Here you are. If it's for anything sexual, we don't want it back, thank you!"

INSET funding initiatives such as T.V.E.I. also gave secondary schools enough funds for larger ones to run their own weekend courses. Also, schools merging into one large secondary institution would run a weekend course for purposes that would probably now be called 'bonding'. Ash Green and Keresley ran such a weekend based at a college in Matlock, for example. The two Dunsmore schools and Fareham High, destined to merge into 'Ashlawn School', also planned such a weekend. But someone, perhaps reluctant to lose precious leisure time, leaked details to the local paper which published a hostile story about a "jaunt at the ratepayers' expense", failing to mention that teachers were giving up a weekend in order to ensure that the merger would lead to a better school.

Warwickshire used Woolley Hall in the West Riding for some of its courses, as did H.M.I. The charismatic C.E.O. of the West Riding, Sir Alec Clegg, corresponded often with officers in Warwickshire. Key thinkers in primary education such as Leonard Marsh were speakers at authority conferences such as those for newly-appointed heads.

There were concerted attempts to bring artists of all kinds to work with pupils in school time and with teachers at weekends. Sculptors, instrumentalists and dancers all led workshops or performed. A regular visitor was Malcolm Williamson, Master of the Queen's Music. Others who came to conduct, compère, perform or lead workshops included Sir Peter Maxwell-Davies, Lennox Berkeley, Moura Lympany, Richard Rodney Bennett, Anthony Hopkins and Guy Woolfenden. The King's Singers and the Alberni Quartet contributed to music education in the county. A particularly well remembered visitor was Maltese composer Charles Camilleri; his visits led to strong links between the county and Malta, with county musical groups visiting to play in Malta. The annual Schools' Proms were county-wide occasions, taking place at Bedworth Civic Hall, and compèred by such names as Richard Baker and Brian Kay.

Local writers with a national reputation such as Andrew Davies, T.V. dramatist, and Gillian Cross, children's author, would frequently visit schools to talk to the children. 'Books for Students' on the Heathcote Estate in Leamington, with some claim to be the largest paperback warehouse in the world, regularly collaborated with the authority to present evenings with internationally known authors such as Allan Ahlberg, Penelope Lively, Judy Blume, Betsy Byars, Michael Rosen and Terry Jones.

Inspection of Schools: The Office for Standards in Education (OFSTED)

A major plank in the drive of the Conservative Government towards accountability was its creation of OFSTED. There always had been inspection in various forms; occasional H.M.I. inspections, regular H.M.I. visits (seldom reported, except to the head and C.E.O.) L.E.A. inspections and regular visits to departments and schools by L.E.A. inspectors. All this was dismissed as too 'cosy' and too private. What was supposedly needed was a publicly accountable system with a bracing injection of lay wisdom and common sense. OFSTED is now very familiar and L.E.A. inspectoral support often devoted to pre and post inspection work.

The Warwickshire inspectorate sought to be 'ahead of the game'. It experimented with lay inspectors and inspections of schools such as St. Gregory's, Stratford and Boughton Leigh Middle well before OFSTED had begun. Lay inspectors were particularly helpful at Catholic schools, given that no member of the inspectorate was then a practising or even lapsed Catholic. This experiment may have been a first in the country. A certain first for the team was the invitation to inspect a grant-maintained school: Great Barr, Birmingham's largest inspectorate. This led the magazine "Education" to note the following: "A Midland L.E.A. which has just completed inspections along the lines of the Schools Act appears to be streets ahead of the rest of the country."

The team recruited two OFSTED-trained H.M.I. immediately on their retirement from the national inspectorate, thus returning to a policy used in 1902 to recruit Warwickshire's first Director of Education. It continues to supply inspectors for OFSTED teams, although much more time is now spent working with schools in preparation for, and in the aftermath of an OFSTED inspection.

The team also responded to invitations to inspect from its own schools, Exhall Grange, for example. The result was a one hundred page report - the last of the old-style professionally accountable reports (aimed at staff rather than the public). Hence its detail. Margaret Maden reported to Committee an estimated cost of £23,000 in staff time. Clearly, in the new world of tendering for contracts against competition, that investment of time and expertise could not continue. The report appeared to have been helpful, however, as Exhall Grange went on to receive from OFSTED reports so complimentary that the school became the first in Warwickshire to be designated a 'beacon' school.

A personal anecdote, also about Exhall Grange. In the week prior to the L.E.A. inspection I received a somewhat intemperate letter from a member of staff demanding answers to all kinds of questions about the purposes and the methodology of the inspection. Reading this at home one evening, I noticed that the teacher in question had written from a home address near to my own home. Keen to show our humane and accessible nature, I wrote a reply, walked round the corner, and posted it through the teacher's letterbox. Within the hour I received another testy, hand-delivered letter with further strident questions. At that moment, I began to see the advantages of a more detached, brusque system.

13

Towards Intercultural Education For All

Postwar immigration, especially in the 1950's and 1960's produced piecemeal responses. Those responses were based on two assumptions : that immigrants would either return to their homelands or be assimilated into the British "way of life". Neither assumption proved to be correct. People remained, but were not assimilated; they sought to preserve the principles of their own ethnic, religious and cultural identity.

Schools were, unsurprisingly, slow to extend their linguistic and cultural understanding. When Giovanna Parisi was asked in a Warwickshire village school to write about her birthplace in the fifties she found that the word 'Sicily' had been crossed out several times, and 'Scilly Isles' substituted.

A D.E.S. Consultative Document in 1977 was the first to advocate a different approach: the recognition and the celebration of a multi-cultural society. This philosophy received strong and cogently argued support from the Swann Committee of Enquiry whose report, in 1985, argued for:

" ….. a truly pluralist society ….. within a framework of commonly accepted values, practices and procedures whilst also allowing and where necessary assisting the ethnic minority communities in maintaining their distinct ethnic identities."

Warwickshire responded speedily to the Swann Report by appointing a County Adviser for Multi-cultural Education : Sam Sharma. A key part of his brief was to promote understanding of different ethnic cultures in schools where there were no ethnic minority groups. As a deliberate step to give impetus to this aim he was given pastoral responsibility in the predominantly "all white" schools in the south of the county.

Sam Sharma was well experienced: he had been a multi-cultural adviser in Walsall for the previous seven years. He arrived with practical knowledge and experience of the need to boost both achievement and self-esteem of youngsters from ethnic minorities by, for example, establishing mother tongue classes which would encourage them to value their home languages and better understand their own religion and literature.

His initial challenge was to establish exactly how and where money allocated by the Home Office to support ethnic minority teaching, known colloquially as 'Section Eleven Funding', was being used. The Home Office expected its funds to be allocated to named teachers and pupils, not spent generally for the good of the school. Unless this could clearly be established, the Home Office threatened to withdraw funding.

Once this had been done, with schools in receipt of Section Eleven money able to name the teacher so funded, Sam was able to move to promote a county-wide understanding of the benefits of "intercultural" education. The Multi-Cultural Support Service was established in 1984. Two years later it became the Intercultural Curriculum Support Service. I.C.S.S. sought to work not just with ethnic minority pupils but with all schools, colleges, parents and voluntary groups.

The concept of "intercultural" education was a broader one, expounded in a policy statement published in 1987 entitled "Intercultural Education for All". The last two words were critical: support units staffed by advisory teachers were established in all four areas of the county. These centres were intended to serve all children and schools, not just those perceived as serving predominantly the black community. This followed widespread consultation, promotion and in-service education. The centres were at Cashmore Middle School, Leamington, St. Andrew's C.E. Middle School, Rugby and Manor Park School, Nuneaton. However, an issue was how best to service the many and widespread small schools of the Southern Area, an area Sam Sharma had come to know well through his pastoral school visiting. After prolonged thought, he hit on a novel idea : a mobile unit with two advisory teachers and a secretary. The unit was a bus laden with books and materials and examples of good practice. That intercultural bus evoked great curiosity. Both the B.B.C. and the Commission for Racial Equality showed enthusiastic interest, and Sam Sharma was invited to Israel to lecture on his work as a means of helping the co-teaching of Arab and Israeli children. The bus propelled many initiatives. An example was at Tysoe C.E. School which "twinned" with the Frederick Bird School in Coventry. Tysoe children attended a Diwali Festival at 'Freddie Bird's', and the latter's children were invited to a nativity play at Tysoe, for example. Shipston High was one of a number of schools to stage an 'Intercultural Week'.

Gradually, schools began to integrate an intercultural dimension into their mainstream curriculum work in language, history, geography, dance etc. Regular Arts Festivals across the county were introduced to "reduce prejudice through intercultural understanding." Schools developed musical groups that performed throughout the county: The St. Giles Bhangra Group was a striking example. The excitement and the widening of horizons not only extended to the so-called 'deep south', they thrived and blossomed there. Intercultural projects brought together schools like Newbold-on-Stour, Shipston and Tredington. Schools such as Bishopton in Stratford hosted events and workshops.

14

Arts in the County

There have been numerous examples of arts initiatives, many bringing artists to work with pupils. The sculptor, Tim Tolkien (yes, they are related) has worked with schools such as St. Nicholas, Kenilworth on a sculpture project, with children at Nursery Hill on a project based on the history of the local mining community and, in consultation with one of the classes, a play sculpture in the grounds of Newburgh School. A local sculptor, Walter Ritchie, has created a piece specially for Thorns School, also in Kenilworth, and based on 'Alice through the Looking Glass'. Ritchie, in particular, has contributed greatly to our school environments, with sculptures in the grounds of Arden Hill, Binley Woods, Abbots Farm Infants, Rokeby Infants, Bawnmore and Kenilworth. On behalf of the County, former County Architect Eric Davies commissioned a number of such post-war works.

A group of Nuneaton schools has collaborated on an area 'sculpture trail': Milby, Weddington, Wembrook and St. Nicolas are all involved. The millennium prompted many projects including the millennium wall in Warwick market place, the result of collaboration among local primary schools. Across the county, Studley Infant School has placed emphasis on learning through creative subjects with an imaginative play area and environmental sculptures. Priors Field School, Kenilworth, for its own millennium celebrations, commissioned a sculpture by Ilona Bryan in the school grounds, based on suggestions from the children. A time capsule lies beneath it. Work at Southam Primary School has included visiting artists working with cardboard, with textiles and 'computer art'. The school has had workshops from the Royal Ballet, The Royal Shakespeare Company and English National Opera, and regularly takes part in the National Gallery Challenge. Exhall Grange has a number of works of art, some donated and some commissioned by former head George Marshall. The founding of the WTAA (Warwickshire Teachers' Arts Association in the eighties) has enabled teachers to participate in workshops and to visit galleries all over the world. It became WRAG (Warwickshire Renaissance Art Group) in 1999. How fitting that an exhibition of teachers' work in 2002 should be in Gaydon Village Hall, the hall being a Bolton King gift to the area.

Arts work across the county was given fresh and strong impetus by the appointment of Rex Pogson to lead the newly-created Warwickshire Arts Zone, and in particular to line-manage the very influential 'Artists in Warwickshire Education', an agency with ten years of experience of placing artists in schools.

Arts Zone

The Arts Zone was devised as a project to act in the role of advocate and animateur for the Arts and Creativity in Warwickshire. The strong foundations of good practice in music, visual arts and drama, and the commitment of Richard Grant, elected members and Eric Wood to the breadth and colour which the Arts could bring to learning, provided a powerful impetus for a profile-raising initiative. The priorities of the Arts Zone (a small agency of two LEA officers), were to bring the Arts closer to the heart of pupil achievement and attainment, school improvement, individual and community regeneration, and creative professional development for teachers and artists working together in schools. The Director of the Arts Zone brought together Artists in Warwickshire Education and Study Support, the rapidly-growing encouragement of out-of-school hours learning. The whole enterprise coincided with a national recognition that open-ended, risk-taking learning is a necessary corollary to the vigorous, core-subject improvement which had been the theme of the 1990's. Arts Zone events ranged from mass events for thousands of pupils (Reading Relays and Millennium Wishes) through specialist festivals in a number of art forms, to large-scale celebrations at Warwick Castle, Charlecote Park, Stoneleigh Park and the Millennium Dome. 'Childcentredress' combined with vigour was the motto, characterised by the spectacular progress of creative work in Early Years, pioneered across the Midlands by Artists in Warwickshire Education.

The Early Years provided an encouraging example of how collaboration could enrich the learning of young children. A project in 2002, based on the pre-school philosophy of Reggio Emilia, set out to explore creative ways of achieving goals for early learning. Artists and advisory teachers worked with small groups of children from schools and from nurseries in South Warwickshire. The project was jointly sponsored by Stratford District Council and by the Early Years Development and Childcare Partnership. The results could be seen to exciting effect in a display in Manor Hall at the end of the year, and the experience was best summed up by participant young Morgan:

"Oh this is so wonderful."

15

Famous Ex-Pupils of Schools in Warwickshire

In this chapter I deal briefly with some of the distinguished people who have received all or part of their education in Warwickshire schools. Some, like Shakespeare, Lewis Carroll and George Eliot are known world-wide. In their cases I concentrate almost entirely on their schooling. With the fairly well-known such as Lytton Strachey and John Masefield I add a little information on their claim to fame. In some cases the people I have chosen are not at all well-known, but they have achieved distinction, or at any rate distinctiveness, in some area of human endeavour. Most choices should be obvious, some are idiosyncratic. Inevitably the list is somewhat arbitrary, depending as it did on how easily available the information was, and the efficacy or otherwise of my researches.

Warwickshire could make the modest claim to have educated pupils who have had more influence on English Language and Literature than anyone else. Shakespeare was voted 'Man of the Millennium'. George Eliot has written "Middlemarch": a novel cited by many as one of the greatest ever. Fowler is still acknowledged as the greatest authority on the rules and conventions of the English Language.

I am not able to say how many other counties could claim to have educated a Prime Minister, two Chancellors of the Exchequer, an inventor, five world sports champions, two comedians, a poet laureate, a leading bookmaker etc. The list goes on. But it has been fascinating to research such a diverse range of talents and to try to answer questions on their education in Warwickshire. Regrettably, I have not always been able to provide full details of their education. Details of their earlier years have often eluded me. Few works of reference name primary schools.

Some of the characters about whom I have written are described more fully in the books by Paul Bolitho, former Warwick Librarian, and listed in the 'Biography' section of the 'Bibliography'.

One reassuringly recurring plot in these life-stories is that of the person who was undistinguished, even a nuisance at school, but who went on to achieve success. Even the most unpromising pupils may go on to bring their schools a small place in history.

Neil Adams

1981 Olympic Judo Champion was born in Rugby but moved to Leamington. He attended Milverton School. One teacher, Mrs Henry, recalls him saying aged nine that he wanted to be an Olympic champion one day. Of his school days, he noted ruefully:

"I am sorry to say that even in those early days my sporting activities took preference over my studies."

He won two Olympic silver medals and a world championship, and was awarded the M.B.E. In a letter to his old school on the occasion of its centenary, he wrote: "Please give my best wishes to everyone there, and remember me to all those unfortunate people who had to put up with that horrible little boy." I have no other details of his schooling.

Joseph Arch

Joseph Arch was one of the key figures in the history of British trade unionism. He was born and educated in Barford in 1826 and lived till 1919. He published his autobiography in 1898 which told the story of his life from school to farm labourer to trade union leader to Member of Parliament. His parents were both Warwickshire people, so: "I come directly of Warwickshire stock on both sides."

He recalled that his mother was a keen letter-writer and an admirer of Shakespeare. She often wrote letters for friends and neighbours who were illiterate and with relatives living afar. She worked before marriage in Warwick Castle. (It was Frances, Countess of Warwick who was later to write the preface to Arch's autobiography.)

Arch lamented the absence of Board Schools in his own area. He was scathing about the predominance of what he called "parsons' schools": "I should like to see them swept away from off the face of the country." He conceded that the local Barford parson's school was "a downright good one", and his teacher was " ..... as excellent a teacher as a poor boy could wish to meet with ....." Arch thanked him for ensuring that he was well-versed in the rudiments at least of " ..... reading, writing, spelling, arithmetic and mensuration ...." He started school at six: "There was no such blessed thing as an infant school. A child could run loose about the village in poverty, ignorance and dirt till he reached the regulation age." He had to leave before the age of nine, but "I did not let the black cloud of ignorance settle on my faculties." Instead, he began a lifelong career of self-education. He stayed in and read rather than going out to play and his mother would give him writing to copy and sums to work out.

He was the first agricultural labourer to become a Member of Parliament, serving as Liberal M.P. for North-West Norfolk from 1885-6 and 1892-1900. He was also a member of the original Warwickshire County Council from 1889 to 1892. He was thus a colleague of Bolton King and had taken much interest in King's experiments in co-operative farming at Radbourne Manor Farm.

He is buried in the churchyard at Barford. His grave has at its head an obelisk erected by members of the National Union of Agricultural Workers.

Eleanor Archer

The daughter of a farm labourer, she was educated at the National School in Hunningham. She devoted her life to work to help the deserving. She was Assistant Collector of Poor Rates in Barford from 1892 until well into the 1920's. She became friendly with Joseph Arch and rented his cottage in Barford. She wrote regularly for local newspapers and began a circulating booklet entitled "The Quiver Manuscript Magazine". She was closely involved with the Viavi Cause, founded in San Francisco, and dedicated to improving the health of girls reaching puberty and of women. The Cause established treatment in line with modern homeopathic principles.

Matthew Arnold

Poet, critic and inspector of schools, he deserves a longer piece than space will allow. He came as a pupil to Rugby late, after some time at Winchester. His father, the legendary Doctor Arnold, was headmaster. All the tensions of being in the school where one's father was a powerful leader are described by Park Honan, one of his biographers. Not easy, particularly for a quiet, reserved boy. His parents were disappointed with his progress, even though he won an English prize.

He became one of the first of Her Majesty's Inspectors of Schools at the very young age of 28. His love of maps doubtless became of practical value as his work took him all over the country. He was away from his family for much of the year. One of his letters to his wife contained the observation: "Next to Liverpool, Birmingham is the finest of the manufacturing towns." His "patch" took him across England from Pembroke to Great Yarmouth. He was an outspoken critic of the Revised Code (payment by results) which he alleged turned schools into a "mere machine for teaching reading, writing and arithmetic." The Bishop of London asked him whether "the exam dictates the instruction?" His answer was simple: "Yes".

Braving both press hostility and the risk of losing his job, he expounded his own approach to inspecting; he praised "teachers who worked harder and were paid less than I did. I saw the cheerfulness and efficiency with which they did their work and I asked myself again and again: 'How did they do it?' "

It was his belief that, if the teachers and children seemed happy, it was probably a good school. Not quite today's view, although Arnold might have nodded approvingly when, almost exactly a hundred years later, heads at a county Primary Heads' Conference, invited to rank 72 possible aims of primary education, put as their top aim that the children be: "Happy, cheerful and well balanced." Apart from travel and inspecting, his work also involved much marking of pupil scripts, as well as the inevitable writing, and some committee work. The hours were long. His writings included essays and many poems, one entitled 'Rugby Chapel'.

He was a member of the Taunton Commission, as was one of his father's successors as head of Rugby, Frederick Temple. Reportedly, they did not always see eye to eye.

Joseph Ashby (1859-1919)

We learn most about the schooling of Joseph Ashby, from his daughter's biography of him, published in 1961. He was born in the year when the "gaunt and large National School" was completed in his home village of Tysoe. Miss Ashby's description was somewhat dispiriting " ….. this barnlike two-armed erection with ecclesiastical windows too high for children to see out of and 'Early English' doors too heavy for little children to push."

Joseph's learning came from a variety of sources: from the stories his mother read, from his explorations of local brooks and hedges, and from watching skilled thatchers and farmers at work. He attended the "new school" from ages 5 to 11 where he soon learned to chant the alphabet and the numbers one to a hundred. Though discipline was tight, the room was not quiet: "Several children would be reading aloud, teachers scolding, infants reciting ….." Reading was painstaking, as pupils had to keep their finger on the word being read no matter how slow the reader.

In 1888 Joseph Ashby met Bolton King. Despite their very different origins, they discovered a common interest in the conditions of people living in villages and collaborated on a detailed survey of part of South Warwickshire. They examined a range of topics: housing, wages, allotments, soils and the effect of machinery on labour. Their detailed report was published in two parts in the Economic Journal in 1893.

Michael Billington

Long-time drama critic of 'The Guardian', and former film critic of 'The Birmingham Post', he was educated at Warwick School. He has published widely, including 'The Guinness Book of Theatre Facts and Feats'. When reviewing at the theatre at Stratford, he has fitted in visits to talk to A level Theatre Studies students at Stratford College. In 'Who's Who', he lists one of his recreations as 'work'.

Geoffrey Blundell

Educated at Studley and at Alcester Grammar, he developed radio microphones used world wide in film-making and broadcasting.

Arthur Bostrom

Arthur Bostrom was educated at the Paddox School and Lawrence Sheriff School. He read Geography at Durham University where he was a leading member of the university revue group. He took a one-man show to the Edinburgh Festival before joining a drama school. An early television appearance in a B.B.C. drama led him to play opposite Robert Hardy, an ex-Rugbeian. He briefly appeared as Sue Pollard's boyfriend in 'Hi de Hi' and that brought him to the attention of another ex-Rugbeian, comedy writer (Dad's Army' etc.) David Croft. This led to his being cast in his most famous part: Arthur Crabtree in "'Allo 'Allo", a long-running television sitcom. He has returned to his old school for various functions and has acknowledged a great debt to two of his teachers: Gerard Bateson and Charles Rankin.

Rupert Brooke

Rupert was educated first at Hillborow, a preparatory school close to Rugby where his father was a housemaster. As the name suggests, this was on the brow of the hill, on the town side of St. Cross Hospital.

Rupert entered Rugby School in 1901, aged fourteen. Most of what we know of his time there came from the memoirs of a contemporary and his eventual bibliographer, Geoffrey Keynes. He was of a delicate constitution and had various illnesses. He was a keen reader, shy and quiet, thereby earning the nickname "Oyster". His early school reports were at best little more than lukewarm: "Work rather below par this term."

His letters made it clear that he was happy at Rugby and he eventually became Head of House under his father. He joined the school Rifle Volunteer Corps. He wrote many poems while at school, one: "The Bastille" which he was asked to read to the whole school. His final report spoke of a dislike of detail but a literary capacity for "very brilliant results". He went up to Cambridge in 1906 ..... after supporting the local election of the Liberal M.P., Corrie Grant. He returned to Rugby in 1910 to be temporary housemaster following his father's death and he stayed for one term. His last visit to Rugby was in June, 1914. In September he was offered a commission as a Sub-Lieutenant. He died on St. George's Day, April 23rd 1915 abroad in Egypt of blood-poisoning. He is remembered in a plot in Clifton Road Cemetery in Rugby, where three members of his family are also buried. The original wooden cross from his grave in the Greek island of Skyros was also brought to the family plot.

Robert Burton

Educated at King Edward College, Nuneaton in the late sixteenth century, Burton was educated at Oxford University and became the keeper of his college library. His most famous work, a lifetime's endeavour, was "The Anatomy of Melancholy", a prose work published in 1621. It is a kind of medical treatise, but also an anthology of observations on the human condition in general. To him has been attributed the preamble: "As every schoolboy knows ....." ...... a preamble these days, if ever it was, seldom linked with what schoolboys (and girls) actually know! But the words survive today as an oft-heard cliché.

Lewis Carroll

Lewis Carroll, author of "Alice in Wonderland" and "Alice through the Looking Glass", has been the subject of many biographies, including three major studies in the latter half of the 1990's. He clearly continues to fascinate. As one of his recent biographers, Cohen (1995) acknowledged, we have only "slender record" of his years at Rugby. Biographers such as Michael Bakewell make much use of phrases like "must have had" and "would have had". The chief sources of information are extracts from diaries he kept, and from the thousands of letters he sent.

He entered Rugby School in 1846. It is unclear why his parents chose Rugby, given that his father and uncle had attended Westminster. Three reasons have been suggested: Westminster's reputation was in decline, Rugby's in the ascendant following Dr Arnold's headship since 1828 and his father was by now clergyman at Croft-on-Tees in the North East, and Rugby was more than eighty miles nearer to home. Lewis, or Charles Dodgson (his real name), did well at Rugby. He won prizes and excelled in Mathematics and Divinity. But diary extracts and two surviving letters suggest he was unhappy: "I cannot say that I look back upon my life at Public School with any sensations of pleasure ...." Apparently, he "spent an incalculable time writing out impositions". In his one game of cricket he was put on to bowl, but taken off after only one ball. The reason given was that " ..... the ball, if it had gone far enough, would have been a wide."

Sir George Catlin

Catlin was that rarity, at least until recently: one whose claim to fame depends mainly on the woman he married. She was Vera Brittain, author of the books "Testament of Youth" and "Testament of Experience", the former serialised on BBC television.

He did become well known as an academic and writer, and was knighted in 1970 for his services to Anglo American relations. His autobiography tells us virtually nothing of his time at Warwick School (1908-12). It was dismissed in the words " ..... and there were schooldays at Warwick." Indeed, there is almost nothing on any of his childhood, although he was to become President of the Old Warwickians. He became an academic, and was knighted for his work on Anglo-American relations. He fought various constituencies as a Labour candidate in the 1930s.

His death in 1979 brought his daughter, Shirley Williams, the then Secretary of State for Education, to his funeral in Warwick. His funeral took place at the church of St. Mary the Immaculate in Warwick. He is buried in Old Milverton churchyard, alongside his father. Vera's ashes were scattered abroad on the grave of her brother, who was killed in Italy during the First World War.

Neville Chamberlain

Few schools can claim to have educated a Prime Minister, but Rugby can claim one. By far the majority were educated at either Eton or Harrow, with a sprinkling at Westminster and two at Glasgow High School. Neville attended a preparatory school at Rugby before going to Rugby in the 1880's. The 1881 census lists a 'Neville Chamberlain' as living at Orwell House, Clifton. Little documentary evidence survives about his schooling. His various biographers have drawn on letters written to his sisters Hilda and Ida, now preserved among his papers in the library of Birmingham University, and on an article in the Rugby School magazine "The Meteor", published on 16th December 1940. They all agree that he was not happy there. He was recalled as "a slender, dark-haired boy, rather pale, quiet and shy" who disclaimed any interest in politics and declined invitations to speak in school debates. His older brother Austen was in his last term when Neville began, and he was a confident speaker whose glory may have overshadowed and daunted his little brother. However, Neville did end up as head of his house and he achieved a "cap" in Rugby Football. He was also a keen member of the Natural History Society. After leaving Rugby, he rarely spoke of his schooling and never returned to the school, though he frequently passed through Rugby on journeys to and from his Birmingham home. Though now recalled as the Prime Minister of Munich fame whose career ended in failure, he was effective in both local government in Birmingham and as Minister of Health.

Sir Austen Chamberlain

Sir Austen's experiences of Rugby were more positive. Though he did not start until he was almost fifteen, he went on to become captain of his house. Fifty years later he was to serve as Deputy Chairman of the Governors. Austen Chamberlain formed what was to become a lifetime friendship with his housemaster Henry Lee-Warner, and they regularly corresponded over the years. A surprising story is that in April 1879 Austen's father intervened by strong letter to insist that his son was not to be caned for trespassing. The school concurred reluctantly and Austen was instead detained at the end of term. During his time at Rugby, Austen became a skilful debater. Though a famous politician of his time, his unique claim to fame was to be the only leader of the Conservative Party in the twentieth century not to become Prime Minister (N.B. William Hague was still in with a chance of sorts till 2002). However, he did achieve high office, being twice Chancellor of the Exchequer and once Foreign Secretary, leader of the House and Lord Privy Seal. He served as minister under four prime ministers and was a member of Lloyd George's War Cabinet.

Sebastian Coe

Former Olympic and world champion in both the 800 and 1500 metres, Coe received some of his primary school education at Bridgetown School, Stratford and some at Dunnington School. His middle name is Newbold, but there seem to be no connections with the Warwickshire Newbolds.

In spite of its title, Coe's biography "Born to Run" makes no mention of his primary education. Nor does his autobiography "Running Free". The latter does mention the family's move to Stratford-on-Avon "because of my father's work". The family lived "on the edge of town" and Seb would regularly run the "two miles or so" into town. He would also choose to jog rather than to walk "beside my sister Miranda's pram." Putting together shreds of evidence : admission registers, teacher memories etc. it seems likely that he attended Dunnington School between the ages of five and seven, while the family lived in Alcester. The family then moved to the edge of Stratford, and Sebastian attended Bridgetown School. There did exist, with luck still preserved, a cricket scorebook at Bridgetown with the words: "S Coe run out 0".

Michael Drayton

An Elizabethan poet and a contemporary of Shakespeare who was born in Hartshill, hence the school there that bears his name. Of Hartshill, he wrote: "Harsell, small town, where first your breath you drew".

However, Polesworth has at least as much claim, for he spent many years there attached to Sir Henry Gooder. Little is known of his education, but in a dedicatory address fixed to one of his 'Heroical Epistles', he claimed indebtedness to Sir Henry for "the most part" of his education. Unlike Shakespeare, he had no local grammar school to attend. The nearest one at Atherstone was not due to open until later in the sixteenth century.

The school bearing his name was opened in Hartshill in 1967, and a monument was unveiled by the then Poet Laureate Sir John Betjeman in 1974. Made of Hartshill quartzite, it stands on Hartshill Green, on the site of Drayton's home. It is a shelter, obviously well-used, judged by the now ubiquitous but unpoetic graffiti.

George Eliot

When George Eliot was born in November 1819, on the Arbury Hall estate on the outskirts of Nuneaton, most children received no education in school at all. Such provision as there was usually depended on the ability of parents to pay. But George Eliot, or, to give her the name with which she was born: Mary Ann Evans, did have parents able to pay. When she was a baby her parents moved to Griff House on the road from Nuneaton to Coventry and her first education was in a "dame" school in a cottage across the road, run by a kindly lady called Mrs Moore. The "school" was described as "a decrepit two up two down cottage" opposite the main gate of Griff House." At five years old she was moved to join her sister Chrissy at a Miss Lathom's boarding school at Attleborough, where the older girls fussed her and called her "little Mama" on account of her sombre demeanour. She was described as "a queer three cornered awkward child who preferred to talk to adults."

In 1828, aged nine, she was moved to another boarding school run by a widow, Mrs Wallington at the Elms, Nuneaton. She had set up the school as a means of educating her own children. At thirteen she moved again, to a school in Warwick Row, Coventry, where she learned English, French, history and arithmetic, and she developed her piano-playing skills. She was also taught to jettison her Midlands accent. She read voraciously, won a prize in French, and impressed her teachers with her excellent composition. She left at sixteen and returned home where her mother was dying from breast cancer.

These are the bare facts about her education, told and confirmed in the many biographies of her, not least by Kathleen Adams, local writer and honorary secretary of the George Eliot Fellowship. We have little direct evidence of her own views of these various establishments, but several of her novels give some clues. It is, of course, unwise to assume that novels are autobiographical. After all, the evidence points to her father being a conscientious, loving parent, but fathers in novels such as "Silas Marner" and "Felix Holt" were often absent and seemingly indifferent. We have a description of Tom's school-time in "Mill in the Floss". He found Latin grammar "complicated", and a "bore" and "beastly stuff". He claimed that doing Euclid brought on toothache, and when her sister Maggie offered help his scornful reply was: "Girls never learn such things."

It took time both locally and nationally to honour George Eliot, but a statue in Nuneaton and a plaque in Westminster Abbey have achieved belated justice.

William Webb Ellis

He is traditionally credited for the invention of the game Rugby Football. The story, commemorated by a plaque in the close of Rugby School is simply told, using the words of the plaque " ….. who with a fine disregard for the rules of football first took the ball in his hands and ran with it ….."

Of course, the claim has on occasions been disputed. One view is that the Webb Ellis story was invented belatedly by a group of old Rugbeians. They cite in support of their view a lack of contemporary documentary evidence, and that Eton, Harrow and Winchester all had distinctive forms of the game of football. But neither the school, nor the town, is likely to part with the version of events that has given the name of Rugby world-wide recognition, any more than Stratford will part with Shakespeare as the real author of all those plays. One of those who gave evidence to a panel set up to establish the origins of the game was Thomas Hughes. He unhelpfully recalled that "the tradition had not survived to my day".

Ben Elton

Ben Elton has achieved fame as a comedy performer, a novelist and a lyricist. His achievements include best-selling novels such as "Popcorn", television series like "The Young Ones", "Blackadder" and "The Thin Blue Line" and collaboration with Andrew Lloyd Webber on a musical.

He studied for two years at Stratford College on a Drama and Theatre studies course after leaving school. He has since publicly cited his teacher there, Gordon Vallins, as the best teacher he ever had, describing him as "inspirational". More recently, in an edition of 'Teacher', he stated: "To me he was a hero."

Dennis Joseph Enright

Enright has achieved fame as a writer and editor of numerous poetry anthologies. He has also pursued a distinguished academic career with professorships locally at Warwick and further away at Bangkok and Singapore. Among many honours bestowed on him were the Queen's Gold Medal for Poetry in 1981 and the O.B.E. in 1991.

He was educated at Leamington College in the 1930's but his memoirs dealt principally with his work between 1956 and 1967 when he worked abroad. He did publish a poetry anthology called "The Terrible Shears: Scenes from a Twenties Childhood" in which we gain glimpses of his education. One poem informed us that the copper, when not in use, was lined with old newspapers and that he thus learned to read upside down. Another recalled bowing heads to "a hurried nurse" and hearing nits rattle on the paper.

One short poem paid tribute to Miss Anthony: "our lovely Miss" who used to charm the listeners with "Wind in the Willows". She was presumably a teacher, but this has to be inferred. There were poems about games in Jephson's Gardens, and an attack on "they" who represented authority in its various forms. Later poems reinforced the notion of a keen reader and book-lover. He told how he once rescued an "old broken-backed Bible" from the dustbin because he could not bear "to see printed matter ill-treated". Fifty years later he was more sanguine about disposing of books, though he claimed that he would still "dive in" to rescue the Bible and Shakespeare.

He clearly enjoyed teaching at a young age and would educate his younger sister with a blackboard "and an overbearing manner". Sadly, the lessons always ended in tears.

He was evidently of humble origins because he wrote of the council house in which he was brought up, and we later learn that he went to Leamington College as a scholarship boy. A particularly barbed poem "Scholarship Boys" reflected on the docility of the lower orders. He apparently did better than expected in 'The School

Cert' but was still advised by the headmaster to leave and get a job before a mistake in the results was discovered. The poem ended with the simple line: "And I almost did."

The theme of not trying to get ideas above one's station ran through several more poems. He recalled that the mother of one of his classmates was "genuinely enraged" when he won a scholarship and later told him that Cambridge was not meant for people such as him. Actor Norman Painting has recalled that Enright's scholarship gave the school a bonus half holiday. The poems form an episodic case study of one small boy from an ordinary family rising to the top of the academic world in spite of all the pressures of the time to know one's place.

Enright died just as this book was going to the printers - on the very last day of 2002.

Harold Flint

One of the many Warwickshire schoolboys to give his life in the First World War was Harold Flint. His story came to be told in unusual circumstances one hundred years after his birth in May 1897. A judge from Worcester, Judge Ian Morris, had seen his scroll and medals for sale in a Warwick antique shop, bought them and then determinedly researched his brief life. Harold Flint was educated at Shrubland Street School and, when his parents moved to Bascote Heath, at Ufton C.E. School. It is uncertain exactly when he was called up, but he served with the 6th Battalion of the Dorset Regiment in battles on the Somme. He was killed in 1917 by an exploding enemy shell, aged just twenty.

Why tell his story? Judge Morris summed it up in the May 2nd edition (1997) of the Leamington Courier: "His story ...... is unremarkable. It is a story of loss which sadly was repeated in parishes and counties the length and breadth of the country. Yet in another sense his story was unique. There was only one Harold Flint."

Reginald Foort

Reginald Foort was educated at Lawrence Sheriff School. His theatre organ career began in Edinburgh in 1925 and he made his cinema dèbut in 1926 at the New Gallery Cinema in London. He went on to become resident organist at many leading theatres. Foort was the first to broadcast on a Wurlitzer organ in Britain, and in 1936 became the first BBC staff theatre organist. He left the post after two years to tour vaudeville theatres with a 30-ton, five-manual pipe organ which became BBC Theatre Organ No.2 after World War II. Foort returned to Rugby in 1938, described in the local paper as "The World Famous Organist". He played at the Plaza Cinema in a fund-raising concert for the B.T.H. Employees' Hospital Fund and gave wartime fund-raising concerts, again in Rugby. Part of his fame came from many jocular references to him in the popular pre-war radio series 'Bandwaggon' starring Arthur Askey and Richard

Murdoch. In 1951 Foort went to live in America, where he remained for the rest of his life, becoming organist of Temple Sholom in Chicago and then of a temple in Miami. His recording output was immense, and he is best remembered for his transcriptions of well-known classical and light orchestral music on the theatre organ. He wrote 'The Cinema Organ' (London, 1932) and composed several light-hearted pieces. He also wrote a school song for his 'alma mater'.

Henry Watson Fowler

Henry Fowler has that unusual distinction: a surname that is immediately recognised as a supreme authority. For his "Modern English Usage" is known simply as Fowler and to this day is quoted when debates on 'correct' or 'incorrect' English occur. Another product of Rugby, he was a quiet, shy boy, not enamoured of most sports, though he achieved some success at swimming and cross-country running. Academically, he excelled, especially in Latin and Greek. In a school debate, he opposed a motion 'that preposterous prominence is given in modern Public Schools to classical studies'.

He became Head of House before going up to Oxford University where he achieved moderate though unspectacular results. He taught for some years at Sedbergh School before going to the Oxford University Press. He served in the First World War, enlisting in the 23rd Battallion Royal Fusiliers. His regiment spent some time at a camp in Leamington before going to fight.

His writings on English usage can be unequivocal: " 'Also is an adverb; the use of it as a conjunction is slovenly, if not illiterate."

However, he is more cautiously pragmatic on some well known sources of heated linguistic debate. For example, the split infinitive is labelled as 'ugly' rather than wrong, and put in its place " ….. it is one among several hundred ugly things." One of his own books was attacked for a preface containing a paragraph that ended in a preposition.

Elizabeth Gaskell

Miss Gaskell was a well-known novelist of the nineteenth century. Her biographers are not agreed on when and where her education in Warwickshire began. Jenny Uglow asserted that she started at a private school in Barford in 1821. The school moved with her to premises in Stratford called "Avonbank" in 1824. "Avonbank" was to the north of Holy Trinity Church. It has long since gone, but a modern housing development close to the Royal Shakespeare Theatre's 'The Other Place' is called 'Avonbank'. The summerhouse, now a brass rubbing centre, also survives in the gardens by the river. Formerly owned by Shakespeare's cousin, Thomas Green, Avonbank was destroyed in 1866, but is described in "Lady Ludlow", a short story by Miss Gaskell.

John Chapple, another biographer, has claimed that no records survive to prove that Elizabeth attended the Barford school, although she did certainly go to Avonbank. Her education would have included Reading, Spelling, Grammar, Composition and some Geography and History. By paying more, her parents could secure for her 'optional extras' such as Music, Dancing, Drawing, Writing and Arithmetic. It is salutary to reflect that her education would cost well over one hundred guineas a year in fees at a time when Joseph Arch's father was earning approximately ten shillings a week (50p), also in Barford.

Her novels included 'Mary Barton' and 'Wives and Lovers'. The former was described by the historian Simon Schama as 'genteel whistleblowing', going even further than Dickens to expose the misery of industrial life in Manchester. The latter regained for her some of her lost fame when it was serialised on B.B.C. television in 1999. It was adapted by local writer and former Warwick University lecturer, Andrew Davies. Miss Gaskell died suddenly in 1865 before completing this novel, so Davies had to extemporise an ending, using copious notes that she had left behind.

Roy Gaveston-Knight

He was known to many as the 'Warwickshire Poet'. Educated at St. Nicholas School, Kenilworth and at Myton, he had poems published regularly from the age of fifteen almost to his death aged 80. He published several anthologies including 'Green Warwickshire'. The first part of his surname testified to his descendancy from Piers Gaveston, favourite of King Edward II, to whom there is a monument near Leek Wootton.

Sabine Baring Gould

His lasting fame is as author of "Uncle Tom Cobley" and "Onward Christian Soldiers". He received little formal education but did attend Warwick School from 1845-1847.

Larry Grayson

He was brought to Nuneaton by his unmarried mother and, after a short while, he was brought up by his elder sister. He was then called William (or Billy) White and lived in a terraced house in Abbey Green in Nuneaton. The house was close to the gates of his school: Abbey C.E. School. It was a modest house, sharing its back garden toilet. However, it was one of the first houses in the area to have its own telephone. People used to come to the house to make calls at two pence a time. Larry would often be in the next room and later claimed that he got much material from eavesdropping on the calls. The house no longer survives and its site is now a car park.

Even when at Abbey School, Larry was 'stage-struck' and would often put on concerts, after school at home in the wash-house. However, little information on his schooling either at Abbey or, later at Manor Park, now survives. His biographer, Mike Malyon mentions that he appeared in the school nativity play aged 8 or 9. Reportedly, he was a shepherd but wanted to be one of the kings when he saw their costumes. Abbey School did have an annual Christmas concert with carols throughout Larry's time there. A contemporary friend recently told me about the time when Larry joined a church choir. The friend asked 'Why? You can't sing!' 'No, but I look nice,' came the reply.

He completed his education at Manor Park where he used to do little performances to his peers for payment by the then popular cigarette cards. He started playing local clubs as a comedian at places such as Ansley and Chapel End, with admission at fourpence for adults and twopence for children. Jonathan Moore recalled that Larry was so hard up that he walked from home to the Gasworks Club in Foleshill because he could not afford the bus fare.

Even after his success, he continued to live at Abbey Green until persuaded to buy a car and a big house to boost his image as a star. He would often walk around Nuneaton and, according to one story, kept salt and vinegar in the glove compartment of his newly-acquired Rolls Royce so that he could stop for fish and chips and eat them on the way home late at night.

There are numerous reminiscences to the effect that he continued to walk regularly round the shops at Nuneaton even when he was appearing at the London Palladium and compering B.B.C.'s "The Generation Game" through most of the 1970s. He returned to Abbey School on several occasions, including once as part of a television documentary with Janet Street-Porter. In spite of his camp style, he remained free from scandal. He retired to Torquay with his sister but returned to Nuneaton after two years. He died on 7th January 1995 His funeral in Nuneaton was " ..... the biggest funeral Nuneaton has ever seen."

He was well summed up by Terry Wogan " ..... a funny, lovely, gentle man". In an equally fulsome tribute, Bob Monkhouse has recalled that Larry's concern for his health had led him to inform admirers that: "In my will I've specified that I have to be buried in the no-smoking section of the cemetery". He is buried in a family grave in Nuneaton under his original name of William White. 'Larry Grayson' appears in brackets underneath.

'Trina Gulliver

'Trina Gulliver has won world-wide recognition in an area not traditionally associated with women: that of darts. In 1997 she became number one female darts player in the world, and has since gone on to win further world championships, for example The Embassy Women's World Championship in 2001 and 2002. In an interview with the Times Educational Supplement, Trina paid tribute to the support given to her by teachers at Southam First and Middle School and Southam High School and the then Mid Warwickshire College. The support she mentioned was not specifically for darts-playing which she began only when fourteen. Rather was it for the encouragement to take part in a variety of sports and to cope positively with setbacks.

'Trina's story is a fascinating one, a story of a very determined trailblazer. Her parents told her that she first started throwing darts when she was two, but she retained no memory of that. There was a dartboard in the family home, so the opportunity was there. No dartboards were available in school, needless to say, but she was able to demonstrate her throwing skills. She held the record for throwing the rounders ball at Southam Middle, and when at Southam High, she represented Warwickshire in the javelin event. Darts were not a school-approved activity then, given their close association with pubs, so 'Trina developed her skills in evenings and at weekends.

She was a courageous individualist in other respects. She was the first female to go through the Carpentry and Joinery course at Mid Warwickshire College. The 'lads' on the course teased her remorselessly, but she braved their mockery, and even won their grudging respect when she outplayed them at lunchtime darts sessions. Ironically, many year later, she returned to the college to teach that same course ..... first, to an all female class, and then, after prolonged persuasion, to teenage males.

Her career has been impressive, but she insists on giving credit to others: to her husband, also a keen sportsman, and also educated at the Southam schools ..... and to her local sponsors: Reeve's Boat-builders of Napton, and Car Consultants of Ufton. Her success has brought her back to her old schools; she returned to the now Southam Primary School, to open a fête there, and to Southam High to present certificates and prizes. She described the experience of a prize-giving speech as making her: "more nervous then when I was playing for England but I loved it." She has also been able to help local youth clubs in Southam and Harbury by donating dartboards. On occasions, she has found herself co-presenting with Southam Mayor Glesni Thomas who taught 'Trina twenty five years ago in the First School.

Her time at school was not wasted. She now writes a monthly column for 'Darts World' and one of her former teachers noted how darts-playing had much improved her mental arithmetic. She still lives in Southam, but her house is no longer big enough to display the more than one hundred singles and pairs titles she has won.

Ernest Thomas Harris

Ernest Thomas Harris was one of the great sea adventurers and war heroes. Leamington-born, and educated at St. Paul's School, Leamington, he won the Pacific, Africa, Atlantic and Burma Stars. He was the only survivor of one boat trip in "one of the little boats" at the evacuation of Dunkirk. He was mined twice and torpedoed once. He "carried" shrapnel in his body for the rest of his life. One of his many achievements was a medal of commendation from the Russian government for his work protecting Arctic shipping routes to ensure that vital supplies reached the Russian front.

Eddie Hemmings

Eddie achieved cricketing fame as a spinner, playing cricket over many years for Nottinghamshire and England. His autobiography: "Coming of Age", told on the first page of early sporting success at "Cashmere (sic) Avenue School" (presumably 'Cashm<u>o</u>re'). This, however, was in athletics when he finished second in the under-8s 60 yard race. Seven years later he came second in the long jump at a Mid Warwickshire inter-schools event in 1963. He recalled as a teenager having little time for academic studies because he was playing cricket for Warwickshire Schools, and even captained England Schools against the English Public Schools XI. But after three pages, his schooldays were dismissed and we learn virtually nothing of his education. He played cricket for England throughout the 1980's, playing in 33 one day tests, for example.

George and Mary Hewins

Two ex-pupils who could never have envisaged fame were George Hewins and his daughter, Mary, both educated at the National School on the corner of Alcester Road in Stratford. George was there in the 1880's and Mary in the 1920's.

Their fame came by an unusual route. George's granddaughter-in-law, Angela Hewins realised the story-telling potential of George, and she and her husband, George's grandson, began to tape his memories. Angela turned their stories into books, both of which were dramatised and performed by the Royal Shakespeare Company. George's life was presented under the title "The Dillen", (the runt of the family). The performance began in "The Other Place" and then moved around the streets of Stratford as various episodes of his life were re-enacted. The performance ended 3^1/$_2$ hours later with a standing ovation each evening. Later, Mary's story was also performed in industrial premises near where she had worked.

Neither Mary nor George was either forthcoming or enthusiastic about their education. He remembered lots of drill, and "bribing" for things such as good attendance and for cleanliness. He recalled " ..... threepence a week to go to school and once you paid they didn't care if you didn't go till next Monday." They "got off" school and "ran wild" as often as possible. He recalls vividly an incident where two mothers of lads who were caned till "the skin was broke" arrived next day to deal with the offending schoolmaster. He escaped through the back door while the "kids stamped with excitement". This incident happened not in Stratford but at a school in Trinity Street, Leamington. His epitaph on school was that it was a waste of time because "you knowed what was going to come."

Ironically he was to return to the school after being seriously injured in the First World War. He was offered the job of caretaker in his old school. The vicar expected to see George in church on Sundays as part of the deal and criticised him for missing church one Sunday to chop sticks for the school fire next day. George resented the criticism as it was made in school as the vicar warmed himself in front of the very fire that George had been preparing.

Mary used to help her father with his caretaker duties. Hence her terse dismissal of her education: "I can't remember anything about school much 'cept cleaning it." She couldn't "writer proper" or "add up". She recalled the regular visits of the vicar ("Why's'e come?"), and the crowds from the Commercial School that used to gather to watch Miss Salt, a young teacher in a very short gym slip as she leapt enthusiastically in netball games. Her friend 'Sis' attended the nearby Board School in Broad Street which Mary thought to be a much better school.

Later, the family moved into the School House on Alcester Road. The new head apparently did not wish to live there. Other memories later included the arrival of wartime evacuees "from Brum mostly" although some never arrived and others returned home quickly. Their school building has gone, but is remembered in the premises on its site .... called 'Scholars' Court'.

Angela Hewins has continued to contribute to the history of Warwickshire, co-authoring a book of memories of the Hugh Clopton School (now Stratford High School), further along the Alcester Road. She was until recently the librarian at Mid Warwickshire College.

Vince Hill

The popular singer Vince Hill was reportedly educated at Wheelwright Lane School. The present head, Cliff Cook, has tried to verify this by examining past records, but has not found conclusive proof. Vince was invited to the school's fiftieth anniversary celebrations but declined. History does not record whether his non-attendance stemmed from other commitments, or from the fact that he never went there in the first place. Nevertheless, local folklore strongly suggests that he did go to the school; his brother and sister still live locally, and he returns to the area from time to time to perform at Bedworth Civic Hall. Like Larry Grayson, his early apprenticeship was working the clubs in Coventry and North Warwickshire.

William Hill

A name famous in bookmaking circles, I understand that for a while he lived in Barnacle, and was educated at Shilton School. A letter to the firm's headquarters, seeking to elicit a contribution on Hill's life for a millennium history of Barnacle failed to produce a reply, but William did make a donation towards the purchase of gates for Shilton Playing Fields, and he officially opened the Fields in 1956.

Thomas Hughes

Probably the best known account of schooldays in Warwickshire is 'Tom Brown's Schooldays', written by ex-pupil Thomas Hughes. No-one who grew up in Rugby could be unaware of Tom Brown. In the 1950's, the novel was filmed in and around the school. Exotic payments were paid to older boys of my acquaintance to appear as extras in the film. I saw the film and read the book several times. But until I began to research this book, I had not known or even wondered what became of him once he left school. His subsequent career was represented on his statue in Barby Road, Rugby, only by the letters 'M.P.'

His school story needs no re-telling. It is still well known and widely available. But his subsequent career, just as interesting in its way, is worth a few words.

He was born in 1822 and was at Rugby from 1833-42. He went on to Oxford and was called to the Bar in 1848. Soon afterwards he became closely involved in the Christian Socialism movement. In the 1860's he was elected to parliament as M.P. for Lambeth, seeking to promote the cause of the working class. Later, he moved to Frome as their M.P. In 1869 he became a Q.C.

In 1870 he made his first visit to America and his experiences in Britain led him to found a Rugby Colony in the state of Tennessee in 1880. The underlying concept for the colony was to eliminate the evils of competition and to foster the co-operative spirit. Sports such as cricket, rugby and boxing were introduced to the colony. Various buildings such as a hotel, church and library were erected. Many young men from the gentry and the middle class crossed the Atlantic to help develop the colony. But the land was rugged and little suited to agriculture, and most of the recruits little suited to the hard work needed to clear and to till the land. Thomas Hughes withdrew from the enterprise, having lost a fortune, and the settlement was sold. Hughes returned to England and became a County Court Judge on the Chester circuit. He died in 1896.

An association has been trying to restore the American Rugby as a memorial to its founder; and the 'Tom Brown School Museum' can be found in Uffington, the Oxfordshire village where he was born.

William Johnson

William Johnson, often known as "Billy", was the youngest of eleven children and the son of a Chilvers Coton miner. He began school at the age of three at a school opened only seven years previously. He was educated at the Collycroft Church of England school on the outskirts of Bedworth from 1852 to 1861 and was elected to the county council in 1889, defeating well-known local landowner Francis Newdigate of Arbury Hall. He was a member of Warwickshire's First Education Committee and served as a local Member of Parliament from 1906-18, again defeating Newdigate.

He fought hard to get pensions for miners in Warwickshire ten years before Lloyd George introduced old age pensions in his budget of 1909. His own father had never earned more than three shillings a day in his life.

He is buried in Bedworth Cemetery and his name is perpetuated by the Johnson Memorial Pavilion in Bedworth's Welfare Park, and by Johnson Road.

Walter Savage Landor

Landor is well commemorated in Warwick. His birthplace survives and is now called Landor House. It has in it the official entrance to King's High School and a stone inscription over the doorway is a permanent memorial to him. It bears the simple message: 'Landor born 1775'. He was sent to boarding school at Knowle at the age of four and a half and to Rugby School aged nine. However, his father was asked to remove him after he had twice "insulted" the headmaster. Apparently he had disobeyed orders. The Head, Dr. James, immortalised by James Street in the town, described him as "rebellious, and he incited others to rebellion." He may have softened in later years for he visited Dr. James, now retired and living in Worcestershire, and "offered him my right hand which he accepted."

He wrote many poems and won accolades from better known poets such as Swinburne who compared him with Milton. His rebellious streak, evident at school, led him into violent disagreements with his father and into political activity. In 1797 he joined Dr. Parr, curate at Hatton, at a mass meeting in Warwick, called to protest against Pitt's proposal for an incomes tax. The meeting began at Shire Hall, but the crowd was so large that it had to adjourn to the nearby racecourse.

His most recent biographer is Jean Field, former King's High School pupil and former teacher at Myton School. She tells the story of how members of his family: two sisters and a brother, helped to found elementary schools in Warwick and Whitnash. Jean has also founded a Landor Society.

Ken Loach

Ken Loach was a film director, famous for films of "social realism" in the 1960's which caused strong reactions at the time. They continue to be discussed and shown to this day. Examples include "Kes", "Cathy Come Home" and "Up the Junction". More recent films include "Land of Freedom". He has won several prizes at the Cannes Film Festival.

Of his early years, he has said: "It was an ordinary life in a semi-detached where my mum still lives, a stable community and a happy family." His early cinema going experience was mainly confined to X rated continental films at the Nuneaton Hippodrome. He would often cycle the 30 miles return journey to Stratford to see Shakespeare plays. These forays were usually to matinées, but the occasional evening productions led to arrivals at home around 2 a.m. During the war he and his mother went to stay with an aunt in Devon. Ironically, the street they stayed in, in Exeter, was heavily bombed.

Born the son of an electrician, in 1936 he attended King Edward VI College in Nuneaton before going to Oxford to study law. There, he partnered Dudley Moore in revues. He once stated: "I want to make films that are real." In 1999, Warwick University awarded him an honorary D.Litt.

John Masefield

Even as a young child his favourite authors included Milton, Hood and Longfellow. He was sent to Warwick School as a boarder before he was ten years old and was at first very unhappy. He tried to run away but was caught and returned by a policeman. He tried to kill himself by eating laurel leaves but "only gave myself a horrible headache."

Thereafter life improved. He made friends and enjoyed some success in cricket, gymnastics and swimming. However, this happier time ended abruptly when his father, a Ledbury solicitor, died aged forty nine. John was removed from Warwick because his mother could no longer afford the fees and he was sent away to join the school ship H.M.S. Conway, a sailing ship designed to provide initial training for boys who hoped to become officers in the Merchant Navy. He came to look back on his schooling with affection: "It was a good school, the masters were a fine lot, and the place had a high tone."

He was to become famous as Poet Laureate from 1930 to 1967, his naval education doubtless the inspiration of "Cargoes". This was a poem committed to memory by generations of schoolchildren through much of the twentieth century. Less well-known are the many novels, plays and children's books he wrote, most of which form the John Masefield collection in the library at Warwick School. Many are first editions. He returned to school in 1928 to present prizes. The School magazine, "The Portcullis" gave a full account of his speech when he told the pupils they would have to decide for themselves whether he was an "old buffer", an "old geezer" or an "old josser" before going on to speak on the spirit of competition.

Katharine Merry

Educated at Dunchurch First and Middle Schools, and at Bilton High School, Katharine showed considerable talent from an early age. She set a world 200 metre record age-12 (25.4 in 1987) and ran numerous U.K. age records including those at 14 for 100m and 200m. She still holds British records for sprint and field events at under thirteen and under fifteen levels. In 1989 she won the A.A.A. girls (U15) indoor 60m with a record 7.35 and then set U.K. girls records for 100m and pentathlon (1318). She won four English Schools titles: Junior pentathlon 1988, 100m 1989; Intermediate 100m 1990, 200m 1991. She had a record six years as a junior international 1988-93, with outstanding success, culminating in two gold medals at the European Juniors. In her first year as a senior she was second at both sprints in the 1994 European Cup. In 2000 she showed consistent world-class form at 400m, starting the year with four successive wins including a personal best 50.05 in Nice. In Sydney she broke 50 seconds for the first time to take the Olympic bronze medal in 49.72 and ran the anchor leg at 49.6 on the sixth-placed 4 x 400m team. Another honour was to captain the British Women's European Team. The list goes on, and it is a formidable list of a sustained series of achievements.

Fred Mulley

It is sad to reflect that a distinguished career can be eclipsed for ever by one unfortunate lapse. Such was the fate of Fred Mulley, a Labour Government Minister in the 1960's and 1970's. He was M.P. for part of Sheffield for 33 years and minister in various departments, including Transport and Education and Science. He attended Bath Place School in Leamington and, briefly, Leamington College, before transferring to Warwick School from 1929 to 1936, as the recipient of a scholarship. Leslie Wells, long-serving teacher of history at Lawrence Sheriff School, was a contemporary of his at Warwick and recalls long cycle rides together into the Cotswolds.

His most famous moment for many was captured in a photograph when he momentarily fell asleep while sitting alongside the Queen at a Silver Jubilee R.A.F. fly-past. He died in 1995 and is buried alongside his parents in Whitnash. For many years he sponsored old boy dinners at the House of Commons and was president of the Old Warwickians in 1969.

James Ormond

Educated briefly at St. Anthony's, Exhall, (now closed), St. Francis R.C. Bedworth and St. Thomas More, Nuneaton, James played for Corley Cricket Club for some years before trialling unsuccessfully for Warwickshire. He went on to play for Leicestershire, gaining his county cap in 1999. He has also played for the England under nineteens tour to Zimbabwe and for the England A tour to Sri Lanka. He made his test debut in the Ashes series against Australia at the Oval in 2001.

Norman Painting

Norman Painting plays the part of Phil Archer in the world's longest-running daily radio serial, described as "a farming Dick Barton". "The Archers" upset many schoolchildren of the early 1950's because it replaced a very popular series called "Dick Barton - Special Agent". This was in 1951. More than fifty years later he is still there. But there is much more to his career than Phil. He was educated at Milverton School, at Leamington College and at King Edward VI School, Nuneaton. He graduated with first class honours at Birmingham University and taught Anglo-Saxon language and literature at Oxford. He worked for a while at Nuneaton Library. He appeared as a youngster in the Co-op Hall, Nuneaton. In the audience was a William Webb, later to acquire fame as Larry Grayson. Grayson recalled this event when they first met properly some thirty years later. He is an organist, a keen gardener and his written output includes scripts for "The Archers" as well as documentaries for television. He was awarded the O.B.E. in 1976. He lists his Archers' pay on his tax return as 'incidental' earnings.

He paid return visits to Milverton and to Leamington College, recalling in particular, as many others have done, a legendary head of the college called Arnold Thornton. He was less than flattering about his schools: "Leamington College had come down in the world from being a minor public school' and "King Edward's was a tense, highly disciplined school. The buildings were cramped and overcrowded". However, he records that he enjoyed his Leamington College days where he played the piano in a swing music group ..... accompanying such contemporary classics as 'Bob White What're You Going to Swing Tonight'. At Nuneaton, the boys were apparently 'earthier' and more enamoured of 'rugger and fisticuffs'.

Sir Henry Parkes

Born in 1815, he was educated at Stoneleigh School till the age of eight, when his father fell into debt. Henry emigrated to Australia in 1839 where he began a career in politics that led to his becoming Premier of New South Wales five times. In 1882, he was knighted by Queen Victoria. There is a story, uncorroborated, that he returned to Stoneleigh in 1880 and visited his old school.

Fred Parrott

Thousands of Warwickshire-educated pupils have gone on to serve the county as elected councillors. I have, invidiously I know, chosen one to stand for all. His name is Fred Parrott. He died as I was completing the book. Educated at Loxley and at Wellesbourne schools, he served at district, town and county level for a total of fifty years, contributing particularly on health and housing. He became the youngest ever Mayor of Stratford. In an obituary, the Stratford Herald noted: 'He never lost his sense of fun'.

Sir Charles Henry Plumb

Sir Charles was born in Atherstone and educated at King Edward College, Nuneaton. His lifelong commitment to agriculture led to his becoming President of the National Farmers' Union in 1970. He later became a Conservative Member of the European Parliament for the Cotswolds and, subsequently, President of the European Parliament. Among honours given to him were a life peerage and an honorary L.L.D. by Warwick University.

Allan Randall

He was born in Bedworth and educated at the Collycroft School. He was famous for his George Formby impressions but Roy Hudd has also recalled his talents as a jazz musician, playing various instruments including drums. One claim to fame was that he appeared with Eric Morecambe at the Roses Theatre, Tewkesbury on the night of Morecambe's last ever appearance. At the end of the show, Morecambe collapsed, and died soon afterwards. The two had spent some time reminiscing earlier in the evening.

Arthur Ransome

Ransome achieved fame by writing classics of children's literature such as "Peter Duck" and "Swallows and Amazons". His own childhood was much less contented than those about which he wrote. He ran away from his first school near Windermere in the Lake District. He came to Rugby School as a day boy in Whitelaw House. His parents lived near the cemetery in Clifton Road. He was bullied at Rugby and his glasses often broken, although his short-sightedness had not been recognised until a teacher at Rugby discovered it. His time at Rugby was summarised by him as " ….. what I can best describe as tolerable years at Rugby."

He joined the Natural History Society and regularly went on cycling expeditions, for example to Lutterworth Church. He read widely, but did not stay on into the sixth form, preferring to go to college in Leeds. While at Rugby he edited a magazine, and composed a piece for the local paper on the death of Queen Victoria in 1901. This piece engendered some scathing comments from a few of his peers.

William Shakespeare

The most famous product of a Warwickshire grammar school is generally believed to be William Shakespeare. I say "generally believed" because we have no certain documentary proof as to where Shakespeare received the education that his plays indicate he clearly had received. Many guides assert that Shakespeare was educated at the Grammar School at Stratford. The school itself is more circumspect. A notice at its entrance states "it is generally believed that Shakespeare was educated in this school".

The school's biographer, former headteacher Leslie Watkins, is equally cautious "….. it is generally taken for granted that he attended the school though no records exist to prove it." Shakespeare's first biographer, Rowe in 1709 took us no further than to assure us that he was educated " …. for some time at a Free School". Even Park Honan, a recent and thorough biographer, says no more than: "As a deputy baliff he (Shakespeare's father) was unlikely to have sent William to any school but the borough one." While we cannot be absolutely certain of his attendance there, we can be certain of what he would have been taught at Stratford, or at any other grammar school he might have attended. This is because a kind of agreed "National

Curriculum" was taught in all of the grammar schools and we have detailed records of what it was.

There was much memorising, and high priority was given to the study of Latin, then the pre-eminent language of Europe. His knowledge of Latin would certainly not have merited the strictures of his contemporary Ben Jonson who claimed that Shakespeare had "Little Latin and less Greek". Though his knowledge of the classics and of religion was strong, his sex education may have been less so. Judged by the dates of his marriage and of the birth of his first daughter, Susannah, he appeared to have had what we used to call "a shotgun wedding"!

But the first priority at school would have been to learn the fundamental doctrines of the Christian religion. School began and ended with daily devotions. As he grew older he would have broadened his studies to include subjects such as logic and rhetoric. The latter would surely have helped his construction of the major speeches of characters such as Mark Anthony and Henry the Fifth. However, the curriculum included no 'modern' history. School was likely to have begun each day at least as early as 7 a.m. but probably at 6 a.m. In the summer months, it would continue, with short breaks, till 5 p.m. Although pupil records do not survive from Shakespeare's day, there is much detail on record about the teachers who taught at the school then .... teachers such as Thomas Jenkins, an Oxford graduate who was there from 1575-9.

A few of Shakespeare's plays provide some indication of his experience at school. The most memorable example comes in the "All the World's a Stage" speech in Act V of "As You Like It" when the second of seven ages of man is described as:

" .... the whining schoolboy, with his satchel
And shining morning face, creeping like snail
Unwillingly to school."

An exchange in Act IV of "The Merry Wives of Windsor" between Sir Hugh Evans, a Welsh parson and a young boy called William Page has the former testing the latter on his knowledge of Latin vocabulary. He is tested on his knowledge of words "in the accusative case" and "your genitive case plural" but is chided for forgetting "some declensions of your pronouns". Mistress Quickly wondered at the wisdom of such learning: "You do ill to teach the child such words - He teaches him to hick and to hack."

Romeo reflected ruefully beneath Juliet's balcony that "love goes towards love as schoolboys from their books". Cremio returned from Petruchio's wedding "as willingly as I'er I came from school" ("Taming of the Shrew"). Clearly, a recurring theme in these quotations is that of reluctance to go to school.

Jim Shekdar

Jim Shekdar attained international fame in 2001 when be rowed alone across the Pacific Ocean in a boat just twenty three feet long with a tiny cabin. As soon as he set foot on land at the end of an epic journey, he received congratulations from Prime Minister Tony Blair for his "tremendous achievement" and from five times Olympic gold medallist Sir Stephen Redgrave who commented: "I'm sticking to ponds, lakes and rivers." Jim attended Leamington College in the 1960's, and joined Leamington Swimming Club. He achieved a national reputation then by playing water polo for Warwickshire and Great Britain. He now lives in the U.S.A.

Sir Bernard Spilsbury

Sir Bernard was born in Leamington and was educated at home and then at Leamington College. He continued his education at Oxford and at St. Margaret's Hospital, London. Paul Bolitho, in his "More Ripples from Warwickshire's Past" described him as "the greatest medical detective of all time."

His work as forensic pathologist in London brought him national fame. Among cases were his evidence at the trial of Dr. Crippen and the ghoulish "Brides in the Bath" mystery. Spilsbury Close in the north of Leamington is so named in his honour. He carried out some 2,500 post-mortems, although only one per cent of these was connected with murders. An exhibition in Leamington Art Gallery in the spring of 2003 paid tribute to his work.

Lytton Strachey

Michael Holroyd, Strachey's biographer, refers rather unkindly to the "traditional philistinism" of Leamington College where Strachey was bullied and nicknamed "Scraggs". His father offered to come and help but advised him "go grin and bear it" unless there were any acts of "indecency". Lytton wrote back to accept his father's advice.

After the first term, matters improved, and Lytton began to become more involved in school life. He joined a glee club, took part in chess competitions and eventually became Head of House. This entitled him to carry a walking stick and wear a tin mitre on his cap. He was seriously ill several times and was allowed to stay in bed and miss early school at seven o'clock. Nevertheless, he went on to achieve much academic success, taking his school certificate examinations early and passing in seven subjects. The college's attempts to turn him into a Christian gentleman were unsuccessful. Letters home show him to be an acerbic agnostic in his comments on sermons he heard. His love affairs or "desperate businesses" with other boys were "almost certainly platonic and inconclusive". He left in 1897 to go to University College, Liverpool.

His most famous work is, perhaps, "Eminent Victorians", published in 1918. The book consisted of a series of essays on "the good and the great" which led many to see him as an irreverent iconoclast. His mocking attitude to religion was more evident than ever. One of his essays was devoted to Dr. Arnold, former headmaster of Rugby, in which he described how " ….. the condescension with which he shook hands with old men and women of the working classes was long remembered in the neighbourhood". He saw Arnold's legacy not in the production of Christian gentlemen but in the notion " ….. that an English public schoolboy who wears the wrong clothes and takes no interest in football is a contradiction in terms."

His life was eventful, including a twenty four hour engagement to the novelist Virginia Woolf. Interest was revived in his life-story when the film "Carrington" appeared. Based on Holroyd's biography, it starred Emma Thompson and Jonathan Pryce. The film dealt in particular with a strange love affair he had with young painter Dora Carrington.

Henry Tandey

Henry Tandey has been described as "the most decorated British private soldier" in the First World War. Within a space of six weeks, he was awarded the Victoria Cross, the Distinguished Conduct Medal and the Military Medal. He was one of fifty holders of the Victoria Cross chosen to line the aisle of Westminster Abbey for the burial of the Unknown Soldier. After the war, he married and became a porter at the Regent Hotel.

So much is certain. Much more is harder to confirm by any reliable evidence. Born and brought up in Leamington, he was almost certainly educated at a local elementary school, but I have not yet traced which, and Paul Bolitho, who first drew my attention to him, does not know either. Nor do we know for certain the truth of the story that in that war he spared the life of a young German corporal, because he was already injured. That young corporal was one Adolf Hitler who never forgot this act of mercy, managed to find out the name of the English soldier who spared his life, and sent best wishes to him via Prime Minister Neville Chamberlain at the end of the 1938 Munich Conference. Among honours bestowed on him, was to become Freeman of Leamington.

Randolph Turpin

Randolph Turpin was born in Leamington Spa in 1928, one of five children. He lived in a damp, vermin-ridden basement flat and his father died from the after-effects of war-time gassing before Randolph was one year old. For a while the family was split up, but eventually they were re-united and came to live in Warwick. He was educated at Westgate School and soon achieved reputation as a fighter (his nickname was "Licker") and a sprinter. He was also an outstanding swimmer. Part of his time at Westgate coincided with the early years of the Second World War. He was often first to the shelters in an air-raid, even though "running" was supposedly banned. He reportedly knew that he wanted to be a boxer at the age of eight, though he was only able to make significant progress towards his aim when he joined a newly opened local amateur boxing club aged fifteen. His biographers say little of his schooling. He was widely respected among his peers, and a leader of the gang in and around his home in Wathen Road, Warwick. A local boy, Maurice Mancini, recalled that he used to go to St. Mary's School "the long way round" to avoid having to pass the Turpin home.

The rest of his story is well-told elsewhere. By July 1951 he had progressed to the point of meeting and beating the legendary Sugar Ray Robinson, so bringing Britain its first middle-weight world boxing championship that century. He was also British, European and Empire Champion. Reportedly, twenty thousand people turned out on The Parade in Leamington to cheer his return home. Only about eight hundred were at Holy Trinity Church for his funeral. He died, almost forgotten, in debt and having killed himself with a .22 calibre revolver. A reporter in the Coventry Standard (May 1966) observed tartly: "Everyone in the fight game was Randy's pal. I wonder where they all were on Tuesday." Belatedly, his extraordinary achievements are being remembered. There is a plaque in Leamington Town Hall and celebrations of the fiftieth anniversary of his achievement of a world championship, included the unveiling of a statue by Henry Cooper in the market square at Warwick.

Tony "Banger" Walsh

Tony Walsh produced his autobiography: "Minding My Own Business" in 1998. It contains but a few lines on his schooldays, first at St. Peter's R.C. school in Leamington, where he was "neither a model pupil nor a trouble-maker". He failed his eleven plus and thus went to Dormer School, later one of the halls which made up Trinity School in Leamington. Lessons were "tolerated" but his real enthusiasm was for sports. He went on to become a wrestler, well known for his television appearances on I.T.V.'s 'World of Sport', and then boss of a security firm based at Cubbington, and "minder" to stars such as Roy "Chubby" Brown.

His autobiography has a foreword by Brown, not a name to make the index of many educational histories, which paid generous tribute to Walsh. Walsh was clearly lukewarm about his own schooling, and one of the achievements of his wealth as he saw it was to get his own youngest son into a private school in Leamington.

Arnold Weinstock

Warwickshire can lay claim to some responsibility for educating the legendary industrialist and long-serving head of G.E.C. (General Electric Company). As a teenager, he was evacuated from Stoke Newington in London. Young Arnold, an orphan, was directed with other evacuees to Rugby Station, and then to the nearby cold, windswept cattle market in order to be placed with a family. The unofficial pecking-order for choosing children: young ones first, then girls, and finally "gangling teenage boys", left Arnold almost to the last, before he was eventually chosen by Harry and Florence Smith and taken to a council house on the outskirts of Churchover. He attended school in Harborough Magna for a few months, a daily return journey of six miles, before moving to Withybrook. He resumed his schooling at Monks Kirby. Relations between Mary Bounds, Head of Harborough Magna, and the Stoke Newington staff were not always easy. She complained in her diary of unnecessary work: 'I had so much tidying that I had no lunch at all.' Matters eased a little at Christmas when the evacuees entertained the local children in the school hall.

In 1941, Weinstock sat his matriculation exams in the parish hall at Harborough Magna. His results, which included a distinction in mathematics, helped to secure him a place at the London School of Economics. As he walked around the villages, especially Churchover, he would probably have been able to glimpse in the distance the taller buildings of the then sprawling B.T.H. (British Thomson Houston) factory, part of the industrial empire he would lead in years to come.

Sir Frank Whittle

Perhaps the most famous Warwickshire "old boy" of the twentieth century was Sir Frank Whittle, inventor of the turbo-jet engine which advanced aviation significantly. Whittle was born in Earlsdon, Coventry, in June 1907 and moved to Leamington in 1916 where he was educated briefly at Milverton Council School before winning a scholarship to Leamington College where he remained till 1922 or 1923. He was a small lad and recalled as "rather quiet and reserved."

He began in the 'A' stream but was demoted to 111B. This galvanised him to work harder. His early successes came in drama, where he played a memorable Shylock in "The Merchant of Venice" and on an occasion where he took up an invitation to talk to his form for ten minutes and "held the boys fascinated for an hour" on the subject of aircraft. His teachers slowly realised his gifts in Science and during his last two years he was allowed to miss games and work alone in the laboratory.

His invention has given him lasting fame and many subsequent honours including the Freedom of the Borough of Royal Leamington Spa, nine honorary doctorates and the rarely awarded Order of Merit in 1986. He returned to Milverton School in 1952 to unveil a commemorative plaque celebrating his attendance there. Of his brief time there, all he could recall was being shocked by being told the facts of life in the playground. On the same day, he also unveiled a plaque at Leamington College. One of his biographers, John Colley, claimed that he was never an angel and was not averse to forging his mother's signature to explain absence or undone homework. He would readily rise to "dares" such as running along the parapets of bridges.

Johnny Williams

Johnny Williams achieved fame as British and Empire Heavyweight Boxing Champion in 1952. He first became interested in boxing at the age of eight when he was a pupil at Elborow School in Rugby. He then went to Murray School because they gave boxing instruction on Friday evenings. War interrupted his training and ".... my ringwork was confined to an occasional after-school night in Mr Taylor's room and contests ..... in boxing booths which then frequented Rugby far more often than today .... If I reach the top, I'll always remember the debt I owe Murray for my early instruction." (N.B. Mr Taylor was the then head of Murray School).

Kenneth Williams

Kenneth Williams, educated at the Eastlands Schools and Lawrence Sheriff School in the late 1950's, was the long-time pianist and vocalist with the Syd Lawrence Orchestra. His piano tuition only began when the family inherited his grandfather's piano. Before then, his instrumental prowess was confined to the recorder. He proved to be a rapid learner and, after one year of tuition, he won an organ scholarship. He taught briefly at the then Herbert Kay School in Rugby before he joined the band. He toured the length and breadth of Britain and made frequent television appearances. He sadly died of cancer in his fifties. Syd Lawrence and the band turned up for his funeral in Rugby where he had continued to live throughout his career. One of his wreaths was in the shape of a grand piano.

Cavin Woodward

Educated at Whitnash County and Oken High Schools, Cavin held for several years a number of world records in long-distance running. It had not been obvious at school that he would do so. He had shown little aptitude for or interest in running until the age of sixteen, when most of his peers left school. His P.E. teacher wanted a team at sixteen plus level and he was drafted in.

He joined a local club after leaving school in 1964, and ran his first marathon in 1969. Since then he has run 218 races of at least marathon distance, many of them longer. He went on to set world records for the fifty miles, the 100 kilometres and 100 miles. To this day those records have only been bettered once; he remains the second fastest runner of all time at those distances. At the time when I spoke to him (2002) he had completed another marathon earlier in the year and was still regularly cycling. A road in Whitnash is named after him in honour of what are almost literally achievements of unimaginable endurance.

"Who's Who in Warwickshire?"

There exists a book called "Who's Who in Warwickshire?" published in 1934. I have seen several copies of it, in libraries and in second-hand bookshops, but have been unable to trace any other editions. I assume that it was a 'one-off'.

I read through it in the hope of tracing yet more illustrious ex-pupils but with limited success. The authors of the book did not choose to disclose or even hint at their criteria for inclusion of the six hundred plus entries. Most listed only their secondary education, in either a grammar or in an independent school. Some listed no education. Others, simply said 'educated privately'. Neither Bolton King nor W. H. Perkins was included, though some headteachers and a few Rugby School masters can be found. I could find only a dozen or so whose education occurred in a Warwickshire elementary school. All had in common experience as a local councillor of some kind, many combining this with being a J.P.

Famous Old Girls

I am conscious that this selection has been dominated by males. That is because I have been largely dependent on male-orientated sources. Many Warwickshire-educated females have, of course, gone on to distinguished careers while not necessarily achieving fame. Here are a few examples:-

Alcester Grammar School

Pearl Jephcott was a key figure in the formation of the Association of Girls' Clubs. In 1942 she published "Girls Growing Up", a standard text of its time. During her time in research at the London School of Economics, she published many other books. After retirement she researched the problems of living in high rise tower blocks.

Back Lane School, Coleshill

Carole Quinton: I have gleaned only sketchy details of her. She won a silver medal in the Olympic Games at Melbourne.

Harris High School

Judy Simpson: nationally successful heptathlete who achieved even greater fame as television gladiator Nightshade.

Rugby High School

These brief biographies are selected from a number which appeared in the school's own Golden Jubilee History (1969).

Irene Begrie: In the 1960's she worked with B.B.C. Television and acted as consultant on programmes for London Weekend T.V.

Mollie Kitchen: Worked for the U.N. Secretariat in London, in New York and in Geneva. She was Secretary for a Commission on Human Rights under the chairmanship of Mrs F. D. Roosevelt.

Julie Hayes: First health visitor in the country to be appointed to work full-time in group practice. Served on government committees.

More recently, the 'Times Educational Supplement' featured
Fiona Reynolds: Educated at Rokeby School and at Rugby High, she is now Director General of The National Trust. She was awarded for the C.B.E. for services to conservation and the environment.

Stratford Grammar School for Girls

Here, I have brief notes only of:

Jo Wine
Commonwealth Long Jump Champion, Sydney Olympics.

Corinna Corfield
BBC Radio 4 news presenter, 'Today' programme.

Claire Bishop
'Midlands Today', news programme.

Sadly I cannot name the school whose head wrote of famous female ex-pupils as follows: "I regret to say that we cannot think of anyone except a case, a few years ago (approx 1997) of an ex student who did a streak in a national televised snooker tournament." He asked me not to identify this young woman's place of education. But the incident adds to the enormous range of achievements of Warwickshire-educated youngsters, and, I have discovered, is widely remembered.

Special School Honours

Our special schools have had some impressive successes in the world of sport. Diane Hitchcox of Ridgeway School participated in the Special Olympics in Louisiana in the U.S.A. in 1983. She excelled in her sprint event, and won the Gold Medal.

Pupils from Exhall Grange have achieved successes galore at national and international level. One consequence was the award of the Sportsmark Gold Award, a distinction given very sparingly by Sport England. The head, Richard Bignell and Sheila Carey, P.E. teacher and former Olympic athlete, travelled to the ground of Manchester United to receive their award.

Exhall Grange School has had many distinguished ex-pupils. At the risk of being invidious, I have selected one more to illustrate the range and quality of career destinations. Adrian Dilworth is National President of UNISON. He revisited his old school only recently, and recalled his times in school from 1961 to 1971. Most staff at that time had had experience of serving in the forces, and the strict routines for stripping beds and folding blankets were memorable evidence of a predilection for military routines. "I've still got very clean shoes", said Adrian. The philosophy was one of tight military discipline and a constant supply of tasks to keep one occupied, whether compulsory prep each evening, or litter picking on Sunday afternoons, or compulsory exercise on the field. Punishments included a "loss of privileges", though Adrian was never sure what the "privileges" were meant to be. Routines were enlivened by regular 'Hell, fire and brimstone' sermons. Adrian started at the age of eight, "crying my eyes out". His work now includes lots of travel and many television broadcasts. His problems with reading print mean that he will, where possible speak "off the top of my head".

Musicians

Warwickshire has produced numerous talented musicians. One example is Emma Bell, who attended Myton School, North Warwickshire College and was a member of Warwickshire Youth Chorale. She has been a soloist with Glyndebourne Opera, Opera North and the English Chamber Opera. Emma was educated at Lillington, Myton, Binswood Hall and North Warwickshire College. She joined the Warwickshire Youth Chorale and went on to achieve fame in the singing world, winning the Katherine Ferrier Award in 2000. She stepped in at the last moment to appear in a Vaughan Williams piece at the opening night of the Proms. Another member of the Youth Chorale, educated at Higham Lane School was Andrew March. He won the Master's Competition for young composers in 1999 and has performed in prestigious venues such as the Barbican.

Postscript

As this book went to the printers, the Parsonage Project at Bedworth staged an exhibition on the town's "Sporting Heroes". The sheer number of locally-born people who had achieved national and international excellence raised the question: is Bedworth unusual? If not, then the totality of county successes would be enormous. Here are some examples, with schools included where known:

Ernie Crutchlow: (Leicester Road and Nicholas Chamberlaine)
Achieved four world cycling championships in the 1970s.

Chris Davies and: (Educated at Ash Green)
Alyson Evans Both represented their country at Bowls
(sisters)

Margaret Ghent: Represented England at netball.

Basil Heatley: (Bedworth Central, George Street and
King Henry VIII, Coventry)
A former silver medallist in the Olympic marathon, and
ex-holder of the world ten mile record.

Keith Knight:	National success in archery.
Ian Neale:	One of five Ash Green pupils in the sixties to represent England in gymnastics.
Adam Whitehead:	(Canon Evans/Canon Maggs) Gold and silver medals in Commonwealth Games in swimming (breast-stroke).

Conclusion

This chapter has been lengthy, and probably too long. Yet my prediction is that most of the criticisms I shall receive will be about the many homegrown products that I omitted.

16

Headteachers

Headship has changed greatly over the years. An early example of a 'job description' for a head comes from the village of Dunchurch, where in 1707 the trustees sought to appoint "a sober, grave, orderly and learned Schoolmaster ..... who shall carefully and diligently teach and instruct the children of the inhabitants of the parish ... in learning the catechism and also to write and cast accounts in the said school."

Records do not usually tell us the qualifications of heads, but a newly-appointed head of Cubbington School noted his credentials: "Certificate of the 1st Division ..... (3rd in order of merit). I hold a full 'D', Five advance sciences, Tonic Sol-Fa Certificate, Drill Certificate and Double First Class Archbishop's Certificate."

It is hard now to imagine how the heads of the past lived their lives. To begin with, they were often appointed at a surprisingly young age. In the late nineteenth century, Mary Fisher was appointed to King's High, Warwick aged just 22. Oscar Summers, former pupil at Tanworth-in-Arden, became head of Lapworth aged 24. George Ball may hold some kind of record, appointed to Pailton as the Master aged 21.

Once appointed, unless they moved on to another headship, and most appear to have been happy or resigned to stay, these heads saw lengths of service that are difficult now to imagine. Mr. Lawrence taught at Grandborough from 1813-1862; a cottage bearing his name honours this record. At Claverdon, Enoch Belcher survived 42 years (1874-1916). At Haselor two heads, Miss Mold and Miss Smith, between them covered 83 years between 1881 and 1964 with just a three year gap between them. Miss Fanny Jacques arrived at Halford in 1870 and stayed 47 years. Periods of service between 35-40 years were common. Mr Strudwick was head of Long Itchington for 43 years (1871-1914). He died just one year after his retirement. The nearest modern example is probably William (Bill) Stubbings, who was head of Fenny Compton from 1945-86. He married a former pupil and became a school governor there on his retirement. Mr. Lole led Wolston School for 45 years. He received a letter of thanks from Bolton King, preserved in the logbook, in 1920.

Yet, in spite of almost a lifetime's commitment, the logbook record of heads' farewells was typically and bleakly succinct; as for Joseph Chandler: "Today I cease my duties as Schoolmaster of the Kineton C of E School after 39 years. I am retiring from the profession."

What is most surprising, given the present-day demands on heads' time, is the number of other roles they performed. This was particularly true of village school heads. The previously-mentioned Fanny Jacques at Halford also played the harmonium for church services and organised a large Sunday school. Mr. Nokes, head of the 'Parish' school at Hill (Leamington Hastings) for 39 years was also church organist, clerk to the parish council and to several bodies of trustees. Clerking duties were a common practice for heads in country parishes. They were often carried out at a nominal fee, sometimes as little as two pence a week. Mr. R. H. Myers, head of St. Matthew's Rugby for 35 years, was at different times a town councillor, county councillor, mayor and J.P. The impressively named Guernsey Walsingham Webb, head at Kineton, was not satisfied with merely being the church choirmaster and organist. He founded a choral society and became conductor of Stratford-on-Avon Choral Society.

Mr. Greenwood, the "schoolmaster" of the school at Newbold-on-Avon at the turn of the century served a mere 18 years. But he also served as choirmaster, clerk to the Parish Council and taught maths and book-keeping at continuation classes at the college. He supported sporting ventures in rugger, swimming and athletics and acted as secretary for the local Horticultural Society. His obituary in the local paper occupied five columns.

Much more recently, the head at Claverdon, Miss Hinchliffe sometimes herself cleaned the outside earth closets. She also took country dancing at lunchtimes and ran a youth club in the evening for youngsters aged fourteen and over. Frank Grant, ex-pupil of Leamington College, died on the eve of his retirement as head of Stoneleigh School in 1967 after 45 years teaching, of which 36 years as Head in Devon and Stoneleigh. He was a Parish Councillor, Parochial Church Councillor, Treasurer of the Village Hall and Captain of Church bellringers.

Yet another example was Edward Beard, head at Long Compton in the late nineteenth and early twentieth century. He found time to father eleven children, write articles for local papers, do income tax work, bind his own books, repair the family's shoes and was a keen photographer. Gilbert Skinner, head of Warwickshire's first comprehensive school, Nicholas Chamberlaine, from its opening in 1952 was Founder-President of Bedworth Rotarians, Secretary of the Parochial Church Council, Chairman of Bedworth Concert Society and served on thirteen committees.

Quite what rules these heads operated under, or at any rate heeded, is not always clear. Log-books gave occasional teasing glimpses, for example that the Head of Long Compton School in the 1920's was often out of school "buying pigs". (The school had developed two acres of land into a small farm.)

Appointments then, as now, could be problematic as these minutes show:

"A meeting of the Managers was held in the Charlecote Schoolrooms on Saturday June 10 1916. There were present Sir Henry Fairfax-Lucy in the Chair, Mrs. Goule, Revd. J. G. Watson, Mrs. J. W. Lea, and Mr. W. Bennett. Lady Fairfax-Lucy was also present. The Meeting was called to interview three selected candidates for the Post of Headmistress. Before the Meeting was held one candidate, Miss Baker, withdrew. When the Meeting was held only Miss Edwards from Spark Hill was present. Later a telegram was received from Miss Cooper, the other candidate that she had missed the connection in London.

On the motion of Sir Henry Fairfax-Lucy, seconded by Mrs. Lea it was proposed and carried that Miss Edwards be appointed Headmistress. At the same time it was arranged that if Miss Cooper came the correspondent should take her to see the Chairman, Lady Fairfax-Lucy and Mrs. Lea. Miss Cooper arrived two hours later and after interviews, as arranged, it was decided that Miss Edwards still be appointed as being the most suitable candidate."

But some weeks later:

"A Meeting of the Managers was held on Thursday 30 July at the Vicarage. The minutes of the last meeting were read and signed. A letter was read from Miss Edwards requesting permission on medical grounds to withdraw her acceptance of the position of Headmistress and this was agreed to. It was proposed by Mrs. Lea and seconded by Mrs. Goule that Miss Cooper (who had previously been interviewed by some of the Managers see minutes of last Meeting) should be appointed as Headmistress in succession to Mrs. Peers. Carried unanimously."

Memories of heads were often unflattering. The head of Westgate early in the twentieth century was recalled as: "A dour spinster who wore thick cardigans and woollen fingerless mittens." At the same time the Head of Whichford was recalled thus: "We were all scared of him. He gave the cane so often. He was nearly 6 ft. with big bushy ginger moustache. He wore a wing collar of a heavy fustian suit, all the year round. The only concession he made to Summer was a straw hat."

There was little or no sense of external control over any matter of internal school organisation; even into the fifties and sixties. I interviewed former Headteacher of Temple Balsall C.E. School (now with Solihull), Arthur Hunt, in charge of the school for fifteen years, who recalled total freedom in curriculum planning: "I made my own approaches ..... I gave them (his staff) a pretty free hand ..... They gave me weekly plans of what they were doing." Even the Vicar rarely called at Temple Balsall, and, apart from a short termly meeting, the managers kept away, with the exception of one lady who attended special events such as prize-givings and sports day. There was the occasional H.M.I. visit. Mr. Hunt could have used the cane but recalls no occasion in fifteen years of headship when he did so. He preferred a judicious mix of conduct marks and stars for punishment and reward. The only parental complaint he could recall was one on his introduction of sex education.

Many teachers still serving will have their own memories of heads who left an indelible impression on the minds of those who served them. A few examples:

Norman Painting, Frank Whittle and others recall Arnold Thornton of Leamington College. Here is one of many accounts:

"He was a legend, a good man living a rich and rounded life. But he was no plaster saint. Like other successful people, there was a touch of the buccaneer about him. He loved being Head. Few who saw him in action could ever forget him, especially at morning assembly. After that pause which all great performers allow to develop before making their entrance, the doors at the back of the hall would open and he would sail in like a great black galleon, with all sails set, beaming and twinkling, sweeping in majesty and at speed the whole length of the hall on to the platform, rotund in grey suit with waistcoat and shiny polished lace-up boots."

Ray Barrett recalled that, as an ailing pupil at the College, he received a home sickbed visit from Mr. Thornton en route to a preaching commitment at Napton: "I am sure his visit did me more good than a dozen bottles of the doctor's bitter-tasting medicine."

Few can claim the record of moving from bottom to top in a post-war secondary school. One recent example was Mick Reyner at Polesworth High. Another was Geoffrey Martindale at Lawrence Sheriff.

Peter Hastings of the Trinity School Leamington left behind him stories galore that continue to be recycled. Whether it was the state of his office: "It looked ransacked!" confided one prospective parent, or the interviews he carried out while flat on his back (failing to explain to disconcerted interviewees that he had back trouble ....) Some stories may be apocryphal. Did he really call on parents and, upon being invited in, stretch himself out on a settee and fall asleep, leaving the bewildered parents to move around quietly and to clamber over him for the best part of two hours? It certainly could be true. For one who eschewed ties and suits, it was characteristic that his retirement wish was reportedly to punt a young lady along the river attired in full evening dress.

Most of the fifty plus years of Exhall Grange's existence has been in the hands of two great characters.

George Marshall worked at Exhall Grange for just short of thirty years. He had become interested in the education of blind children while training to be a teacher at the Birmingham Teacher Training College, where he used to go to help at a local blind school. He taught at nearby Stockingford County School before applying for a deputy headship at Exhall Grange. Soon after his arrival, he became acting head: the third headteacher in little over two years. Soon after that he was confirmed as head teacher and remained until his retirement in 1981. For thirty years he dedicated himself to his school in particular and to the education of blind and partially sighted children nationally and internationally. He became a consultant in "low vision education" to countries as far away as New Zealand, Malaysia and Hong Kong. He was president of the Partially Sighted Society of Great Britain and chairman of the College of Teachers of the Blind. His various publications included "Eyes and Vision", published in 1968 and reprinted five times in the next ten years. Clearly, these commitments placed a heavy workload upon him. He was awarded the O.B.E. in 1976 for services to special education. His memory is perpetuated by the George Marshall Centre - headquarters of the Warwickshire Association for the Blind, in Warwick. (Awards of honours to Warwickshire heads have been sparse, but another receiver of the O.B.E. was Molly Roberts, Head of Campion School.)

Richard Bignell became Head of Exhall Grange in September 1981. By the time of his arrival his own life-story would have made a good book on the education of the visually impaired. He was brought up in Downend in South Gloucestershire, birthplace of the legendary cricketer W. G. Grace. He attended the local primary school till he was nine. He then attended a school for the partially sighted at Exeter some 90 miles away before successfully taking the eleven plus exam for a mainstream grammar school. However, medical opinion did not support this so he went to the Grammar School for the Blind at Worcester. At that stage he could read print; indeed he went through a degree course at Bristol University without special help.

As Richard slowly realised that his sight condition was degenerative, so he came to recognise the value of Braille to those in a similar position to himself. When he moved to teach at the Royal Normal (later National) College for the Blind at Shrewsbury, his conviction was strengthened by observing the difficulties of pupils who were transferred there.

Richard's next career move was to the headship of the John Hinde School in Shepherd's Bush, London, but by then he was well aware of Exhall Grange. He became head of the school in 1981 and since then has led the school to national fame and to the award of 'Beacon' status.

'Tug Wilson was head of Coleshill School from 1958-83 and was a former prisoner of war at Stalag Luft Three of 'Wooden Horse' fame. He is reputedly the model for the violin-playing prisoner represented in that film. He did not try to escape but did take part in the daily gymnastics designed to mask noises of digging. Stories of his eccentricity abound, stemming chiefly from his preferred mode of travel even when on duty, that of cycling, in shorts. On one famous occasion he arrived late and wet at a heads' conference at Honiley Hall. The speaker suddenly stopped in mid sentence and remarked to him: "I've just realised where I've seen you before. I passed you coming here." One waggish head interposed: "I'm surprised you managed to pass him."

Primary School Heads

But what of primary heads? Did they not include "characters"? They certainly did, although again the stories may have been apocryphal. Was it true that two heads in the Bedworth area decided that their assemblies needed livening up and gave each other permission to stage an incident during the other's assembly. The climax was when one arrived in gorilla costume and wrestled the other to the ground in front of hundreds of astonished but delighted children. Certainly memorable, though history does not record whether the learning objectives for this event had been clearly defined.

Some Warwickshire events have made it to the columns of the Times Educational Supplement via the writings of Gerald Haigh, himself former head of Henry Bellairs School in Bedworth. He is a regular columnist and often cites Warwickshire stories in his articles.

Sue Bullen, head of Corley C.E. School, used to keep a goat in the school grounds. At the height of the budget crisis in the early nineties, the goat managed to seize and eat all the school's budget papers. It died the next day!

There are many more one could mention: Stan Breeze (Gun Hill, Arley) who would use his considerable skills as a cartoonist to capture the highlights of a weekend conference ...... Merlin Price (Northend and then Henley Junior and Infant) who wrote several children's novels but was almost refused entry to a book-signing event, because the assistant didn't believe he could be the author for whom they were waiting, and many, many more.

There are many recorded instances of heads employing members of their own families in school. Such arrangements did not always work well. Early in the twentieth century Ernest Grace at Little Packington employed his daughter Annie. They often fell out over some alleged or real misdemeanour on her part. For long periods, they would not be on speaking terms and he would use notes to rebuke her for lateness.

It is not surprising that heads figured regularly and prominently in the memories of their pupils. There were their stock sayings: "I'll warm their jackets", for example (Mrs Eaves, Stockingford Council). Mr Bennett, head of Leicester Road, Bedworth in the 1930's, used to tell puzzled pupils at assemblies that he had seen 'Indians' in school: "I know they are Indians, because I have seen their smoke signals in school, and when I catch these Indians ...." Just one of the countless ways that numerous heads have broached the vexed topic of smoking in school.

New Heads rapidly established their own style and ways of working in school, especially when they were strong individuals. An individual style was increasingly evident in log-book entries. One example is the opening sequence of entries from Peter James, newly-appointed head at Bishop's Itchington in 1971:

"Sept 1 1971: Today I, Peter James, took over as head of the school.
Sept 7 :   Reported phone out of order
Sept 8 :   Ditto
Sept 9 :   Ditto
Sept 13 :   Phone repaired and failed again
Sept 14 :   Phone failed
Sept 15 :   Phone failed"

Until the 1980's, the concept of 'leadership' was largely confined to ways of ensuring that the system, whatever it was, ran smoothly ..... what we would now probably call 'management'.

Though the training of heads had developed considerably, newcomers could feel awed by the nebulous and yet to be discovered responsibilities of the job. The annual L.E.A. course for new heads normally began in January, so heads starting in September could face particular difficulties, as the opening days of the following headship reveal:

"**Sept 4 1989**
'I am now in a position of responsibility with very little idea of what the job entails. 400 dead wasps found on the library floor'.

Sept 5
'Yet another 300 dead wasps on the library floor.'

Sept 6
'I spent most of today with Neil M. at Warwick Hospital ..... broken wrist due to falling over.'

Sept 7
'Nits letter out.'

I trust that the new qualifications for potential and for serving heads will ensure that they can now manage these tiresome but typical distractions.

Footnote

I regret the bias towards males evident in these cameos. I have drawn on diverse sources, and have found 'eccentricity' to be more evident in males, at least as revealed in reminiscence.

17

Directors of Education and County Education Officers

Bolton King (Warwickshire Director of Education 1904-28)

The story of Bolton King's appointment and achievements as Director of Education have been told in chapters 3 and 4. It is as well, for there is so much that could be said of him that it is difficult to know what to omit. He achieved much as a scholar, a politician, an administrator and a writer. He himself took great care to document in some detail his work in Warwickshire in reports to Committee. His work received extensive coverage in the local and sometimes too the national press. Finally, an excellent scholarly biography of him exists, published as an occasional paper by the Warwickshire Local History Society in 1978.

Where to start? Perhaps with his name. The rest of his family, ancestors and descendants, treated Bolton King as a surname; he used it as his whole name at all times, including on the family vault after his death. Even in the 1881 Census, he was listed as Bolton King only, while his sisters were Charlotte and Louisa Bolton King.

He was born at Chadshunt near Kineton in 1860 and reportedly retained a Warwickshire accent. He came from a family with a commitment to public service: his father was Liberal Member of Parliament first for Warwick and then South Warwickshire. He was also High Sheriff for the County. Bolton King was educated for four years at a school known variously as Hunter's School, Kineton and as Kineton Lodge School. It was a "classical" school, an early form of prep. school. In 1872, at the age of twelve, he entered Eton, where he was Captain of the House, and at Oxford where he gained a first class Honours in Classical Moderations. For eight years he lived at Toynbee Hall, a settlement in East London whose intention was to bring the life of the university to bear on the life of the poor. Toynbee Hall survives today, and is well worth a visit. Over the years it attracted many distinguished figures, for example Clement Attlee. John Profumo, former Stratford Member of Parliament went to work there after his parliamentary and ministerial career ended in a scandal. Records of Bolton King's work there survive, testifying to his work, for example on organising European tours at accessible prices with extensive courses of study, designed to encourage the less well off to enlarge their horizons.

He returned to Warwickshire, where he established cottages and a reading room in the village of Gaydon. He also provided a building in Kineton as a Liberal Club "where a man could spend a comfortable evening, could have his pipe and read the papers or books, or have his game of cards." To this day his initials (just 'B.K.') can be seen in an inscription on the building. In 1889 he stood at Hillmorton in the first County Council elections. He was defeated. Anticipating events in less than a decade, he wrote in 'The Schoolmaster' in 1893 that rural schools should come under the County Council rather than under Parish and District Councils. He opposed Lord

Willoughby de Broke at Kineton and was defeated by just 39 votes. He became an Alderman and in 1901 stood as an anti-Boer War Liberal candidate in a parliamentary by-election at Stratford. He was defeated after a stormy campaign. One national paper reported "an atmosphere of terrorism in Stratford." In consequence, he wrote a letter to the Birmingham Post in July 1901, protesting at the way in which the police handled, or failed to handle riotous meetings. He received support from a leader in the same paper. But his defeat in politics was to prove to be a victory for the quality of leadership in local government, as he led the county through nearly a quarter of a century of immense growth.

Retirement

His retirement earned two full columns in the local paper. He was presented with a crayon portrait of himself at County Hall and a smoker's cabinet from Attendance Officers.

The Hon. Mabel Verney (his long time opponent) was away in "Devonshire" but she paid generous tribute to one who "so brilliantly filled the post of Director of Education in Warwickshire." The Chair of School Committee, Sir Michael Lakin recalled him as a man with a "single-hearted, single-minded sense of duty." Alderman MacGregor spoke warmly too: "There can be no county in England with happier relations than those existing between Warwickshire and its teachers. He has consulted the teachers in everything." Bolton King in his reply observed modestly: "I have tried hard to do what I could for Warwickshire children." He added "..... The Education Committee has gone on the one and only way to make good schools. That is by trusting the teachers and by reducing officialdom to the minimum."

After retirement, he was able to devote more time to his great love, that of gardening. He had always supported the school garden and, more than once, he had set out to visit schools, laden with plants and seeds. His own garden at 42 Coten End, Warwick was so large that part of it was used for the site of the new Coten End school buildings. A plaque in the reception area testifies to this.

An editorial in 'The Times' following his death in 1937 began: "If a history of education in Warwickshire during the twentieth century is ever written, the name of one man will be outstanding, in the early chapters. We refer to Bolton King." He was praised for his " ..... remarkably high degree of efficiency," and his "tact, kindliness of heart and charm of manner which smoothed over all difficulties." The editorial concluded "..... he left Warwickshire with one of the foremost education systems in the country."

An unattributed office tribute said:

"Mr Bolton King was loved by every member of the staff. Every day when he brought the letters round he would say 'Good Morning' and he never left the office in the afternoon without calling in every room and saying 'Good Night'. He would pass St Mary's Church clock at 8.45 a.m. every morning and check the time against his own large silver watch."

The Warwick Advertiser noted in particular how with scrupulous equity he balanced "his passion for education" against "the limitations brought about by financial constraints". It also mentioned: "Happiest memories of the office bicycle rides he used to join." These took place at weekends, and included the whole office staff - all seventeen.

Bolton King was cremated, and his ashes buried in the family vault at Chadshunt. The Benediction was pronounced by the Bishop of Birmingham. There were in attendance representatives from Gaydon (where he had cottages and a reading room built), County Hall, Heads, Teachers, Unions, the Office, Education Committee and from other parts of the County Council. Ironically, his long-term adversary, the Honourable Mabel Verney died within days of his death. Their obituaries were published side by side.

Chadshunt Hall

Chadshunt Hall, the Bolton King family home, still exists. It is situated near Kineton, standing back from the road to Gaydon, behind the small local church and its graveyard. Its recent owner, Martin Dunne, showed us many features in the house largely unchanged since Bolton King's time of residence. He is reasonably certain that the best example of this is the ground floor lavatory! The garden also remains largely unchanged both in design and in its views on all sides. Only a distant hum of traffic intrudes.

The church is there, now used only on a few occasions each year and still relying on candles. The Bolton King family pew is there but Bolton King himself is not there. He is buried in the churchyard, next to his parents. Though they and his wife all have their first names inscribed on the tombs, Bolton King himself has just those two words: Bolton King.

William Hughes Perkins
(Director of Education 1928-45 and County Education Officer 1945-50)

Born in Cumberland in 1885, William Hughes Perkins became Director in 1928, from an appointment as Secretary of Elementary Education in Lancashire. His salary was £1000 per annum. He must have been a strong candidate, for he received nearly three times the votes of his nearest challenger. Yet the field included two with Director experience in boroughs. Perkins was aware of the reputation and achievements of his predecessor, sufficient for Committee to have persuaded Bolton King to stay on well beyond retiring age (he was born in May 1860). By one of those nice little coincidences the school Perkins attended from eleven onwards, Buxton College, was to have as a future head one Ralph Bolton King, son of Perkins' predecessor.

Perkins entered Manchester University aged sixteen and had obtained a first in Chemistry by the age of nineteen. He taught briefly as an Assistant Lecturer in Chemistry at Leeds University and served in the First World War with sufficient distinction to gain an M.C., an O.B.E. (Military Division) and the Croix de Chevalier of the Legion of Honour. He was a keen mountaineer and took an active interest in the Youth Hostel Association. He was appointed Organiser of Day Continuation Schools in Lancashire at the end of the war, appropriately, given that he would eventually find the longest surviving such school in Rugby. He then became Secretary for Elementary Education, still in Lancashire. He worked himself hard. A Divisional Inspector said: "Nowhere do I find a Director of Education at work at 8.00 p.m. save in Warwickshire". Yet he could see a life beyond the job. An office colleague recalled: "W. H. Perkins never forgets that actual office work is only a small part of life." Other colleagues spoke of his "untiring efforts, his attention to detail, his readiness to discuss things and his devilish ingenuity in picking holes in a weak argument."

He sometimes exasperated colleagues by insisting on retaining masses of papers in his own room, spread out on desks and tables. He knew where things were, but others had difficulty in locating papers. He could be absent-minded, asking secretaries if they had seen his spectacles, which he had abstractedly pushed up into his hair. They praised "a family feeling in the office ….." An early colleague was Joan Browne, Principal of the then recently opened teacher-training college at Canley. She recalled a "very outgoing" man who "visited regularly and responded to invitations to college functions with alacrity."

There are stories of his management style ….. of his reputation for dealing with all kinds of matters himself. He had tables around the edge of his office on which were all of the department's key files. The process of agreeing the estimates for expenditure on education each year was a simple and brief one. A metal grille halfway along the upstairs corridor in the office divided the Treasurer's Office from the Director. The Treasurer would ring Perkins to ask him to estimate his needs for the following year. Within a short time Perkins would ring back and they would agree a figure. Michael Ridger, a later County Education Officer, was just one who has wondered aloud whether the elaborate procedures subsequently introduced ever introduced results much different from those Perkins would have obtained.

He was praised for his calm, tactful ways of defusing conflict. A note in the Baginton Parish Magazine recorded his courteous, equable handling of a stormy meeting with parents on the future of the school. The Rector recorded that he "put the matter before us with great clearness and remarkable patience."

He took a keen interest in promoting the use of the wireless in schools, even driving out himself to take a replacement wireless to Combroke when the school was contributing to schools' music broadcasts. This enthusiasm led to his being Vice Chairman of the Schools' Broadcasting Council. Soon after his arrival he was granted leave in July 1930 to act as Visiting Lecturer at a Summer School in Columbia University, New York.

He liked to maintain an enigmatic expression in meetings, letting others speak before intervening to resolve or to mediate. At interviews, the same inscrutability was recalled, as was a tendency to fire the unexpected question. Miss Briselden, applicant for the headship of Rugby High, recalled being asked whether sixth form Arts students should be taught Einstein's Theory of Relativity "in a general way" (Perkins had a Master's degree in Science and cared much about its teaching). Miss Briselden could not afterwards recall the answer she gave, but she did get the job. One of his secretaries could only recall one question of his at her interview : how to spell 'parallel'.

On his retirement in 1950 he was praised by Committee for continuing " ..... the Warwickshire tradition with unfailing resource and distinction ..... (he) so successfully combined progress with economy." At a function at King's High School, Warwick, he was presented with a cheque and a Chippendale chair. Over 1000 teachers had contributed towards the gift. He asked that his epitaph be: "He done his damnedest and angels can do no more." He returned to the office occasionally and was chief guest at Rugby High School prize-giving in 1952. Michael Ridger recalls receiving a note of good wishes from him when he took the job in 1971, and Perkins reportedly lived into his nineties.

Northleigh Aneurin Y Yorke-Lodge
(County Education Officer 1950-63)

Mr. Yorke-Lodge replaced Mr. Perkins in 1950. He would not have needed too much induction into the ways of Warwickshire for he had been Deputy to Perkins in the county since 1947, and Perkins was reportedly keen to see Yorke-Lodge as his successor. Another Oxford-educated leader, he had clearly impressed as deputy. An ex-barrister, he had worked as an education officer in Blackpool. Committee accepted the advice of a sub-committee that: "Council couldn't do better than appoint him to succeed." Indeed, they needed persuading by the Ministry of Education even to interview another candidate.

Many memories survive him. His senior organiser, "Bill" Wilson recalled "a man of few words; getting to know him wasn't easy." Joan Browne found him "less easy to know than his predecessor, but a colleague of integrity." One of his secretaries thought he was "rather reserved". One organiser described him as "a quiet little figure who kept himself to himself." Colleagues in the office recalled Yorke-Lodge as a man with "a wonderful brain" and "a man of high principles". He refused refreshments at public functions because he believed one should not take advantage of the availability of public money. He worked very hard, often not taking his full allocation of leave.

Even if away ill he would arrange for the post to be brought to his home. He would then dictate replies to the messenger-secretary. If out in the country he liked to sit outside to eat his lunch. If in the office at lunchtime he would walk to Cape Road bridge to watch the trains. He was a keen collector of antiques, with a reputation for attending every antique sale in the county, and some outside.

Many recalled him well and confirmed his liking to visit every school once a year, often for no more than fifteen minutes, usually in a Morris Minor. These visits were still recalled by long-serving heads and teachers in the 1980's. He would dash in, speak briefly to the head on any pressing matters and then leave, reassuring, or reminding them that: "You're captain of the ship." Logbooks such as those of Hampton Lucy confirm the regularity of these visits. He would also fit in extra visits for occasions such as the death of a key person in school. The Radford Semele logbook noted such a visit "to express sorrow" in 1958.

His lasting achievements included the re-organisation of elementary schools into primary and secondary and the promotion of Warwickshire "High Schools", an innovation described elsewhere. Some claim that he was an early exponent of the now fashionable "specialist schools" and envisaged Avon Valley (then Newbold Grange High) as a centre of excellence in agriculture for example. I have been unable to verify this. But he did have a strongly held belief that every child should have the chance to make the best of his talents in the schools. He did have to manage a major building programme to cater for a rapidly increasing school population.

An indication of the widespread regret at his going was this editorial by the headmaster of the then Murray School in the school magazine:

"During the last weeks of the term Mr. N. A. Y. Yorke-Lodge, the Director of Education for Warwickshire, visited the school. It is with regret that we learn of his impending resignation. We would like to add our small tribute to him for the tremendous work he has done in Warwickshire by inaugurating and bringing to fruition the Warwickshire High School scheme."

At a farewell event at Oken High School he received a cheque and a Royal Doulton china jug. Heads paid tribute to "their great friend from the Shire Hall." He reciprocated, speaking of "a long tradition of friendliness between the county education office and the schools." Sadly, he died soon after retirement from a brain tumour.

Christopher Chenevix Trench (County Education Officer 1964-71)

Born in India, he was educated at Shrewsbury School and Oxford University. He came from a family with a tradition of service to education, including a brother who was headmaster of Eton.

Christopher Chenevix Trench came to Warwickshire in 1963. He came from Kent, where he had been Deputy County Education Officer. He had served there since 1957, and among his distinctions was the award of the M.B.E. for his work as Major in the Army Education Corps. He did not travel round the county so often as his predecessor. Unless C.T. chose to visit, most matters would be dealt with by central edict or by the area office. He had a reputation as a gentle person with great charm. He saw the possibilities of a stronger advisory service and began to increase the size of the team and eliminate from its multifarious jobs some of the more mundane, clerical tasks. He had been influenced by his experience in Kent, and by the strength of advisory support in neighbouring Birmingham. He championed the cause of the High Schools by urging building programmes that would give them all new and better-equipped buildings. He also launched the programme of consultation and planning that would bring first and middle schools to the county.

He was a strong supporter of games and sports in schools and regularly secured funding to aid developments such as the building of tennis courts in secondary schools. He particularly championed the introduction of fencing. His support, both financially, and to his P.E. organisers Barbara Gibson and Don Woolley, led to the provision of courses at evenings and weekends. Schools across the county from Hartshill to Stratford and Rugby regularly attended. Participants included everyone from probationer teachers to one secondary head of whose training performance Barbara observed: "Vicious wasn't in it!"

He never stood on ceremony, and most recall him as just "Mr Trench". He himself never used 'Chenevix' other than when signing letters. He would sometimes make his own fire in the morning and would occasionally make his secretary a cup of tea if she seemed unduly pressurised. He was on various committees which took him to London but would then return to the office at the end of the day and work late into the evening. An additional pressure was that County Council and Committee meetings became much longer during his period of office. He also did much local voluntary work for the Adult Education Centre at Westham House and was a governor for the Royal Shakespeare Theatre.

He died suddenly one weekend in July 1971 while working in his garden. That morning he and his wife had been to Warwick, he to buy cakes and his wife to buy a coat for a forthcoming function at Buckingham Palace. He came home, mowed the lawn and then collapsed. The local paper headline was blunt: 'Education Chief Dies Suddenly'. In a tribute, the then Chairman of the Education Committee described him as "popular and highly respected". He added: "He had a feeling of real concern for children, for his staff and committee members." As the news reached colleagues and friends throughout the county there was a shared sense of dismay and disbelief, such was the warmth and strength of his personality.

The funeral was a private ceremony at Norton Lindsey church. A memorial service of thanksgiving was held at St. Mary's, Warwick, at which the Bishop of Coventry preached, eight days after the funeral. He is buried with his wife on the slope of a hill in Norton Lindsey churchyard. His wife outlived him by nineteen years. She arranged for a tree to be planted in his memory at their Cornwall home ..... at the spot where her husband used to sit and look out over the valley to the sea beyond.

Postscript

I have been able to speak to a number of staff who worked for both Yorke-Lodge and Chenevix Trench. They speak supportively of both, but remark on the contrast between the two in their ways of working.

Mr Yorke-Lodge kept his desk clear, having only the piece of paper he was working on at that moment. Mr Chenevix Trench had his desk piled high and was wont to say as he searched through his papers: "We'll find a dead typist under here one day".

Y.-L's annual visits to schools led him to refuse all invitations to functions such as speech days. Thus, he was scrupulously equitable to all schools. C.T. freely accepted such invitations, usually in the evening, but made no attempt to visit in the way that his predecessor had.

Y.-L's forays led him to believe that he needed no briefings from his advisers; he relied on his own visits for his views on the schools, which he offered without prompting to colleagues. C.T. would seek briefings from Bill Wilson, his Senior Adviser. When the Secretary of State, Ted Short, spent a day in Warwickshire in 1971, visiting new schools in the Rugby and Chelmsley Wood area, he ensured that he was extensively briefed before he accompanied Mr. Short.

Y-L rarely socialised and kept his private life away from the office quite separate from work, particularly after his promotion to be County Education Officer. But he missed little; he would spot an office romance quickly. Some recall him being better at knowing names than his successor, though rather more formal with them.

Though C.T. often worked late, he adopted a slightly more relaxed style. He kept an edition of Plato in the original Greek in his office, into which he would occasionally dip for intellectual stimulus. If he had a quiet lunchtime he would set out to complete the Times Crossword. He and his wife once joined Warwickshire schoolchildren on the S.S. Uganda for one of its then regular educational cruises.

Y-L was very 'correct' in his dealings, but C.T. would be prepared to be more unconventional at times in moving matters on. For example, he had made regular representations about a faulty hinge on the front door of the office. Nothing was done until he resorted to sending a light-hearted poem to the Chief Architect. Whatever it said, it worked.

Y-L liked a fire on chilly days but would always ask for it to be lit. However, having summoned someone to light the fire he would kneel to help by placing a newspaper in front of the fire to draw up the flames. At least once the paper went up in flames too.

All spoke warmly of a friendly office atmosphere under both gentlemen. Both showed support and compassion when anyone in the office was in trouble or when tragedy affected schools. Their working methods and their personal style were very different, but both earned great respect and loyalty from their staff.

Frank Browning

Frank Browning became Acting C.E.O. until a successor to Chenevix Trench could be appointed. He was close to retirement and not seen as a long-term appointment. He served almost the whole of his professional life in Warwickshire in a variety of posts, and made what Michael Ridger called: " ..... an enormous contribution to the service of education in the county." He was responsible for the development of schooling in Chelmsley Wood, a major development at the time.

Michael Ridger (County Education Officer 1972-88)

Michael Ridger was educated at Wellingborough School and at Queen's College Oxford, where he was an Open Exhibitioner in Modern History. He taught history in grammar schools and comprehensive schools in Worcestershire, Devon and Coventry between 1951 and 1959. He taught at Caludon Castle in Coventry in the late fifties, giving him early experience in comprehensive education, though in a school that was still streamed.

His administrative work included time as an Advisory Officer for secondary schools in Lindsey and five years as Senior Assistant Education Officer in Hertfordshire. He came to Warwickshire from Sussex where he had been Deputy Director of West Sussex County Council. He was selected from twenty-one applicants.

During his seventeen years he had to manage a major contraction in the service following falling rolls and the oil crisis. Nevertheless, he secured the establishment of teachers' centres and the re-organisation of schools in the Central and Northern areas. An example of growth in the advisory service in his time comes in these figures:

1974 : 12 advisers/4 advisory teachers
3 residential courses
37 non-residential courses

1988 : 19 advisers/73 advisory teachers
48 residential courses
200+ non-residential courses

With his active encouragement the team gained in strength and influence.

He also supported the development of the careers service and youth services at a time when they were regularly identified as targets for making savings in the budget. He also championed the cause of arts education at a time when its value was questioned.

I was able to interview him for this book at his home in Leamington. He was characteristically self-deprecating about his own work, but full of mischievous and irreverent stories about working in the education service in the county. However, whenever I began to make any notes he would say: "Oh no. Good Lord! You can't possibly print that." Thus, this biographical sketch is much shorter than I would have wished. However, Chapter 8 describes some of the major developments over which he presided.

On his retirement in 1988, the Committee paid tribute to his skill, humanity and creativity as an administrator, and "a welcome lack of pomposity". He was praised for his "personal accessibility ...." and "a genuine capacity to listen".

Michael Ridger followed many of his predecessors in finding time to contribute to education at regional and national level. For example, he served for three years as Chairman of the Midlands regional group. He chaired an ACC/AMMA working party on the four term year and served on national committees relating to adult education and to sports councils. He retains in retirement a mischievous sense of humour, a sharp mind and a sprightly gait.

Margaret Maden (County Education Officer 1989-95)

As we come closer to the present day, it becomes harder to write with detachment. I worked closely with Margaret Maden for four years. Four years is not long, but she had the capacity to wreak from every minute sixty seconds of hard work - from herself and from her colleagues. This is a relatively lengthy piece, partly because it includes many memories of how the 'Office' was re-organised, and how the L.E.A. managed a daunting volume of change.

Educated in Blackpool, she began her teaching career as a geography teacher in a multi-racial comprehensive school in Brixton - an early example of her readiness to face challenges. She then lectured in a College of Education before taking a deputy headship at a comprehensive school in Bicester. For eight years she was head of Islington Green Comprehensive. She then became Director of Islington Sixth Form Centre which drew its clientele from more than thirty North London schools. For a short period she was Principal of Tertiary Development and Planning with the Inner London Education Authority. She was appointed to Warwickshire as Deputy County Education Officer.

Margaret Maden's reference from the Inner London Education Authority would surprise no-one who knew her well, especially this sentence: "(she has) the rare gift of being able to attend to meticulous and tedious detail without losing sight of the overall pattern of action." She was described as " ….. a headteacher of excellence ….. remembered with respect, gratitude and affection."

She can recall vividly her first impressions upon arriving for interview for the Deputy post in 1987:

"I can remember the very first time I walked in for interview. ! thought, 'what a dump - reception area full of packing cases, one dim light bulb, neon flashing intermittently - no-one was there to say hello - to anyone'. One of the first things I did when I got there was to get that whole area refurbished, put in a proper counter, and regular receptionists - I did a couple of hours myself on duty sometimes and thought it was very interesting, who was coming in and going and the expressions of some of my nearest and dearest staff as they came in was quite wonderful to behold. Gasp! Was she checking on them? No, I just needed to see what went on from the point of view of someone in a remote management job.

I was also struck (dumbstruck, almost) by the lack of women - except cleaners, part-time 'clerks' and a handful of Advisers as I recall. Coming from London, this was a bit shocking and whilst I was half prepared for the monochrome ethnicity (just slightly relieved by Sam Sharma), the overwhelming maleness at senior officer level and councillors was a bit weird. I certainly did what I could about the appointment of high quality female officers once installed.

Peter Collinson, the Education Department wag at that time, commented that my appointment was like 'Maradona joining Port Vale'. I puzzled over this, wondering whether I should be flattered by the comparison with an Argentinian (male) footballer - albeit in the period before the 'hand of God' incident, mercifully. Then I thought 'why Port Vale?' and gradually concluded that the secret weapon of Warwickshire C.C. - and several other Councils at that time - was its ultra humility and recessive approach to public affairs. No showing off, no conceit or vanity. Nowadays, of course, such an approach is unthinkable."

Two years after her arrival in Warwickshire, she was promoted to the position of County Education Officer. She was one of twenty one applicants, four of whom were interviewed. Her predecessor and 'boss', Michael Ridger, wrote an informal reference for Chief Executive Ian Caulfield in which he spoke of: " …… an unusual capacity for innovation ….. a capacity for hard work …..". He praised "her vigorous and determined response to the challenge of the Education Reform Act" and added a characteristically perceptive caveat: "If at times she seems impatient, this is partly a reflection of her quite exceptional ability."

Margaret has her own memories of the Education Reform Act:

"For the record, the big GERBIL (The Great Education Reform Bill, later ERA 1988 et al) project landed on my desk as soon as I started at Warwick in September 1987 (Kenneth Baker had slipped it in during the summer hols.) Michael Ridger said 'Over to you, Margaret, I don't like the look of this lot'.

In spite of the enormous demands made on her time by national legislation and a major programme of local re-organisation, she found time to respond to invitations to speak all round the country. She contributed to books; she served on the National Commission on Education; she wrote regularly for the Times Educational Supplement, using her author's earnings quietly to fund a variety of small and beneficial projects. She kept up at all times a programme of visits to schools and would often return to the office with indignant demands for explanations of lapses in service. Among her many abilities was being able to remember the names of hundreds of people. However, she was never entirely confident that she had fully grasped the intricacies of office life:

"So I got to know Northgate Street though I am not sure that I ever did, because it seemed to be rabbit warrens in there. Even in my last years I was still discovering staircases I had not entered before. One line could be that it is all rather charming and eccentric (which it is) or it is all inefficient. I could never quite resolve this because the anarchist in me believed that it is good for staff to have their own space, their own territory and to work in a rabbit warren, eccentric cubby hole type place; I am sure it was a fire risk. The place was absolute murder if anyone was disabled, you just could not access many of the offices, even with just an arthritic knee, stairs were winding and twisted."

Though a strong leader, she was not hierarchical; she was far more likely to deliver a dressing down to one of her senior colleagues than to a humble clerk or cleaner. One man, brought back from retirement in his seventies to help in a crisis in the INSET office, was astonished when Margaret came across to his office to thank him for his support. He recounted her visit with (literally) tears in his eyes.

She gave priority to improving communication with schools and within the office. The latter was propelled by the inception of "Views", a cheerful news-sheet designed to keep everyone in the office informed.

And one final piece of history from Margaret Maden herself:

"The only other chunk of this particular history I would like you to think about a bit more is the school re-organisation project, although you may have already covered this in some other bit of your work. Nonetheless, it's worth chucking in my own recollections and observations, even if repeating what others have already said and written.

This was the biggest school re-organisation of the post-1944 Education Act period, according to the DES anyhow. It was the last, really, of the traditional 'rational planning' model. After this, the notion of 'school effectiveness' drove and dominated school planning. Warwickshire stuck to older principles, like location, size, quality of buildings and related these to newer educational criteria, especially Key Stages of the National Curriculum.

Eric Wood's meticulous work, leading an extraordinarily impressive team of front-line (and backroom) officers, was quite stunning. I wasn't 'out there' as much as others, but even so, I logged up 87 public meetings in just over two years and (almost) successfully stuck to an overall vow of silence as others, more neutral and coolly bureaucratic than I, did the business."

She moved on to Keele University to take a chair in Education, following Tim Brighouse who had chosen to return to L.E.A. work in Birmingham. Her account of her final meeting of the Education Committee when fulsome tributes were paid to her work was characteristic of her lack of self-regard. She devoted most of the account to a scathing 'Good Riddance' speech from one acerbic county councillor, attacking her alleged fondness for closing small schools. Far from being slighted, she recounted the attack with positive glee. Margaret not only grasped nettles, she searched tirelessly for new ones to seize.

Eric Wood (1995 -   )

At the time of writing Eric is in post and looks certain to remain there for a few years yet.

He attended school in Staffordshire and went on to Manchester University. He taught at different levels from nursery to adult, still in Manchester, before deciding to make a move to local authority administration. His first post was as professional assistant in Barking. He then returned to Staffordshire, where he moved through the ranks from assistant education officer to acting deputy. He came to Warwickshire as Deputy in 1989, and, with the support of the three main parties, became County Education Officer in 1995.

With a wife as teacher, two daughters going through the schools and an extensive programme of school visits and consultation meetings, there has never been any chance that he would "forget what it is like". I do not think it too fanciful to suggest that he would have found it relatively easy to work with Bolton King or Manchester University alumnus, W. H. Perkins. All three might have followed political careers, but put aside their affiliations to work with politicians of all parties. All have combined pragmatic good sense with unyielding principle.

Margaret Maden recalled her insistence that her new Deputy should be someone with experience of a major re-organisation and added: "We couldn't have done better, could we?"

Appendices

Appendix I

The First Ten Years : A Report (1903-13)

Ten years on from its inception, Bolton King wrote a summary of the work of the Education Committee over that decade. It was produced on July 1, 1913, exactly ten years on, and a few quotations show the sense of pride and conviction in what had been achieved. They also show how, ninety years on, many of the same issues continue to generate debate and concern. Paragraph one challenges the 'empty vessels' model of education still popular today, and goes on to exhort the value of 'first hand experience'. Paragraph two questions the value of formal grammar.

Elementary Curriculum

"These 10 years have seen something of a revolution in the aims of elementary teaching. Up till then the educational policy of the country had been to staff the children's brains with facts, little matter how undigested and how soon forgotten, and neglect alike the training of character and the training of the mind. However much this may have been mitigated in practice by the wiser influence of individual Inspectors and Teachers, it wasted much of the effort of 30 years of national education. The abolition of payment by results and the freeing and broadening of the curriculum have allowed Local Authorities to foster new and better aims. The children now are taught to think. It has become comparatively unimportant whether a child has accumulated so many facts of History or Geography or can work sums in Arithmetic which he will never be called upon to do in after life. It is of prime importance that his brain should be trained to observe, to reason, to learn how to use the knowledge that will come to him in after life. Perhaps the most striking example of the new spirit is in the use made of Nature Study. In country schools particularly, but in town schools as well, the children are directed to the best and most obvious material at hand - the study of the world around them. Flowers, stones, the seasons, the main processes of farm and garden, the life of birds and trees have to a large extent taken the place of books, and country life has gained a new interest. So to in Geography lists of mountains and rivers disappear. The child begins with the Geography of his own parish and county, and Geography becomes a living and intelligible thing.

At some schools the exchange of letters and picture post-cards with children in colonial and foreign schools has given a personal touch to this. The teaching of History, perhaps the most difficult of all school subjects, has advanced less, but tables of dates and like monstrosities are beginning to disappear. The history of the child's country is becoming more real, he hears less of kings and statesmen and battles and more of the life of the people, and he has gained something in which patriotism can take root. The teaching of English has radically changed.

Formal grammar - an almost meaningless exercise - is going fast. Lastly, Arithmetic is brought more and more into touch with life, and the child begins to see how he or she can use it for the practical purposes of a farmer's, or a carpenter's, or a house-wife's business; he realises that figures are not abstractions, and have to do with things; he learns how to measure and calculate timber and house-walls and land.

Appendix II
Warwickshire County Council
Chairmen of Education Committee

Technical Education Committee
1892-93	Councillor Eilsee
1893-04	Alderman Bolton King

Education Act Committee
1903-04	Alderman J. S. Dugdale

Education Committee
1904-07	Alderman Dugdale
1907-27	Alderman J. Broughton Dugdale
1927-42	Alderman E. Parke
1942-50	Alderman Major M. Nickalls, MC
1950-57	Alderman W. Howard
1957-58	Alderman D. Gee
1958-61	Alderman E. Alderson
1961-67	Alderman J. Steele
1967-74	Alderman H. Doughty
1974-76	Alderman M. Hammond
1976-81	Councillor R. Kettle
1981-82	Councillor P. Thomas
1982-85	Councillor J. Little
1985-86	Councillor P. Blundell
1986-89	Councillor I. Bottrill
1989-91	Councillor G. Jones
1991-92	Councillor L. Rouch
1992-93	Councillor Mrs. R. Styles
1993-97	Councillor J. Airey
1997-	Councillor R. Grant

County Education Officers
1903-04	Gerald Fitzmaurice
1904-28	Bolton King
1928-50	William Hughes Perkins
1950-63	N. A. Y. Yorke-Lodge
1964-71	C. J. Chenevix-Trench
1972-88	Michael Ridger
1989-95	Margaret Maden
1995-	Eric Wood

Appendix III
Education Acts

Here is a summary of the key Acts of recent years that the authority was required to implement. Each Act or event affected every single school in the county:

1981 Act   This required LEAs to make provision within mainstream schools for children with special educational needs. It was estimated that 20% of children would have such needs at some point in their career. This Act introduced the process of 'statementing'.

1986 Act   This further redefined the membership of governing bodies. It increased the number of parents, reduced the number of L.E.A. nominees and gave new duties and new powers to governors.

1988 Act   Known as 'ERA': the Education Reform Act, its impact was massive. This was the Act that introduced the National Curriculum with its associated key stages and end of key stage tests. It delegated budgets to governing bodies (known as L.M.S: Local Management of Schools).

It established Grant Maintained Schools and City Technology Colleges.

It further increased parental rights over school admissions.

There was more, much more, but these provisions alone transformed the daily lives of teachers and their pupils. It also changed the basic power structure within education.

1992 Act   The key theme of this Act was greater accountability, achieved through a range of measures: the establishment of OFSTED, published reports and test results, league tables etc. It also removed sixth form colleges and Colleges of Further education from L.E.A. control.

1993 Act   This was relatively minor: a tidying up Act. It did introduce more measures to encourage schools to opt for grant-maintained status.

1995 Act   Sir Ron Dearing was brought in by the Government to simplify an over-detailed National Curriculum and its associated complex procedures for assessment and record-keeping. It followed a widespread boycott of tests by teachers in 1993 and reflected the uncertainty of a government with a disappearing majority.

1997 Act	Enabled OFSTED to inspect local authorities and teacher training courses. It created QCA: the Qualifications and Curriculum Authority.
1998 Act	School Standards and Framework Act. This imposed a duty on L.E.A.s to improve standards in their schools. It also introduced Education Action Zones.

1997 saw the First Labour Party election victory since 1974. In what the Times Education Supplement called "a torrent of activity", a small selection of its initiatives included:

- Extra funding to reduce infant classes to 30.
- Tough targets for eleven year olds in literacy and numeracy.
- Introduction of baseline assessment.
- Introduction of National Literacy and National Numeracy Strategies.
- Summer schools to boost achievement for target groups.
- Introduction of 'value-added' measures of pupil and school performance.
- Home-school contracts.
- The future of selective (grammar) schools to be determined by local ballot (i.e. no government action).
- Performance-related pay.
- Publication of OFSTED gradings for teacher-training courses.
- Introduction of 'Citizenship' into the revised 2000 National Curriculum.
- Curriculum 2000: major changes to courses and examinations post-sixteen.

Appendix IV
A Note on Former Schools

It is happily unusual for schools that are closed to be eliminated from the scene altogether. The buildings live to fight in another incarnation. The most common fate is to become a cottage or a house. Examples can be found everywhere, but usually in villages such as Bearley, Burton Hastings, Cherington, Dunchurch, Great Wolford, Lea Marston, Nether Whitacre, Newbold-on-Avon, Preston Bagot, Ullenhall and Wootton Wawen.

At Nether Whitacre at the start of the new millennium, the old school, though a private home, retained its outside toilets and some of the playground markings. Nearby at Baxterley, the school buildings seem to have merged with adjacent farm buildings. They now serve as a workshop for the Merevale Estate. At Shustoke, the old school now offers a particular form of accommodation: almshouses. At both Nether Whitacre and Shustoke at the time of writing it was still possible to see on outer walls signs of their past function: targets for playground games etc. Alcester, too, has given its old church school site to the elderly in the form of a retirement complex. Kingsbury Elementary School is also a housing development, but retains the school bell-tower.

Also popular is to make the old school some kind of village centre. This seems particularly helpful, given that school closures are often seen as 'tearing the heart out of the village'. Among numerous examples are halls or clubs in Austrey, Birdingbury, Over Whitacre, Ladbroke, Lapworth, Oxhill, Radway, Shotteswell and Wellesbourne. A variation on this theme is at Eastlands, Rugby, where part of what was once three schools has become a Caribbean Community Centre: the rest have been turned into offices for a firm. In Leamington too, Bath Place is now a community centre. The old school at Whitnash is a church centre. For a while, the former Long Lawford School provided Rugby with a Teachers' Centre, but that is now a private house. A former Atherstone School is now an Arts Centre. The Technical Schools in Leicester Street, Leamington, now form the Newbold Centre; the school façade with the Boys' and Girls' entrances has been preserved. At Bulkington, the Village Centre now includes a hall, surgery and police base. The Stour Valley Museum at Shipston is housed, I am told, in an old school building, but I have been unable to verify this. The erstwhile St. John the Baptist C.E. School in Leamington is now a centre for the disabled. Bilton C.E. School is an evangelical church.

Some buildings continue to serve educational needs. Schools at Astley, Grendon and Wroxall are now nurseries, as are those at Farnborough and Harborough Magna. Much of the old Borough School buildings in Warwick have been taken over and adapted by King's High School. The old St. Mark's School at Bilton, Rugby, has too moved into the independent sector, being now a private school. Ironically, at the time of writing, local schools are full and there are plans to build a new L.E.A. school at nearby Cawston. The old school at Great Alne now houses a Pupil Reintegration Unit.

More adventurously in terms of innovative use are those developments such as at Kineton where the erstwhile school is now the local surgery, and at Preston-on-Stour and at Alderminster where the school building is part of a shopping development. At Fenny Compton, the first school building is now a centre for picture framing; In Astley it once served as a studio for an artist, John Letts, sculptor of the George Eliot statue in Nuneaton Town Centre.

Often, the old and the new work in partnership. The former Polesworth School buildings became Tomlinson Hall, a sixth form centre. Old and new cohabit perfectly well at The Dassett, Cubbington, Lillington and Wilmcote. Until new buildings were opened, pupils and staff at Newton Regis would have to walk through the churchyard in order to travel from the old school to the extra classrooms.

At the time of writing schools such as those at Napton, Bidford, Northend and Butlers Marston still await a new future. Some, sadly, are no more. At Keresley, Hillmorton, Rugby (Murray and High) and Stratford (the church elementary school) the school buildings have been replaced by housing developments. Sometimes the school is remembered by names of developments: Scholar's Court at Stratford and Old Murrayian Close at Rugby are examples. Rugby High School for Girls is remembered indirectly by cul de sacs bearing the names of great women achievers : Brontë and Curie. This is the third girls' High School building in less than one hundred years; the original building is a private house. The former Wolston High School has been replaced by a development that includes small houses for one parent families. St. Michael's School in Warwick has been demolished, but its name has been inherited by a new hospital built on the same site.

A special mention for the school at Chilvers Coton, built in 1735 as a free school for the poor children of the parish. It was sponsored by the Newdigate family and survived in its own right until 1954, and as part of Swinnerton School for a few more years. After a functional and inglorious period as a depot for the Council Parks Depot, it became the Chilvers Coton Heritage Centre, containing many intriguing displays and a Victorian schoolroom.

Finally, it seemed fitting that the Coleshill Civic Society should have hired the former Back Lane School and used the schoolroom for its exhibition on three hundred years of schooling in Coleshill.

Appendix V
A Note on Names of Schools

The naming of schools is a notable example of diversity of practice across the county. Most are prosaically named: after the local area, e.g. Abbots Farm, Milby and Sydenham, or after the road or street in which they are to be found, e.g. Clapham Terrace, Hob Lane and Wheelwright Lane. Next door to Wheelwright Lane School is Exhall Grange School, named after a large house which stood on the site until the 1930's. Two schools bear the name of a river: Avon Valley and Blythe.

Fashions change in names as in everything else. Ash Green may hold the record for school name changes:

1928 : Exhall Ash Green Central School
1954 : Ash Green High
1974 : Ash Green Comprehensive
1984 : Exhall
1992 : Ash Green G.M. (Grant Maintained)

Saints are commonly used, with All Saints, and St. Mary's being particularly popular across the county. The saints Benedict, James, Joseph, Paul and Peter all have two schools which bear their name. Two schools are named after a Saint Nicholas; the 'h' in 'Nicholas' is retained in Kenilworth but absent in Nuneaton. The spelling apparently depends on your preference as between two different European traditions. The same St. Nic(h)olas is honoured by both. Four catholic schools are named after 'Our Lady', and there is one instance each of saints such as Andrew, Oswald, Anne etc.

Authors are honoured, particularly George Eliot, who has one school bearing her name and another bearing the name of one of her most famous novels: Middlemarch, both in Nuneaton. Two special schools have chosen authors: Brooke in Rugby, and Marie Corelli (once a best-selling novelist and a favourite of Queen Victoria) in Stratford. Marie Corelli donated land for the use of schools across the road from Broad Street School. Hartshill honours a famous son, the Elizabethan poet Michael Drayton. They have also chosen to honour a distinguished eighteenth century Quaker, Nathaniel Newton. He left money in 1741 to found a school so that boys and girls should learn to "Read, Write and Cast Accounts". That school was a Quaker School, now gone, but Newton's beneficence is remembered.

Bedworth is distinctive in naming four of its schools after local rectors: Nicholas Chamberlaine, Henry Bellairs, Canon Evans, nephew of George Eliot, and Canon Maggs (the last one lived long enough to learn that a school had been named in his honour). So well-served was Bedworth in church schools, that no non-church school was deemed necessary until 1902 when George Street School opened. More recently, and slightly confusingly, a non-church school named after a saint was opened to serve a housing development: St. Giles at Exhall. In 1996, the school canvassed the local community about a possible change of name. Bob Jelley, the head, favoured 'Banana Bridge Junior' after a nearby pedestrian fly-over, but nearly everyone else supported the retention of St. Giles, including members of the Sikh community. The liking for church schools probably dated from Chamberlaine himself whose original bequest was crucial in the early development of schools in the town. Only the Provost Williams School, a relatively recent naming after a long-serving and popular figure at Coventry Cathedral, is comparable to this Bedworth tradition. Provost Williams is buried at St. Leonard's, Ryton-on-Dunsmore.

Since first writing this section, I have found that Henry Bellairs School has merged with Hob Lane and lost its name. Bellairs himself had fought and won a medal at the Battle of Trafalgar before coming to Bedworth in 1821. However, his name is perpetuated by Bellairs Avenue.

Rugby has chosen to honour some ex-headteachers: Henry Hinde and Herbert Kay, for example. Henry Hinde was head of the Paddox School and his daughter, Mary, also became a head in Rugby. Herbert Kay was head of Long Lawford School in the inter-war years. The school that bore his name was amalgamated with Westlands to form Bilton High. Rugby retains an Eastlands and a Northlands but did not have a Southlands. Other schools honoured local figures with Rugby School connections: Lawrence Sheriff, founder of Rugby School and Colonel Harris, schoolmaster, magistrate and member of the Divisional Executive. St. Matthew's/Bloxam Rugby comprises what was once two schools. The Bloxam school bears the name of Matthew Bloxam, a nineteenth century antiquarian and local benefactor. It was principally on the evidence of one Matthew Holbeche Bloxam that the story of the origin of Rugby Football at Rugby School rests.

The Boughton Leigh and the Newdigate schools were named after distinguished land-owning families in their respective areas. The Boughton Leighs are in Wetherell Way, named after a former alderman and headteacher at Binley Woods. The eponymous Boughton Leigh family lived in Brownsover Hall, now a hotel occasionally used for teacher courses. Stories abound of ghosts etc. at the hall ..... ghosts of figures such as One Handed Boughton, whose hand was severed in mysterious circumstances. His story has led facetious teachers to speculate whether he was the originator of the concept of "first hand experience" in Warwickshire schools. The family did much voluntary and charitable work both locally and in nearby Newbold-on-Avon. Sir Francis Newdigate owned Arbury Hall and started a coal-mine in the Nuneaton area. The family played an active part in local and national affairs from the arrival of Sir John in the late sixteenth century. Another Newdigate, Sir Richard (1644-1710) lived at Arbury Hall, and took an active interest in affairs at King Edward's, Nuneaton.

Greville School, Alcester, adopted the family name of the Earl of Warwick, before surrendering it in a merger with Bidford High.

King Edward VI, a very popular choice in Birmingham, has also given his name to the grammar school at Stratford and the sixth form college (once a grammar school) at Nuneaton. Edward died young, before he reached full adulthood, but his name lives on in schools across the Midlands.

Herbert Fowler was the son of George Herbert Fowler. The family lived in Arley Hall and helped to finance the development of the coal-mine once to be found there. George's son, Herbert, was killed by a sniper's bullet in the first World War. Herbert Fowler Junior School is so named in his memory.

Twice mayor of Nuneaton and an Honorary Freeman of the Borough, Alderman W. T. Smith probably held more public offices than any other Nuneaton citizen. Born at Overseal, Leicestershire in 1878, the son of a railway guard, Alderman Smith moved with the family to Nuneaton before his first birthday. He was educated at Attleborough Church of England School, and at the age of 17 years obtained work with the London and North Western Railway Company. His most outstanding public service was probably in the sphere of education, being a worthy successor to the late Alderman R.W. Swinnerton, for many years Chairman of the Nuneaton Education Committee. Alderman Smith was appointed Chairman of the Committee in 1940 and held the office until his death. His only son, Mr. W.L. Smith became head of Queen's Road School.

Swinnerton School merged with Attleborough to make Wembrook. It had been named in honour of the First Chairman of Nuneaton Education Committee. Educated at Atherstone Grammar School, he too devoted much of his life to public service. A tablet in St. Nicolas Church pays tribute to his work in " ..... many offices of public trust, and (he) rendered valuable service in the County, Diocese and Town."

Aylesford and Newburgh Schools in Warwick honour past owners of the land on which they now stand.

Some schools honour distinguished citizens of long ago. Lawrence Sheriff actually founded Rugby School more than three hundred years before the school bearing his name opened. Clinton School honours Sir Geoffrey de Clinton, who was responsible for the building of Kenilworth Priory. The man responsible for the building of the Clopton Bridge in Stratford, Sir Hugh Clopton, once had a school named after him. He was described as "a charitable gent". It became part of Stratford High. Oken School honoured Thomas Oken, a sixteenth century merchant and benefactor. That school too became part of a much larger school: Myton.

Thomas Jolyffe School perpetuates the memory of a fifteenth century priest and schoolmaster, a key figure in the early history of King Edward's, Stratford. A collage in the Grosvenor House Hotel honours him. It is made of thousands of tiny pieces of paper and depicts a scene in the school courtyard in Jolyffe's day.

Bishop Wulstan R.C. School in Rugby has chosen to honour a bishop from almost a millennium ago. A school governor, Alan Parish, has published an account of his life. He was born in Long Itchington, probably in 1008. He became a priest and a schoolmaster (surely one of the earliest), working mainly in Worcestershire. His devout and philanthropic work led to his being made Bishop of Worcester, a position he held for 32 years. Though he eventually became a saint, it was decided to call the school Bishop Wulstan to avoid confusion with other schools in the Midlands.

Finally, there is no connection between Wood End School and current C.E.O. Eric Wood ..... at least, not yet.

Footnote: Street Names.

It is rare for street names to honour educationists, with the exception of Rugby School headmasters, at least five of whom are thus remembered in Rugby: Arnold, James, Percival, Temple and Wooll. However, Everard Way in Clifton commemorates long-serving head Roy Everard, a rare tribute.

One exception I wish to mention is a former colleague of mine at Dunsmore Boys' School : Trevor White. In an impressively active life he taught five subjects to O Level, was a town councillor and deputy mayor, a Grade One starter in athletics and much more. He was killed in a car crash returning with pupils from a visit to Scotland. He is remembered by the approach road to Rugby Sports Centre which bears his name. His mother was head of Wood Street Infants School, Rugby.

A Note on Sources

There is an enormous and daunting variety of sources of information. I have divided them for purposes of convenience into separate categories, but of course there is overlap.

1. School Documentation : Introduction

Most schools will have had all kinds of documentation: logbooks, admission registers, architect plans etc. After a period of time, many schools have placed these documents in the County Record Office at Warwick. Some schools keep them on the premises and use them in teaching as historical documents. Some have been damaged by floods or by storage in damp basements. Many, sadly, have disappeared without explanation. Occasionally, the records of some church schools, for example the minutes of managers' meetings, are lodged with the Church of England Centre at Earlsdon, Coventry. Punishment books are fascinating, but those held at the Record Office are confidential until seventy five years have elapsed.

2. Local Newspapers

These, especially in the early part of the twentieth century, provide detailed accounts of county council meetings. They will often record a sequence of meetings over issues affecting the life of a school, for example the threat of closure or re-organisation. Again, for the first half of the century they will often record in some detail the speeches of visitors to union meetings. For secondary schools, the report of the annual 'Speech Day' will typically provide an insight into the particular school's preoccupations and alleged or real achievements.

3. School Histories

There are far more of these around than library shelves would ever suggest. Many schools have taken the opportunity of a (e.g.) centenary to produce a history. But it often will not have occurred to that school to place a copy in the local library or the Record Office. Copies have usually been cheaply produced and may be disintegrating. The bibliography will show how many I have managed to trace. In major libraries such as Warwick, more flimsy publications are stored in boxes rather than on shelves.

4. County Council Committee Meetings

These are well bound, well indexed and stored in a basement in Shire Hall. They contain useful policy statements, annual statistics, issue papers and summaries, for example on children's health or on plans for comprehensive re-organisation. To assess how important/controversial they were seen to be at the time, they need to be studied in conjunction with contemporary local newspapers.

5. Reminiscences: Published and Oral

Many local history groups, or groups such as the Women's Institute, have collected and published reminiscences. These are often fascinating, although not easy to check. They complement other sources well because the memory tends to select topics that would not normally find their way into official documents, for example:-

a) heads and teachers : personality, mannerisms, sayings etc.
b) dress e.g. the school uniform of the time
c) food : school dinners
d) playtime and dinnertime games, and the journey to and from school
e) the classroom stove, its uses, abuses and smells

6. Other Sources

Many schools, usually secondary, hold a set of school magazines. These can be particularly useful for a better understanding of the impact of national events on the daily lives of schools: wars, financial cutbacks, major strikes etc.

The County Record Office and local libraries hold copies of useful theses on the history of education in Leamington, Nuneaton and Warwick.

The most difficult period to cover that I have found is the recent past, not because of a shortage of documents. Precisely the opposite. One can take a number of major events as seen at the time: The Technical and Vocational Educational Initiative, the Elton Report, the creation of OFSTED, Grant Maintained schools and write extensively on them. The harder part is to be sure which will have a lasting impact, and which will rapidly be forgotten. The last thirty years have seen more than their fair share of half-baked initiatives and reinvented wheels. As I write, the KS3 Literacy Strategy is resurrecting all the old debates prompted by the 1975 Bullock Report's demand for "a language policy across the curriculum". Schools will have shelves or box files full of these documents, though lack of storage space often leads to eventual journeys with laden cars to the local 'tip'.

7. Local History Groups

I have been enormously aided and intrigued by the work of many enthusiastic and industrious local history groups. At the risk of being invidious, I select as examples Alcester, Kineton, Polesworth and Rugby, but there are many more.

8. Millennium Village Histories

The millennium prompted a number of villages to write a (usually updated) history. Examples include Combroke, Leek Wootton, Stretton-on-Fosse and Stretton-on-Dunsmore.

9. The Attic

Where people have been painstaking and judicious in clearing out the attic or wherever, some valuable and almost unique records: sets of exercise books, reports, old text books, correspondence etc. have come to light. A few have found their way into the Record Office.

10. Statistical Records

Many schools still hold their 'Stock and Stores Account Books' in which, for example, one could find the number of needles and thimbles ordered in a particular year, should one so wish!

Admission registers are held by schools for most of the century: a good starting-point for those, for example, seeking to convene a reunion of past pupils. They also provide other information. They indicate how many evacuees joined a particular school, and how long (officially) they stayed. One can work out the percentage of pupils transferring to secondary schools in the days when most pupils stayed at an all-through elementary school until they left at fourteen.

11. Diaries

Keeping diaries was popular, particularly in the last two hundred years. Not all were completed either regularly or in detail but those that have survived such as the diaries of Adelaide Pountney, telling of her years in Leamington (1859-64), can give us information about education. Adelaide taught regularly at Sunday Schools in the area.

12. Log Books

These deserve more commentary because they contain so much. They were a legal requirement for elementary schools from 1862 onwards. Visiting H.M.I. would call for the logbook on any visit. Clear rules were listed for their regular completion. Heads were obliged to confine themselves to the factual: attendance rates, staff absence, arrival of parcels, visits from the clergy or inspectors etc. Inspectors' reports were often copied into them. Most heads adhered to these rules unfailingly, refraining from any personal comment even when completing thirty or forty years' service.

The Wolston logbook covering the 1920's included some revision to the guidance for heads. This included specific suggestions as to what to record, for example the "introduction of new books and apparatus".

There seems to have been a gradual change in the form of words deemed acceptable to record the reason for staff or pupil absence on health grounds. How often now would one find or use the phrases much deployed in the first half of the century:

"absent with a cold"
"absent with a chill"
"absent with a bilious attack"

Words like "influenza" or "flu" and the all-purpose "virus" now lend a little more weight to explanations, without adding any precision.

There is much less use of upper case letters than hitherto. In the past, school subjects and words like 'teacher' received a capital. Another example of a decline in deference, perhaps?

Most heads ceased to complete logbooks in the 1980's once the drive to accountability required so much more paperwork, including detailed reports to parents. The most up to date logbook I have seen is that at Arden Hill School. The head, Chris Stain, has not only maintained a logbook which enabled her to record the arrival of the new millennium, but has used a word-processor rather than the traditional pen to do so. The Arden Hill logbooks, like those at Quinton, often include photos, correspondence and newspaper articles.

N.B. Log books at the County Record Office are confidential until thirty years have elapsed; for hospital schools the period is one hundred years.

13. Parish Magazines

In recent years, the local parish magazine has often incorporated school news, especially in villages. Here is an example from 'The Dove', parish magazine for St. Nicholas, Austrey and Holy Trinity, Warton on recent news from Warton Nethersole's C.E. school:-

> " 'Pottermania' struck Year 6 at Warton with the release of 'Harry Potter and the Philosopher's Stone' before Christmas. Popcorn and drinks (which cost more than the cinema tickets) were consumed as we visited UCI as a class. Book and film reviews have been written with great enthusiasm and books have been devoured at a greater rate than ever before!"

14. The L.E.A. and the Board

The Public Record Office at Kew retains a voluminous blue file full of correspondence between the L.E.A. and the Board of Education in those early years. They show the L.E.A.'s caution in checking all kinds of details with the Board. But the Board too was learning its role. Each letter received from Warwickshire was passed round various civil servants before a composite reply was drafted. Copies of those letters, together with notes in the margins, are all carefully preserved. I do not know where else other than Kew it would be possible to find an authentic signature of Gerald Fitzmaurice or Bolton King.

One letter to the Board from Bolton King in 1906 ran on for five pages, listing in detail points that 'I am directed by my Committee to observe', all on the teaching of practical subjects. Two months later, a seven page letter made the suggestion that '..... demonstration and practice (in Cookery) be combined in one lesson.' In 1909, Bolton King took up the case of Ansley Council School who wanted to know whether the participation of its boys in a cricket league could be counted as 'organised games'. A reply two weeks later tersely refused. It gave no reason, though it might have been that the powers-that-be were keen in subsequent decades to emphasise games-training rather than playing.

15. L.E.A. Circulars

There are examples albeit sporadic, of schools pasting or copying letters from 'the office' into the logbook. Quinton School has a file of L.E.A. circulars for the 1950s and 1960s which provides glimpses of the time.

Bibliography

Trying to ensure that I have read everything of possible relevance has been challenging, time-consuming, and great fun. The bibliography is deliberately full and detailed. My hope is that I can save some time for those who follow me.

Inevitably, some texts are much more valuable than others. A few texts provide an ideal introduction: O'Shaughnessy on Leamington, Powell on Kenilworth, Saville on Alcester, for example. Local History groups are an invaluable source of both published and oral information. The Record Office has copies of theses which give helpful accounts of the development of education in places such as Leamington, Nuneaton and Warwick.

Many texts cited do not include key details: publisher, date of publication, author etc. I have included all I can find. Texts are normally listed alphabetically by author's surname.

Keeping up to date has been a constant pre-occupation. Of all the texts listed, approximately 150 have been published since I began researching in 1995. Of those, more than fifty have been published since the start of 2000.

BIOGRAPHY

"Neil Adams : A Life in Judo" by Neil Adams (Willow Books: 1986)
"The Dictionary of British Educationists" by Richard Aldrich and Peter Gordon (Woburn Press)
"Our George" by Joan Allen (Bethany Enterprises: 1990)
"Sir Robert Morant" by Bernard M Allen (MacMillan and Co: 1934)
"The Autobiography of Joseph Arch" (Macgibbon and Kee: 1966)
"From Ploughtail to Parliament: an autobiography" by Joseph Arch (Cresset Library: 1986)
"Thomas Hughes" by Edward C Mack and W H G Armytage (Ernest Benn Ltd: 1952)
"Joseph Ashby of Tysoe" by M K Ashby (Cambridge University Press: 1961)
"John Masefield: A Life" by Constance Babington Smith (Hamish Hamilton: 1978)
"The Turbulent Years" by Kenneth Baker (Faber and Faber: 1993)
"Lewis Carroll: A Biography" by Michael Bakewell (Heinemann: 1996)
"Little Girls Don't Grow into Farmers" by June Ball (Peter Drinkwater: 1989)
"A Dear and Noble Boy: The Life and Letters of Louis Stokes 1897-1916"
ed. R A Barlow and H V Bowen (Leo Cooper: 1995)
"Peasants and Parsons" by Ray Barrett (Robert Hale: 1991)
"The Genius of Shakespeare" by Jonathan Bate (Picador: 1997)
"Dr Jephson of Leamington Spa" by Eric G Baxter (Warwickshire Local History Society: 1980)
"Vera Brittain: A Life" by Berry and Ostridge (Chatto and Windus: 1995)
"The Tragedy of Randolph Turpin" by Jack Birtley (New England Library: 1975)
"The Countess of Warwick" by Margaret Blunden (Cassell: 1967)
"Whittle 1907-1996" by Paul Bolitho (Warwickshire County Council: 1998)
"Bolton King: Practical Idealist" by R Bolton King, J D Browne, E M H Ibbotson
(Warwickshire Local History Society: 1978)
"The Life of Arthur Ransome" by Hugh Brogan (Jonathan Cape: 1984)
"The Toynbee Travellers' Club" by Joan D Browne (History of Education: 1986 Vol.15)
"The Formation of an Education Administrator" by Joan D Browne (History of Education: 1981 Vol.3)

"The Art of the Possible" by Lord R A Butler (Hamish Hamilton: 1971)

"Walks with Writers" by Elizabeth Cader-Cuff (E Cuff: 1999)

"Margaret Thatcher" (Volume 1) by John Campbell (Jonathan Cape: 2000)

"For God's Sake Go" by Sir George Catlin (Colin Smythe: 1972)

"Elizabeth Gaskell: The Early Years" by John Chapple (Manchester University Press: 1997)

"John Dagley of Chapel-end" by Gordon Chilvers (Bethany Enterprises: 1990)

"Running Free" by Sebastian Coe with David Miller (Sidgwick and Jackson: 1981)

"Lewis Carroll: A Biography" by Morton N Cohen (MacMillan: 1995)

"Weinstock" by Alex Brummer and Roger Cowe (Harper Collins: 1998)

"Dr Parr: A Portrait of the Whig Dr Johnson" by Warren Derry (Oxford University Press: 1966)

"Neville Chamberlain (Volume 1 1869 - 1929) by David Dilks (Cambridge University Press: 1984)

"Arthur James Balfour" by Blanche E C Dugdale (Hutchinson & Co: 1988)

"John Masefield" by June Dwyer (Ugas: 1987)

"Shakespeare in Warwickshire" by Mark Eccles (University of Wisconsin Press: 1963)

"The Terrible Shears: Scenes from a Twenties Childhood" by D J Enright (Chatto and Windus: 1975)

"George Eliot: The Last Victorian" by Kathleen Evans (Fourth Estate: 1999)

"The Life of Neville Chamberlain" by Keith Feiling (Macmillan and Co: 1946)

"Landor" by Jean Field (Brewin Books : 2001)

"Loach on Loach" ed. Graham Foller (Faber and Faber: 1998)

"Low Seams and High Vistas" by Albert Fretwell (Albion Press: 1994)

"Whittle: The True Story" by John Golley (Airlife Publishing: 1987)

"The Squire of Arbury" by Eileen Gooder (Coventry Branch of the Historical Association: 1990)

"George Eliot" by Gordon S Haight (Clarendon Press: 1969)

"The Autobiography of Arthur Ransome" ed. Sir Rupert Hart Davis (1967)

"Friends and Apostles: the Correspondence of Rupert Brooke and James Strachey 1905-14" ed. Keith Hale (Yale University Press: 1998)

"Rupert Brooke" by Christopher Hassall (Faber and Faber: 1964)

"The Handsomest Young Man in England" by Michael Hastings (Michael Joseph: 1967)

"Coming of Age: A Cricketing Autobiography" by Eddie Hemmings (Stanley Paul: 1991)

"The Dillen" ed. Angela Hewins (Elm Tree Books: 1981)

"Mary After the Queen" by Angela Hewins (Oxford University Press: 1985)

"Matthew Arnold" by Park Honan (Weidenfeld and Nicolson: 1981)

"William Shakespeare" by Anthony Holden (Littley, Brown and Co: 1999)

"Lytton Strachey" by Michael Holroyd (Vintage: 1995)

"Tom Brown's Universe" by J R de S Honey (Millington Books: 1977)

"Shakespeare: A Life" by Park Honan (Oxford: 1998)

"Neville Chamberlain" by H Montgomery Hyde (Weidenfeld and Nicolson: 1976)

"Anthony Crosland" by Kevin Jeffery (Richard Cohen: 1999)

"The Chancellors" by Roy Jenkins (Macmillan: 1998)

"Rupert Brooke, Life, Death and Myth" by Nigel Jones (Richard Cohen: 1999)

"George Eliot's Nuneaton" by Peter Lee (1999)

"Thomas Hughes 1822-1896" by John E Little (John E Little: 1972)

"Randy" by Peter McInnes (Caestus Books: 1996)

"The Warden of English" by Jenny McMorris (Oxford University Press: 2001)

"George Eliot: a Literary Life" by Kerry McSweeney (Macmillan: 1991)

"The Cross of Skyros" by Peter Miller (1994)

"Two Feet and a Thumb" by Tim Montgomery (published by the author: 2001)

"A Life of Matthew Arnold" by Nicholas Murray (St. Martin's Press: 1997)

"Norman Painting: Reluctant Archer" by Norman Painting (Granta Editions Limited: 1982)

"The Life of St. Wulstan Bishop of Worcester" by Alan Parish (Bishop Wulstan School: 1995)

"Patrick Gordon Walker : Political Diaries 1932-78" ed. Robert Pearce (The Historians' Press: 1991)

"The Family Guide to Shakespeare and his Life in Stratford-on-Avon" by Rosemary Phipps (Pitkin Guides: 1994)

"The Mysterious Miss Marie Corelli: Queen of Victorian Bestsellers" by Teresa Ransom (Sutton Publishing: 1999)

"Forever England, the Life of Rupert Brooke" by Mike Read (Mainstream: 1993)
"With the Rank and Pay of a Sapper" by James Sawbrook (Paddy Griffith Associates: 1998)
"We'll All be Union Men: The Story of Joseph Arch and his Union" by Bob Scarth
(Industrial Pioneer Publications: 1998)
"A Square Mile of Old England" by Aubrey Seymour (Roundwood Press: 1972)
"The Oxford Guide to Women Writers" by Joanne Shattock (Oxford University Press: 1993)
"Bold Man of the Sea" by Jim Shekdar (Hodder and Stoughton: 2001)
"A Life of Education" by Brian Simon (Lawrence and Wishart: 1998)
"A Brush with Life" by Frank Sidney Smith (Weidenfeld and Nicolson: 1993)
"John Masefield" by Stanford Sternlicht (Twayne Books: 1977)
"Dictionary of National Biography" Vol 16 ed. Leslie Stephen (Smith, Elder and Co: 1988)
"George Eliot" by Ina Taylor (Weidenfeld and Nicolson: 1989)
"The Uncrowned Prime Ministers" by D R Thorpe (Darkhorse Publishing: 1989)
"The Journal of William Charles Macready" ed. J C Trewin (Longmans: 1967)
"Elizabeth Gaskell" by Jenny Uglow (Faber and Faber: 1993)
"From Oaks to Avocet" by John Walling (Riparian Publishing: 1994)
"Minding My Own Business" by Tony "Banger" Walsh (Curtis/Walsh: 1998)
"Thomas Oken" by Shirley Wallis (no further details)
"My Cricketing Life" by P B Warner (Hodder and Stoughton: undated)
"My Life and Times" by Tom Watson
"Shakespeare: The Evidence" by Ian Wilson (Headline: 1993)
"One of Us" by Hugo Young (Macmillan: 1989)
"Mr William Johnson MP: A Brief Sketch of his Career" (no other details)

CENTRAL AREA

"Kecks, Cowpats and Conkers" by Francis Allen (Brewin Books: 1995)
"150 Years in the Life of Lapworth School 1828-1978" by Gerald Asbury (1978)
"Emscote 1887 - 1987" by Pat Borrill, David Bradshaw, Sue Lawrence and Lynne Tandy (1987)
"150 Years of Education in Tachbrook" by P R Calcutt (B. Ed. thesis: 1976. No further details)
"Images of England: Royal Leamington Spa" compiled by Jacqueline Cameron (Tempus: 1999)
"Willoughby: A Warwickshire Village" by W J Carlisle et al (1988)
"Royal Leamington Spa" by Lyndon F Cave (Phillimore: 1988)
"A History of Norton Lindsey and District" by K F Chapman (self published in 1994)
"Milverton Combined School 1887 - 1987" by Amanda Clarke (1987)
"Westgate School: The First One Hundred Years" by Amanda Clarke
"Royal Leamington Spa: A Century's Growth and Development" by H G Clarke (Courier Press: 1947)
"The Leamington School Board 1881 - 1903" by John H Drew
(M.A. thesis: University of Warwick: 1974)
"Remember Kenilworth" by John H Drew (Barracuda Books: 1984)
"Insights into Bishop's Itchington" by M E Dronfield (Medfield: 1998)
"History of Leamington School of Art 1866 - 1914" by John Eldon Duce
(Dissertation in part fulfilment of the Advanced Diploma in Art Education)
"A Complete History of Leamington Spa" by T B Dudley (P and W E Linaker: 1901)
"Cubbington C E School 1780-1980" by David Evans and John Goodfellow (1981)
"She Dyed About Midnight" by Jean Field (Brewin Books: 1992)
"Beneath the Great Elms" by Jean Field (Brewin Books: 1997)
"Kings of Warwick" by Jean Field (Brewin Books: 1995)
"St Margaret's Church Whitnash" by Jean Field (1992)
"Royal Leamington Spa: Images from the Past" by W G Gibbons (Jones-Tands: 1995)
"From Humble Village to Splendid Spa: Leamington 1800 - 1850" by W G Gibbons
"Royal Leamington Spa" (Part 1: Social Life) by W G Gibbons (Jones-Sandes)
"Warwick in Times Past" by P J E Gates (Countryside Publications: 1982)
"Old Southam in Photographs" by Alan Griffin (Fielden Books: 1995)

""Lest We Forget: The Southam Men in the Great War" by Alan Griffin (Brewin Books: 2002)

"A History of Radford Semele" by Rev. Laurie Parsons revised by Anthony Hartshorn and Don Simpson (Radford Parish Church Council: 2002)

"Charles Dickens and Leamington Spa" by Bryan Homer (Jones-Sands: 1991).

"Southam School: The First 25 Years 1957-1982" (ed. E M Rumasy and G A Hayward)

"A Portrait of Kenilworth in Street Names" by Geoff Hilton (published by the author: 2000)

"Leamington Spa as an Educational Centre" by W H Harland (Borough of Leamington Spa Education Committee)

"Coten End, Past, Present and Future" by David Howe (WCC: 1997)

"Central Hospital Remembered 1852 - 1995" by Margaret Hunt, Jennifer Dayton, John Bland (South Warwickshire Mental Health Services: 1998)

"Remembering A Child's Face" compiled by Sue Jack, Sally Shillitoe and Ellen West (Long Itchington Book Project: 1996)

"Icetone : The Story of a Warwickshire Village" by Peter James (1980)

"A Maker of Magic: The First Fifty Years of the Talisman Theatre 1942 - 1992" by Peter James

"The Development of Education in the Borough of Warwick During the Nineteenth Century" by G James (M.Ed. Thesis Leeds University: 1971)

"Grandborough: Portrait of a Warwickshire Village" by Canon Idwal Jones

"Birdingbury" by Canon Idwal Jones

"Elementary Education and the Lower Classes in the Borough of Warwick 1876-82" by Andrew Land (1985)

"A History of Warwick School" by A F Leach (1906).

"The Book of Warwick" by Charles Lines (Barracuda Books: 1985)

"Graciously Pleased" ed. Jenny Long and Andrew Barber (Magnaset Ltd: 1988)

"Doreen : A Village Lass" by Doreen Lowe (The Memoir Club : 2000)

"Round About Napton" (1984) by Peter Mann and John Cain (for Napton School Association: 1984)

"John Joseph Murcott: Recluse of Whitnash 1818-1894" by Elizabeth M McIntyre (1997)

"In the Beginning: St Austin's School (1893-1914)" by Elizabeth Meaton

"History of Royal Leamington Spa" (Written for the Leamington Spa Courier 1887-9 by George Morley)

"Portrait of a Parish" by Archibald Payne (The Roundwood Press: 1968)

"Dale Street: A Tale of Two Worlds" by Revd. J Edgar Noble, Revd. R Corner et al (Trustees of the Methodist Chapel: 1916)

"A Spa and Its Children" by Frances O'Shaughnessy (1979)

"The Kingsley School: A Dream Realised 1884-1984" by Anne B Parry (Council of the Kingsley School: 1984)

"A Short History of the Parish of Radford Semele" by Rev. L Parsons

"Broadwell: The Story of Nonconformity in a Warwickshire Village" by Arthur Olorenshaw (Trustees of the Methodist Chapel, Broadwell: 1963)

"Cubbington: Reflections on Village Life" by G F Peppitt (The Pleasaunce Press: 2000)

"Kenilworth at School" by Joyce Powell (Odibourne Press - 1991)

"A Year in the Life of two Warwickshire Villages" (Norton Lindsey and Wolverton) by Mary E Rhodes

"Budbrooke Past and Present" by E Richardson (1993)

"Life at the Poplars 1910-20" by Mary Robertson (1984)

"The Three Sisters' School" by Mary Rock

"Random Papers" ed. Daniel Roth (Leamington Literary Society: 1985)

"I Wouldn't Have Changed Things" by Alfred Spicer

"The History of the Benedictines of St. Mary's Priory, Princethorpe" by Sister Frideswide Stapleton (1930)

"The Warneford: A Hospital's Story" by Craig D Stephenson (South Warwickshire Hospital General Trust: 1993)

"Leamington Spa: A Photographic History" by Graham Sutherland (Black Horse Books: 2001)

"The Life and Times of Warwick Hospital" by Maureen Thomas (Warwick Hospital: December 2000)

"King Henry VIII's Charity" by E G Tibbits (Warwick County Record Office)

"Looking Back Again" by Eileen Tisdale (Odibourne Press 1990)
"In Search of Ufton" by the children of Ufton C.E. School (Children's Village Survey Project: 1968-9)
"Leamington College 1902-1977" by F Williamson
"History of the Parish of Baddesley Clinton" by John M Winterburn (self-published)
"A History of Lillington" by John M Winterburn
"Portrait of Lapworth" by Joy Woodall (published by Joy Woodall 1986)
"Leek Wootton and its Hamlets" (Leek Wootton History Group: 2001)
"Looking back at the Sisters' School" by Mary Rock (Feldon Books)
The untitled published speech of the Rev. Edward Thring, delivered at the prize-giving at the High School for Girls, Leamington (Sept. 1896)
"The King's High School Warwick 1879-1979" (published by The Governing Body: 1979).
"Ladbroke: The Village" (1985)
"Leamington High School for Girls: Records and Recollections 1884 - 1934" (The Courier Press: 1934)
"Leamington College 1902 - 1952" (The Courier Press)
"The Leamington We Used to Know" (Leamington Literary Society: 1977)
"More Looking Back" (Leamington Literary Society: 1980)
"A Last Look Back" (Leamington Literary Society: 1983)
"The History of Chesterton and Kingston"
"Hungry Harbury" (Harbury Society: 1980)
"Southam Through the Centuries"
"A History and Description of the Parish of Whitnash (Whitnash Press: 1865)
"Borough Church of England School 1815 - 1965. A Collection of Memories" ("A Few Friends": 1965)
"Baginton After the Bromleys" (Baginton History Group: 1995)
"Barford in Past Years" (Barford Parochial Church Council: 1992)
"Leaves": Magazine of Blackdown High School (1974)
"Shrubland Street School 1884-1984" (published by the School: 1984)
"Leamington School Board Triennial Reports 1984 - 1902" (published by the Board)

EASTERN

"My First 80 Years" by A.V. Baillie (John Murray: 1951)
"Centenerary of Parish Councils" by Councillor Mrs D Bancroft (For Clifton-upon-Dunsmore Local History Group: 1994)
"More Than a School" by W E Blackshaw (Bilton Grange Trust Ltd: 1995)
"1756 Acres: A History of the People of Pailton" by Roy Bourne
"A Century in Churchover" by Doreen Bradbury and Mary Short (Churchover Social History Group: 2001)
"St. Mathew's School Rugby 1852-1952" by Cyril A Brook and Charles G McLeod.
"Clifton-on-Dunsmore" (Clifton Local History Group)
"Newton" (Clifton-upon-Dunsmore Local History Group: 1999)
"Rugby: A People's History" by Tom Cuthbert (published by the author: 2002)
"A Brief History of Churchover" by C G Down (published by the author: 1997)
"All About Dunchurch" (Dunchurch Staff College: 1976)
"Rugby's Railway Heritage" by Peter H Elliott (Anderson Publications: 1985)
"Two Warwickshire Village Schools: Implementing the 1870 Act" (M.Ed. Thesis by Janice Fielden, Warwick University)
"Bygone Days of Newbold-on-Avon" by Sheila C Frewin (published by the author: 2001)
"End of an Era: Rugby Tales" by R Green
"Rugby Memories" by Mike Green (Stylus Press: 1996)
"Rugby College of Technology and Arts: Junior Technical School 1942-57 Junior Commercial School 1944-57" by Brian Venn Griffin (published by the author: 2001)
"A History of Stretton-on-Dunsmore C.E. School" by T A Gullick

"A Pictorial History of Ryton on Dunsmore" compiled by Barbara Harris, Jill Johnson, Sylvia Lamb, (Ryton 2000 Committee)

"Clifton upon Dunsmore: The Story of a Warwickshire Village School" by K M Harrop (Clifton-upon-Dunsmore Local History Group: 1983)

"A Local History of the Village of Hillmorton" (Hillmorton County Middle School: 1974)

"Looking Back" by Keith Judge (Keith Judge Publishing 2000)

"A History of the Parishes of Long Lawford and Little Lawford 1754-1995" by Keith Judge

"The Rugby Lions: A History of the Rugby Football Club 1873-1991" by Dennis Keen (Dennis Keen: 1991)

"From Learning to Earning: Birth and Growth of a Young People's College" by P I Kitchen (Faber and Faber: 1944)

"Rugby Sketches" by Nelly Leeder Brooks (1941)

"Brynca's Low: A History of the Village of Brinklow" by Diane Lindsay (Brinklow History Group: 1995)

"St. Matthew's Rugby" by John Lenton (1987)

"Leamington Hastings Almshouses and Poor's Plots" by G I MacFarquhar

"History of Bilton" by R Norton

"Rugby at War" by M Pettigrew

"Rugby: Growth of a Town" by Andy Osborne and Eddy Rawlins (1988).

"How the Game Began" by Eddy Rawlins (Eddy Rawlins: 1990)

"Rugby High School Golden Jubilee 1919 - 1969" (Compiled and edited by G F Randall: 1969)

"The Story of St. Andrew's Parish Church Rugby" by C G Richards and C E Pearce (1951)

"Rugby : A Beacon in the Urban Crisis" (Rugby Borough Council and Rugby Community Relations Council: 1977)

"Rugby: Aspects of the Past" and "Further Aspects of the Past" (1977) (Rugby Local History Group)

"Aspects of the Past: 3" by Rugby Local History Group (1991)

"Aspects of the Past: 4" by Rugby Local History Group (1998)

"Aspects of Twentieth Century Rugby" by Rugby Local History Group (2001)

"Rugby & District" (Rugby Local History Research Group: 1995).

"Rugby As It Was" Rugby Local History Group (Hendon Publishing: 1979)

"St. Luke's Hospital and Rugby Union Workhouse 1809-1993" (Rugby Local History Group: 2001)

"A Short History of the Cawston Estate" by R F Smart (T N Technology Ltd: 1967)

"History of Princethorpe Priory" by Sister Frideswide Stapleton

"Stretton on Dunsmore : The Making of a Warwickshire Village" (Stretton Millennium History Group: 2000)

"A Brief History of St Marie's Church" by Derek and Lucy Thackray (1987)

"Rugby: A Pictorial History" by E W Timmins (Phillimore: 1990)

"Rugby Past and Present" by Rev. W O Wait (1893)

"Lawrence Sheriff School 1878-1978" by L V Wells, A Russell (published by Governors of LSS: 1978)

"History of Leamington Hastings" by The Revd. C E Wigram

"A History of the Methodist Churches in the Rugby and Daventry Circuit" ed. Ron Wilson (Rugby and Daventry Circuit of the Methodist Church: 1993)

"Never A Dull Moment" by Eileen Wilson Smith (1992)

"Obituaries of Rugbeians" Volumes 1-5 (John Walker & Co.)

"Rugby & District" A Second Selection (Sutton Publishing: 1997)

"Rugby Education Week" (Handbook)

NUNEATON/BEDWORTH

"The Quakers of Hartshill" by Joan Allen

"Another One Hundred Years: 1890-1990" by Joan Allen (Bethany Enterprises: 1992) (This book about Hartshill and Oldbury)

"A History of Nicholas Chamberlaine School" by Thomas Anney (1994)

"Keresley, Keresley Newlands, Corley and Exhall: The Notes of Historical Researches" by Frederick Charles Archer (1965)

"Bulkington Memories" by Mary Ashmore (Bedworth Civic Arts Society)
"Childhood Memories" (Bedworth and Warwickshire Genealogy Society Edition 3: Sept. 1992)
"A Tale of Bygone Days" Part One 1915-43 by A Bazeley (1991)
"History of Education in Nuneaton" by Arnold Bickerstaff (Thesis submitted for M.Ed: Nottingham University 1967)
"Ansley Remembered" by John Bland and Colin Hayfield (1989)
"Galley Common Remembered" by John Bland and Heather Norgrove (1990)
"Arley Remembered" by John Bland and Colin Hayfield (1987)
"Nuneaton Past and Present" by John Burton (Sutton Publishing: 2000)
"Around Bulkington in Old Photographs" by John Burton (Sutton Publishing)
"Bedworth in Old Photographs" by John Burton (Sutton Publishing: 1988)
"Notes for a History of Stockingford" by Rev. P Croft (Nuneaton Public Library: 1967)
"What House Will You Build Me? Hartshill and its Parish Church 1848-1998" by Bob Cretney
"Mummy What Did You Do in the Strike?" (Coventry Miners' Wives Support Group: 1986)
"Starving in Bedworth: Will Not Pay the Loan" by Tony Davis (1990)
"On Stepping Stones from Stockingford" by Gordon Peter Eaves
"A Rough History of Exhall Juxta Coventry" by N B Edmonds.
"Reminiscences" by Lily Elmer (1986)
"It Grew By Industry" by Dennis Essex (Bedworth Civic Arts Society)
"Notes on the History of Nuneaton" by C G Gardner (Nuneaton Public Library: 1958)
"The Development of Education in the Nuneaton Area" by J L Glazier (Thesis for Certificate of Education: Queen's College Cambridge, 1949)
"Luther" by Mollie Harrell (Brewin Books: 1994)
"Millennium Snapshots of Fillongley and Corley" compiled by Marie Hopkins and Susan Moore (Fillongley and Corley Local History Group: 2000)
"A History of Exhall Grange School" by David Howe (Exhall Grange School: 2001)
"Images of Nuneaton" by Roger Jeffery (Breedon Books for Nuneaton Weekly Tribune: 1995)
"Bedworth: A Short History" by A H Lawrence
"Two Hundred Years: 1784 - 1984" by Aubrey Mann
"The History of the Old Meeting Sunday School, Bedworth: Two Hundred Years 1784-1984" by Aubrey Mann.
"Nuneaton : The Growth of a Town" by Dennis Milburn (Nuneaton Library and Museum Committee: 1963)
"Nuneaton Remembered" by Dennis Milburn (1963)
"A History of Nuneaton Grammar School 1552-1908" by E Nason (1936)
"Skylark Fields: A Forties Childhood" by Alan Sheasby (Warwickshire Books: 1990)
"Bedworth History" (Vol 2) ed. Dr L Orton
"History of Nuneaton Technical College and School of Art" by R Payne (Project: Wolverhampton Teachers' Training College: 1966)
"Scenes from George Eliot Country" by J Parkinson (Richard Jackson: 1988)
"Story and History of the School of Art" by Jack Savage
"A Brief History of Arley" by Maureen Stephenson
"A Brief History of Ansley" by Maureen Stephenson
"King Edward VI School Nuneaton 1552-1952" (various authors Sumner, Bastock et al)
"Pigs in the Playground" by John Terry (Farming Press: 1986)
"Ducks in Detention" by John Terry (Farming Press: 1990)
"Rabbits on Report" by John Terry (Farming Press: 2001)
"Just Among Ourselves" by Barbara Thomas et al (Keresley and Coundon Women's Institute: 1988)
"From Leicester Road to Race Leys 1912-2000" compiled by Hazel Towle and Veronica Hughes (Race Leys Infant Community School: 2000)
"Nuneaton: a History" by E A Veasey (Phillimore: 2002)
"Keresley Faces" (W C C Libraries and Heritage: 1997)
"Nuneaton Infant School (Vicarage Street) School Log 1864-95" (Warwickshire Family History Society: 1998)

"Wolvey: A Warwickshire Village" (Wolvey Local History Group)
"Wolvey: A Warwickshire Village" Book 2 (Wolvey Local History Group)
"Memories of Another Day" ed. Christopher Wood (M T Promotions: 1997)
"Schools of Nuneaton" (Commissioners' Reports for 1840: H.M.S.O.)
"Barnacle: A Millennium Celebration" (Barnacle Village Books: 2000)

NORTH WARWICKSHIRE

"Atherstone through the Lens" by M J Alexander and J L Sulter
(Atherstone Local History Research Group: 1992)
"Atherstone" (Atherstone Local History Research Group)
"We Remember" (Atherstone Branch Royal British Legion: 1995)
"Shustoke Remembered" by John Bland, Rita Callwood and Colin Hayfield
"Maxstoke Remembered" by John Bland, Rita Callwood and Colin Hayfield
"The Story of Coleshill" (Coleshill Civic Society: 1995)
"A Short History of Polesworth" by Adam Craig (A Craig: 1998)
"Charity Education in Polesworth" by David Davies (M.A. thesis: Warwick University: 1981)
"The History of Alvecote" by Petter Edden and Hilary Jones (1968)
"Low Seams and High Vistas: Baddesley Ensor of Yesteryear" by Albert Fretwell
(Heart of Albion Press: 1994)
"Dordon" by Harvey H Fox (1992)
"Coleshill Remembered" ed. Bruce Gascoigne and Colin Hayfield (Spring Hill Publications: 1990)
"Temple Balsall" by Eileen Gooder (Phillimore: 1999)
"Water Orton in Times Past" by C W Green (Countryside Publications: 1984)
"The Story of Kingsbury" by Carole Haines (Kingsbury History Society: 2001)
"A History of Kingsbury School 1686 - 1986" edited by Carole Haines (Kingsbury Historical Society)
"Warwickshire Miner" by Len Hare (1986)
"Around Kingsbury" (Kingsbury Historical Society)
"Changeful Years Unresting: Polesworth School 1881-1981" by L S Moss (1981)
"Kingsbury Remembered" (Kingsbury Local History Society: 1992)
"Polesworth History" (Polesworth History Society)
"Polesworth Local History Scrapbooks" Vols IV and V
"Some History of Nether Whitacre" by Rev T Y and J C T Price
"Some More History of Nether Whitacre" by J C T Price (1988)
"Some More History of Nether Whitacre Part 3" by J C T Price (1990)
"The Big School: A Celebration" by Annette Sweet (Baddesley Ensor Local Pride Group: 2001)
"The Church, Manor and Grammar School of Atherstone" by Sarah A Walters (1985)
"The History of Atherstone" by Brenda Watts and Eleanor Wingard (Mercia Publications Ltd: 1988)
"A New Look at Polesworth History" by Jean Wood (1993)
"A Pot Pourri of Polesworth Memories" (compiled by Jean Wood)
"Old Polesworth" (Volumes 1 and 2)

SOUTHERN

"Alcester: A History" (Alcester and District Local History Society: 1986)
"A Short History of Alcester's Schools 1490-1912"
(Alcester and District Local History Society Occasional Paper No.7)
"Coughton: Aspects of Its History" (Alcester and District Local History Society: 1988)
"Kineton in the Great War 1914-21" by Gillian Ashley-Smith (Brewin Books: 1998)
"Compton Verney: A History of the House and the Owners" by Robert Bearman
(Shakespeare Birthplace Trust: 2000)
"The Changed Village" by Ursula Bloom (Chapman and Hall: 1945)
"A Wellesbourne Guide" by Peter and Rosalin Bolton (P and R Bolton: 1991)

261

262